Man, Motives, and Money

Psychological Frontiers of Economics

$$$$$$$$$$$$$$$ $$$$$$$$$$$$$$$$$$$$$ $$

Man, Motives, and Money

Psychological Frontiers of Economics

$$$$$$$$$$$$$$$ $$$$$$$$$$$$$$$$$$$$$ $$

ALBERT LAUTERBACH

SECOND EDITION

Cornell University Press, Ithaca, New York

PRINTED IN THE UNITED STATES OF AMERICA BY THE

VAIL-BALLOU PRESS, INC., BINGHAMTON, NEW YORK

Acknowledgments

THROUGH suggestions and criticisms many people have helped in the research and writing that led to this book. It would be quite impossible to acknowledge or even to identify every one of these contributions, but I wish to express my appreciation of the especially important share of two persons: Joseph Wilder, M.D., vice-president and cofounder of the American Association for the Advancement of Psychotherapy, and George Katona, professor of economics and psychology at the University of Michigan and director of the economic program at the Survey Research Center, Institute for Social Research, at the same university.

The directors and staff members of the Institute and the Center were most helpful during the year I spent in Ann Arbor working on this study with the help of a grant from the Carnegie Corporation of New York. Needless to say, no one but the author is responsible for any shortcomings of the book.

Some passages in the first and fourth chapters were taken, by permission, from articles by the author in the *American Journal of Economics and Sociology*, issues of October 1950 and October 1952. I am likewise indebted to Professor Robert Mossé, University of Grenoble,

France, for permission to use passages from the English text of an article that George Katona and I jointly contributed to the *Bilans de la connaissance économique*. Harvard University Press generously agreed to let me use, in a section of Chapter IV, much of my contribution to its volume on *Totalitarianism*, edited by Carl J. Friedrich.

Permission to quote from works copyrighted by them was very kindly granted by the following publishers: The Brookings Institution, Chanticleer Press, The Dryden Press, The Free Press, Harcourt, Brace and Company, Harper & Brothers, Harvard University Press, Houghton Mifflin Company, McGraw-Hill Book Company, The Macmillan Company, Penguin Books Ltd., W. W. Norton & Company, Random House, Rinehart & Company, Charles Scribner's Sons, Simon and Schuster, and Yale University Press; also by the American Political Science Association, the Carnegie Corporation of New York, *Fortune* Magazine, the Metropolitan Life Insurance Company, the National Planning Association, *The New York Times*, and *U.S. News & World Report*.

The second edition gave the author an opportunity to do much streamlining in the text and to eliminate certain passages, footnotes, and appendixes which seem less relevant from the perspective of 1959. Some new materials and bibliographical references were incorporated in the revision, but no major rewriting was attempted. The author received many valuable suggestions from reviews of the first edition, both laudatory and critical, and is very much aware of the need for more extensive studies in this field. The present occasion, however, is confined to a new edition of a book that has been out of print in its original version.

A. L.

Sarah Lawrence College
Bronxville, New York
March 1959

Contents

Introduction

WHEN little Kathy fell into an abandoned well in San Marino, California, the engineer who directed the vain attempts to rescue her said to a reporter of the *New York Times*, "You couldn't get men to work this hard or fast for money." When asked about the money to pay for the extensive work done by scores of men and tons of bulldozers, he replied, "I haven't even heard the word mentioned."

This happened in a country that emphasizes belief in the profit motive as the chief driving force of human behavior, certainly in the field commonly classified as economics—that is, activities which have something to do with the relationships and arrangements of revenue, cost, exchange, work, utility, choices, substitutions. Could it be that some of us have been too simple, complacent, or hypothetical in our thinking about supposed patterns of economic relations, too uncritical in generalizing limited experiences in our own period and area into dubious laws of economic behavior in general? For, with a little thought, almost any of us could easily cite many examples of disregard of immediate profit considerations other than the one mentioned initially.

This study is chiefly designed to focus the attention of the reader upon the psychic processes that determine, underlie, or accompany important happenings in economic life. In particular, it endeavors to bring out the complexity, variability, and elasticity of the motivations that guide economic decisions and actions in our own period; the cultural and sociohistorical relativity of many such motivations; and the changing effectiveness of various possible incentives for efficiency and productivity, along with the changing valuation and definition of efficiency and productivity themselves.

The prevailing value system of American culture in the early twentieth century assumed that the profit motive or, more broadly, the quest for pecuniary or material rewards either was or needed to be recognized generally as the decisive and perhaps exclusive force that encouraged productive efficiency. The latter, in turn, was widely identified with great quantity and cheapness of material output without much attention to ethical valuation, social distribution, or human cost.

Some changes in this value system have occurred in recent decades even while productive efficiency has been progressing rapidly. It is one of the main purposes of this study to supply further evidence that there is no good reason to assume any narrow, rigid, or immutable basis of motives for productive efficiency, however the latter is defined specifically. Certain incentives, which today either are not fully utilized or are not even known to be effective, may gain in importance at some future date compared with the profit-maximization motive of the "economic man"—the man who has long been recognized to be a mere hypothetical device in economic analysis.

This study thus supplements my earlier typology of patterns of social control in economic life.[1] An attempt is here made to examine, in the light of cultural and sociohistorical change, a number of time-honored psychological arguments against any such control. The alleged incompatibility of social control, especially under conditions of democratic freedom, with human nature, rational thinking, or the requirements of "economic" behavior is likewise touched upon.

The main kinds of problems in this general area that will be discussed are the following:

1. To what extent does business behavior in our existing society actually follow those rules of economic decision making which economic analysis has assumed or developed? What other—noneconomic—factors influence such behavior and its underlying motivation? How are business decisions actually made? What personal factors are con-

ducive to business success under varying forms of enterprise? Is the aggregate result of such decisions and achievements likely to encourage economic stability or not?

2. Assuming that a substantial degree of economic instability, intentionally or not, is a concomitant of a private business economy, to what extent and in what ways has such instability prevented individuals and groups from acting "economically"? To what extent is economic instability likely to persist, increase, or decrease under other institutional arrangements, such as extensive government intervention; and in what ways, if any, can economic reforms hope to reduce the social causes of personal insecurity?

3. To the extent that any such hope is legitimate, does economic reform of any desirable type presuppose a different kind of human being from the one that we have known thus far, especially in Western democratic countries? What personality traits are conducive to a person's active interest in the various types of economic reform, and which reform types, if any, are psychologically hopeful under the conditions of Western societies of the twentieth century?

Question 1 is the principal topic of the first two chapters of this book. Question 2 is discussed mainly in the third chapter, and Question 3 in the fourth chapter. The final chapter attempts to pull all of the preceding discussion together and then to outline tasks for further studies in this general field.

Admittedly all of the questions just mentioned are ambitious ones, and no one individual could possibly hope to have the knowledge, wisdom, or integrating power to offer a comprehensive answer to all of them. Moreover, the time has not come to formulate a general theory of economic psychology. Yet the need is great for a discussion of such insights as are available today, without awaiting analytic perfection and full integration. The chief justification for this study is the need of students, teachers, public servants, businessmen, and others for a list of pertinent questions and challenging hypotheses for further research in important areas of economic psychology. In order to find a reasonably foolproof answer to any one of the many questions raised, painstaking factual research by many scholars and institutes will be necessary over a long period and in full intellectual freedom. Certain elements of such research, however, are available already.

The author is fully aware of the fact that he raises many more questions than he can even begin to answer. He does so in the hope that this otherwise debatable procedure may stimulate specific research along related lines by individuals and agencies. To the extent that answers or hypotheses are ventured, the evidence is in the main confined to factual data and surveys that have been worked out by others and to the substantial quantity of economic, sociological, psychological, and anthropological literature that has been examined. The rest is admittedly hypothesis or speculation. The reader who wants to be shown right away will undoubtedly find just as much fault with this book as the author has often found with earlier hypotheses and speculations, especially those based on camouflaged or unconscious motives. If, however, this study succeeds in encouraging fresh thinking in this crucial field of studies, it will have accomplished its purpose.

Man, Motives, and Money

Psychological Frontiers of Economics

Chapter I

The Motivation
of Business Activity

"THE business of America is business." This famous statement by President Coolidge aptly summarizes the prevailing climate of ideas in the United States during his period and, to a lesser extent, in our period. Perhaps this statement also postulates implicitly that the business of economists is an inquiry into business, on the basis of "no-nonsense" assumptions concerning profit maximization, the constancy of market reactions, and the implied framework of both institutions and motivations.

It is the purpose of this chapter to examine (in line with Question 1 of the Introduction) the sociohistorical setting of the type of human activity that is ordinarily characterized as business, the personality factors involved, and the variations which business activities and their underlying motivation appear to undergo depending on the period and locale concerned. This should not be interpreted as an attempt to replace the economic analysis of business phenomena by a psychological one. We are *not* going to assume that incentives to invest, for example, depend only on the personality traits of the investor and not at all on the tax structure, or that business depressions merely reflect emotional reactions of people so that the inventory situation is not worth study.

Practically, every business action is both economic and psychological depending on the angle of observation. Pricing a pair of shoes at ten dollars obviously entails some purely financial effects upon the firm, but it also assumes certain attitudes and reactions of the consumer concerning readiness to spend, to shop around, to follow the fashion, and so forth.

It would, therefore, not be easy, nor would it be especially rewarding, to disentangle "economic" factors from "noneconomic" ones in each case. The emphasis in this particular discussion, however, as distinguished from more conventional interpretations of business processes, will be on motivational and personality factors in business, including self-assertive elements in competition. This emphasis, we repeat, should not convey the impression of minimizing those business factors which are of an impersonal character, such as aggregate income or tax legislation. Rather is it intended to put the spotlight on emotional and cultural influences in business behavior which have often been neglected, even at the risk of displeasing groups that might prefer glorification to dissection. It will be shown, in particular, that actual or expected profit is seldom the ultimate determinant of business activity in the psychological sense, even though profit is ordinarily the most direct and conscious incentive for such activity.

Business, in the broadest sense, may be defined as the regular or prolonged pursuit of any kind of gainful activity, but especially as initiative in pursuing gain through the media of production, trade, or credit operations. In most societies the gain is typically calculated, measured, or expressed in terms of money, though there are notable exceptions.

Within this general concept, there is an endless variety of approaches to and practices of business. One might argue that even the giving-away practices of the Sioux or Kwakiutl Indians, for instance,[1] may represent a kind of business, for such practices may involve the expectation of greater generosity on the part of other people or of rewards through improved social status. In some other societies the expectation may be of rewards after death. This, however, would mean stretching the concept of business pretty far. The culture of the Indonesian island of Alor, on the other hand, considers manipulation of finances the main occupation of men, while women are in charge of the essential rice production; the rather predatory control of the men over meat foods and certain cultural requirements connected with family events and feasts are combined into a socioeconomic setup in which debt, interest, profit, and wealth are the basic elements determining social status and prestige. In its rather obsessive preoccupation with money, the Alorese culture represents a kind of unwitting parody of Western capitalism, as do certain primitive societies of an exploitive type such as the Ifugao in the Philippines.[2]

At the same time, the evaluation of certain activities which according to *our* prevailing standards represent business, varies greatly from culture to culture. What one population perceives as greedy profit making, another may perceive as a religious ritual, or vice versa. Bargaining practices, while outwardly similar, may be rooted in different motivations or value meanings depending on the sociocultural setting.

Anybody who has done shopping in a number of different countries will know that . . . in one society the pleasure may be in skill in bargaining, so that the vendor feels defrauded if his first asking price is paid without demur; in another the vendor may feel gratified if he has passed off an imperfect article at a high price, while in yet another he may get greater satisfaction from an experienced and discriminating buyer who manifests his appreciation and knowledge of the vendor's skill and taste; and so on, with a very great number of variations and permutations.[3]

In other words, the traditional approach of many economists and historians in comparing "similar" business practices of various countries and periods as if they were isolated self-propelling phenomena easily leads to ethnocentric misinterpretation. Actually a seemingly objective pattern of business behavior, such as tough bargaining, usury, gambling, generosity, or sloppiness, may reflect great differences in attitudes and frames of reference.[4]

Our policy makers have begun to realize the full range of cultural problems that are involved, for example, in programs for the advancement of underdeveloped areas. Such programs often attempt to spread industrialization, efficiency, and businesslike management, according to Western standards, to populations with entirely different scales of value; they might attempt to remake these populations in the image of a free-enterprise twentieth-century America, thus potentially destroying earlier value systems. To what extent can we take it for granted that *every* population both wants and is able to be more "efficient," more wealthy in the Western sense? A United Nations study formulates this problem as follows: "Even when people know that a greater abundance of goods and services is possible, they may not consider it to be worth the effort. . . . Alternatively, people may be unwilling to make the effort to produce wealth if the social prestige which they desire is more easily acquired in other ways." [5]

It might, of course, be argued that a wide expansion of capitalist industrialism *has* occurred over the last two centuries, and that its economic and technological features have actually spread from England to the Continent, to North America, and to some other parts of the world. But it will soon be shown that, even when seemingly identical institutions or practices prevailed, they did not lead to full equalization of doing business in the United States and western Europe, not to mention other areas.

The relativity of what superficially looks like a general, international spread of business behavior—or, more accurately, the variations in the cultural and sociohistorical setting of business practices—have often eluded observers. If "the neglect of the businessman by historians" has been rightly charged,[6] it can probably be explained by the fact that contemporary business in America seldom likes the idea of being seen in a historical or cultural context; for such approaches imply that, since business came to us some time in the past, it might disappear again some time in the future, a thought which tends to cause malaise to many of those concerned.

Yet no other approach can hope to achieve an understanding of the actual motivation that guides business activity in our own society. A purely formal "theory of the firm" or speculative generalizations about "behavior of the firm," without regard to the cultural and institutional setting of the firms in question, can make only a very limited contribution to our understanding of business. The mere choice of accounting methods (which determine in part how much cost should be assumed and how much profit has resulted from business operations) inevitably involves the motivational patterns and basic values of those who do business. In order to promise conclusiveness, any study of the motivation of business activity in our period must start with the development of business mentality in the contemporary sense.

Variations of Business Mentality

If we employ the concept of business, not in the very general sense that was discussed initially but in the more specific context of Western capitalist society, the rise of business mentality out of the disintegrating feudalism of the late Middle Ages in Europe is rather clearly definable in terms of period and locale. Max Weber, Werner Sombart, R. H. Tawney, and others have contributed much to our understanding of this process, especially of the religious influences involved such as Calvinism and Puritanism.[7]

The reasons why the great and lasting victory of the capitalist spirit and institutions occurred in England, and not in Venice, Florence, Luebeck, or Bruges, all of which had an important head start over the British Isles, have also been explored extensively, though the impact of cultural differences may have been somewhat neglected. Very different cultures, it is true, proved susceptible to a capitalist *Wirtschaftsgesinnung*, to use Sombart's famous term. The difficulty, however, of reconciling it with older and more deeply rooted patterns of perception and sociocultural norms, including those of an ethicoreligious character, turned out to be far greater in some countries than in others. The amount of ingenuity that was required and supplied in order to produce the necessary rationalizations—for a transition from a mediaeval sin-of-avarice attitude to the new virtues of profit making and wealth accumulation, for example—varied enormously, and so did the degree of inner security and external stability of the new economic leadership.

In view of such cultural differences, the spread over large parts of the world of *some* form and degree of capitalist business mentality during the last century or two is certainly amazing. Yet we should not take it for granted that "capitalism" or "business," even when the legal regulations or the terminology employed are identical, necessarily means about the same thing everywhere and at all times. Sombart, who saw in the "capitalist spirit" a changing combination of two very different elements—the acquisitive, adventurous enterprise spirit and the calculating, rational bourgeois spirit—was careful to point out that the timing, durability, intensity, and extent of this combination, as well as its incubation period and its mixture with precapitalist elements, were all subject to enormous variations.[8]

Actually the entire history of attitudinal, institutional, and policy changes under capitalism is largely an account of such variations. The adjustments in the setup and practice of capitalist business, which have been going on continuously ever since the Great Industrial

Revolution, if not longer, have largely been adjustments in the prevailing motivation of economic activity, both private and public. This change occurred under the impact of the social, ethical, and emotional problems and conflicts which, with great variations in timing, form, and intensity, had arisen in every country as the result of earlier practices.

Ever since these beginnings both the underlying philosophy and the specific practices of business have been undergoing profound, though not identical, changes in every country concerned. These changes have tended to outpace completely the adjustment of the terminology concerned, thus leading constantly to semantic twisting of the real problems. In some countries the business principle of profit maximization was temporarily or permanently distorted into a slightly sophisticated version of primitive robbery. Elsewhere it was hampered by survivals of attitudes from the feudal age, such as disdain for competition, calculation, or newly acquired property.

In other words, the climate of business, the value system and the social atmosphere in which it is conducted, the conscious or nonconscious impulses which typically guide business activities, have all been subjected to great variations in the course of each country's historical development. This was true even when the external framework of institutions and the accompanying terminology seemed to be stable to the point of rigidity.[9]

In the United States such changes in the climate of business have been characterized by a relatively fast transition from rugged individualism to the practice or, at least, widespread recognition of social responsibility on the part of business. *Fortune* magazine has described the Age of William Howard Taft as follows, "Its material pride in money, bigness, statistics, and, on the other hand, its high-minded blinking of the realities of human nature were presently to issue in cynicism and despair." [10] Two World Wars with the great depression in between were bound to affect the economic climate profoundly even though the official language of business groups and conventions remained largely that of the Age of Taft if not of earlier periods.

Along with a changing attitude toward social responsibility came a shift in the practice of competition. Still in full swing is the controversy about whether competition as such has declined or has merely changed its forms during the last few decades. There is little doubt, however, concerning the profound effect of the growing differentiation and complexity of merchandise, the standardization of the merchant, and the spread of chain stores. There are indications that the basic will to compete is far less strong than earlier generations rightly or wrongly thought it to be in their own period. Some of the stanchest spokesmen for free enterprise—a concept to be discussed later—now believe that "business will not long remain competitive, if left to its own devices." [11]

Assuming there is some truth in this statement—and the history of both American and foreign business lends much support to this assumption—we ask why this should be so. One possible answer, which has been given by some economic theorists, is that profit maximization often requires oligopoly or monopoly rather than a competitive situation. This answer, however, assumes that profit maximization always guides actual business behavior. In the absence of any such preconception we must allow for other possible influences, especially the often overlooked differences between "free," "competitive," and "private" enterprise. We must further allow for the propensity of many an individual businessman, company, or trade group to perceive its special interests more distinctly or emphatically than those of the business community as a whole and then to rationalize these special interests into general needs, to present its own pressure-group desires as a representation of social utility if not necessity.

In addition, the growth of corporate enterprise in America has affected the nature of business leadership faster and more thoroughly than elsewhere. One remarkable feature of this development in recent years has been the simultaneous growth of corporate big business and of the total number of business units; this number now exceeds 4.3 million. It is still fairly easy for the independent little fellow to start a business of his own, but there is a distinct possibility that it may not survive the first year or that during its lifetime it may depend economically upon one or more big enterprises. At the same time, business leadership in large corporations—and, in an important degree, in the business community as a whole—has passed into the hands of professionally trained executives and hired managerial experts, who usually have little if any ownership interest in their companies. Business leadership, therefore, has largely been divorced from ownership.

Within the large corporation, decentralization of decision making, at least below the policy-shaping level, and the necessity of group decisions in managerial activities have encouraged further changes both in the personality types required and in the motive patterns (including effective incentives) of the decision-making individuals.[12] Last but not least, government regulation has come to be a conditioning factor of considerable importance in business leadership by, for example, discouraging the rise of new robber-baron practices. It would be most surprising if the institutional changes mentioned had not been accompanied by shifts in the motivation of business leadership and, indeed, in the whole pattern of doing business.

Business in America and in Europe

Actually American business has come to represent, in various respects, a specific pattern that has no equal in other countries though it is approximated in one or two. This applies, first, to its consumer-mindedness and service orientation, or perhaps we should say to its long-range approach to business practices; second, to the skilled managerial methods of its growing corporate empire; and, third, to the opportunity that is still left, despite the corporate growth, for entry into some kind of business—at least as long as there is prosperity and no major war occurs. In other words, although business in the sense of capitalist enterprise is by no means an American invention, America has come to be the seat of a very specific concept of business that is almost nonexistent today in the countries which are historically associated with the rise of capitalism. This difference has often been pointed out in a spirit of either uncritical glorification or unqualified disapproval; the purpose of this discussion is purely analytical.

It is unnecessary to restate here in any detail the sociohistorical roots of these differences: the quality of the immigrants, Puritan influences, the pioneer spirit, the melting pot, the wide-open spaces, the frontier, the natural resources, the protection and isolation by two oceans; and, on the other side of the Atlantic, the legacy of feudalism, absolutism, and guild restrictions, the narrow national frontiers, the overlapping century-old hostilities among populations, the cultural diversity, the scarcity and maldistribution of good land and many other resources, the assets and liabilities of colonialism, and so forth.

The eastward spread of capitalist business from England occurred

in most countries under vigorous encouragement by the governments
and heavy protection by private restrictive arrangements. Power, prestige, and emulation were important factors in the international location of industries. This whole process, however, was impeded, not only
by institutional barriers such as national frontiers and governments,
but by a diversity in cultural values which made "business" at Palermo
or Bucharest a very different proposition from "business" at Rotterdam
or Coventry. At the same time, the disintegration of feudal institutions
was seldom accompanied by an equally thorough discarding of the
feudal mentality. The depth of the psychological cleavages between
classes in Europe can in some degree be explained as an adaptation of
the predatory and oppressive features of feudalism to the new capitalist institutions—an adaptation far beyond the purely economic requirements of the upper class, especially after the initial phase of
capital accumulation was over. This applied particularly to certain
antilabor practices that persisted even if they impaired productivity
and profits.

The exploitive features of capitalism thus stood out nearly everywhere in Europe. These features occurred in varying degrees, of
course, though they were generally worse in eastern and southern
areas. European capitalism managed to arouse widespread hostility
toward its social order—a hostility that admittedly varied, in quality
and intensity, from country to country and, to some extent, from one
social group to another. In the United States, on the other hand, the
connotation given to the concept of capitalist business by the great
majority of all social groups remained affirmative. This means that in
Europe business has long been conducted in a far more defensive
and insecure atmosphere than it has in America, though American capitalism has not been completely free from such insecurity as will be
shown later.

These variations in background and atmosphere are bound to result
in attitudinal and motivational variations of great significance. Likewise, differences in the basic aims of business help to explain the
difficulties encountered until recently in establishing economic co-
operation among European nations. Such differences also help to
explain the impatience of American businessmen with the slowness
of their European colleagues in creating one big market based on high

standards of productivity and consumer service, even at some sacrifice of workmanship—in short, their failure to remake Europe promptly in the image of either the real America or an idealized one.

In France, for example, a very large sector of business is characterized by family connections. Typically, the *maison* represents the material basis for the prestige and status of the family. Conversely, the *maison* depends on the financial capacity and credit rating of the family and, therefore, has little desire to grow. It is an enterprise for limited objectives. The desire for protection of the family really underlies the stubborn clinging to governmental protection of business; competition and bigness have an immoral connotation. Moreover, French firms have to deal with extremely individualistic customers. American business concepts may be objectively superior to the French, but many of them would be completely lost on a population and business community with such different values.[13]

Such considerations apply in an even greater degree to the business concepts of large areas of eastern Asia, Latin America, and the Arab world. To many of them may be applied what *Fortune* magazine said about the European businessman: "Inwardly he knows of only one justification for being in business at all, namely, to get out of it—by accumulating as fast and as decisively as possible the sort of wealth that establishes status." [14] In America, being a businessman—or, at least, being a successful one—means status. In England it used to up to a certain point. In most other countries being wealthy (or else being in the government, in the aristocracy, or in the sciences and arts) may mean status, but business as such seldom does. Conversely politics, civil service, teaching, and the armed services in peacetime have traditionally meant low status in America. Typically only those who had too little initiative or ability to succeed in business were expected to go into these activities, although some changes in this attitude appear to have occurred in recent years.

Some of the things that have often been said about the "genuine" capitalism in North America as compared with the restrictive pseudo-capitalism in Europe and other parts of the world undoubtedly represent rationalizations, if not advertising stunts. The sixty years of uphill struggle to enforce American antitrust laws, the existence of price fixing and price leadership in American business, the socially protective function which some restrictive policies—both governmental and private—have had in wartorn Europe and in newly industrialized countries, all these facts should be considered in any criticism of the foreign business mentality from the American point of view. Few people will deny that business in America does not always live up to its official principles of competitiveness, service, and productivity.

Yet the difference is genuine. The fact that social mobility and, with it, economic opportunity are so much greater in America than in Europe admittedly has two sides: the self-assertion *and* the insecurity of the parvenu characterize the analogy in economic reality to the Horatio Alger story. The typical atmosphere in which the motivation of the American businessman originates is thus fundamentally different from the motivational setting of business in most other parts of the world, and research findings about the factors that make the American businessman tick are not necessarily applicable to his confreres abroad—or vice versa.

Who Is the Businessman?

But who exactly is "the businessman" in America? In order to avoid misleading generalizations it is necessary to distinguish carefully among the various types of economic activities that are summarized in the term business. It must be assumed as possible, at least, that the motivations and behavior patterns vary considerably according to the company setting, type of activity, and position of the individual concerned.

The total number of operating business firms in the continental United States at the end of 1957 was 4,323,000, considerably more than in 1944 when it was 3,022,200. Of the 1957 total, the distribution of firms was as follows: contract construction 487,000; manufacturing 309,000; wholesale trade 302,000; retail trade 1,879,000; service industries 768,000; all other 578,000. The annual rates of entrance and discontinuance have hovered in recent years around 8 or 9 per cent.[15] The greatest numbers of business units, largely small ones, exist in retailing, the service trades, and construction; and the annual turnover rate represents close to one firm in eleven for the business community as a whole. Within this figure, there must be a constant coming and going on the level of small independent proprietors along with relative stability among large corporations; but there must also be a sizable turnover of managing business personnel in the corporations, which, of course, does not show up in these figures. In short, an unknown but sizable proportion of persons usually classified as businessmen does business in a changing or unstable setting, and the dividing line between businessmen and other people is not a rigid one.

This is also true for other reasons. There is wide agreement on the owner-manager as representative of the classic type of businessman, though far too little is known on the exact relationship between the consumer role and the business role in unincorporated or family-type enterprises. It is also pretty generally accepted that the top executives of a corporation should be included in the concept of businessman. There is less certainty concerning members of a board of directors, and considerable doubt concerning divisional or departmental managers, supervisors, and, especially, farmers.

There is clearly some element of business activity in the functions of all these groups, but additional factors enter the picture in each case, such as the close family link of farming and, for that matter, of some types of urban small business. American farmers, in particular, differ significantly from European or Asian peasants. For the latter, land represents status, security, and native culture in an incomparably stronger degree than for the former. The peasants' identification with business activity is weak; often there is a feeling that peasants are the mainstay of social and economic life while other people are more or less parasitic.

It is quite possible, we repeat, that the various groups that are partly or wholly associated with business are motivated differently in their market behavior, which thus cannot be expected to be standardized. Such qualifications apply in an even greater degree to various fringe groups. One of these groups consists of members of the profession—lawyers, physicians, accountants, consulting engineers. Although professions are largely thought of here as special ways to do business for profit (much more definitely so in the United States than in Europe), some special codes and motive patterns obtain. Another such group consists of parttime businessmen: workers or teachers who utilize their leisure time to do business as mechanics, electricians, carpenters, farmers, motel owners, or salesmen. Even greater qualifications apply to such quasi-business activities as the management of cooperatives, some types of business unionism, and the management of autonomous government enterprises.

Last but not least is the stockholder. If he holds a purely inactive ownership interest in a corporation, is he a businessman in a sense or not? If so, at what level or proportion of stock ownership does this role begin? A study by the Brookings Institution [16] came to the conclusion that in 1951 there were 6,490,000 individuals belonging to 4,750,000 family spending units who owned shares in publicly available stocks. Approximately one of every sixteen adult persons owned shares in one or more stock issues, and there were one or more share owners in one-tenth of all families. In addition, owners of privately held issues were estimated at 3,000,000 in 2,300,000 families. The 6,490,000 owning public stocks accounted for 30,300,000 shareholdings, which means that the average stockholder held shares in four or five companies. Men slightly outnumbered women and tended to have larger holdings. The proportion of shareholders in the various age groups rose with age up to sixty years. Educational and income levels were related to the incidence of share ownership. Some 76 per cent of all shareholders belonged to family units earning less than $10,000 a year, but this proportion does not, of course, express the relative importance of their holdings as compared to the large holdings in the upper income groups despite the latter's small share in the total population.

Finally, the proportion of share ownership was highest among administrative executives (45 per cent) and operating supervisory officials (19 per cent); but this also means that even among managerial personnel the majority did not own stocks. Among the professed motives for the acquisition of stocks, desire for profit-value appreciation ranked first (28 per cent); income from dividend yield followed with 22 per cent; 20 per cent had inherited their stocks or acquired them as a gift, and 10 per cent had just followed the advice of their brokers or attorneys.

These figures would seem to imply a warning against uncritical identification of stock ownership as such with activity in business. Another possible approach to circumscribing business is a look at personal characteristics of the business population. Data from the 1958 Survey of Consumer Finances indicate a certain correlation between business ownership and high income groups, but even so the majority of persons in the high-income brackets do not own or co-own business. As an economic group businessmen, both self-employed and managerial, are certainly better off than other groups, but this advantage has been somewhat reduced by postwar developments. There are indications of considerable differences between the self-employed and managerial groups in evaluating individual financial situation and income outlook.

Evidently the concept of business includes activities and units of a widely varying character, which all meet on the market in different positions and with different driving forces. "The firm" thus means a varying pattern or combination of interpersonal relations—among its personnel as well as between the latter and the suppliers, customers, and competitors. The internal structure of the firm represents an endless variety of patterns of hierarchy, delegation, responsibility, authority, control, communication, organization, specialization, "channels," bureaucracy, with all their advantages and drawbacks. From another angle, the firm represents a varying combination of sociocultural and interpersonal processes, in which dominance, dependence, role expectations, isolation, anxiety, status rivalry, co-operation, processes for handling stress (including the picking of scapegoats), and change mechanisms are especially important. These processes have been rather widely explored and need only be mentioned here.[17]

Historical developments have diversified the firm in the sense that many business units are still carried on with the same setup and motivation that prevailed in past decades or centuries, while others have established entirely new forms of organization and motivation. Generally speaking, there has been a tremendous growth of "organization" in business no less than in political or social life. This organizational growth has tended to meet certain emotional needs (for example, some of those for security and self-assertion, respectively) while creating some new ones, such as those arising from conflicts of loyalties or from the impersonal character of big organizations. This process has also tended to diversify and complicate some important areas of business decision making, such as decisions whether or not to start or expand an enterprise; to reduce or discontinue it; to let personal or family factors overrule purely financial considerations in running a business; to emphasize liquidity and self-financing; to keep adjusting the technological and managerial organization of the firm; to run labor relations in an authoritarian way; to adopt novel pricing, production, and marketing policies; to emphasize nonprice factors; and so forth. The complexity of such decision making and the diversity of decision patterns according to the type of firm and management have been almost steadily increasing.[18]

The effects of historical changes in the pattern of competition have been similar. It has been pointed out already that the structure of American business ranges all the way from the one-man store to the "private socialism" of giant corporations. We need not be concerned here with the moot question whether big business is getting bigger all the time or whether it just remains about as big as it grew to be some time in the past.[19] The interesting thing is that the business community today appears to be characterized by a peculiar dichotomy of solidarity and conflict at the same time.

These limits of identification within the business community emphasize the motivational innovations which the rise of the big corporation has brought into economic life. The old-time small enterprise shows none of the complexity of a corporate structure in which business may be done, in one way or another, by the board of directors or, at least, its chairman; the stockholders; organized interests such as customers, suppliers, consultants, underwriters and lenders, labor, and government agencies to the extent that they influence the conduct of business in the company; and, last but not least, the executive management from the president down through an elaborate hierarchy to the level of the supervisor if not the foreman.

Executive management has increasingly come to represent a professionalized leadership group. Initiative plus capital resources or credit rating suffices less and less to start or run a big enterprise; the expert with administrative, technological, or financial training (or some combination of these qualities) is taking over. The differences in personality and background between the first, second, and third generation of corporation presidents in some of the great automobile companies illustrate this change.

The attitude of a hired executive toward the corporation is likely to differ in quality from that of a business owner toward "his" firm. The financial incentives involved are, on the whole, expressed in terms of salary and perhaps bonus, not in terms of profit. The nonfinancial incentives include such elements as power, prestige, emulation, creative urge, group identification and loyalty, security needs, and service, in degrees or combinations which differ from those that prevail among the older business types.

Personal ambitions become transmuted into a powerful desire to serve the business enterprise itself as an independent and living entity. . . . The owner-enterpriser may be more willing to gamble his own money than the chief executive of a great corporation may be to jeopardize the financial empire of which he is trustee. The goal of business leadership is still profit-*making* but not profit-*receiving*.[20]

There are some indications that executive management tends to be less daring and more cautious in its business policy than were the great individual enterprisers of the past, and that it is also characterized by greater conservatism in its social and political attitudes than the owner-manager group, but these indications remain to be tested. Certainly the growing influence of the executive group in the councils of business organizations has been accompanied by such effects. In other words, the new business leadership is apparently both more expert and more conservative than the older one. Internally, executives often feel under pressure to justify continuously their presence and function in the company while the business-owner can adopt a self-purpose attitude toward his company: *L'état, c'est moi!* At the same time, the sense of belonging to a great organization may lead executives to identification processes that are absent in older-type enterprises for anyone but the owner.

"The decay of entrepreneurial faculties," which Alfred Marshall deplored long ago as a result of the growth of firms,[21] largely represents the emergence of a new motivational structure, for better or worse, along with a wide survival of the old one within the same national economy. It is true that some of the big corporate enterprises have grown out of the ranks of small family units (Henry Ford could be cited as an example), but this has by no means been the general rule, especially in recent years. Certainly the supply of large corporations is relatively inelastic compared with that of owner-manager units. Thus far, at any rate, we have been facing a mixed structure of private business types ranging all the way from the grocer at the corner to General Motors. With it goes a mixed motivational structure in which big corporations and the new system of executive management occupy an extremely important and leading role.

The communication problems, working pressures, and hierarchic self-assertion patterns of the new managerial type have been widely discussed. Oswald W. Knauth claims that we face an actual change from free to managerial enterprise, the latter being "a system of production and distribution, unified by policies and controlled by managers, whose main idea is to administer the business that concerns them in the interest of continuity. . . . What has hitherto been deemed eminently proper and ethical now subjects them to unexpected criticism and opprobrium." Continuity of both demand and operation has now become by far the main driving force of business management. Johannes Alasco, on the other hand, sees managerial enterprise too on its way out and believes that the newest type of private enterprise is based on immaterial, intellectual assets.[22]

Regardless of whether or not one wishes to accept any of these theories, the recent development of corporate business and its executive management, along with a wide survival of older business forms and mentalities, requires a restatement of the entire question (which was raised in the Introduction under 1) of effective personal reasons for doing business.

Why People Want to Do Business

The traditional answer to the question why people want to do business (whenever any such question was raised) has, of course, been profit. This answer, needless to say, continues to receive much credit today. But a good many people begin to feel that it really is not much of an answer. This is true even if we disregard, for the purpose of this discussion, the basic conceptual differences between the meanings of profit in economic theory, in accounting, and in business practice. Strictly speaking though, a distinction should be drawn among profit goals as a guide for policy decisions, profit measurement from accounting data, and profits as a control device in a complex business structure.

The purpose of managerial activity today, insofar as it concerns corporations, clearly is no longer to assure profit for the managers except possibly in the indirect and almost incidental sense of bonuses. The corporation executive is in business in order to make profit all right, but not for himself. Moreover, even the profit drive of the corporation as a whole is sometimes neglected over considerable periods in the interest of its continuity, security, or standing, for the corporation is assumed to outlive any of its executives and, indeed, to be potentially permanent.

Both the owner-manager and the corporate executive are now widely assumed to pursue profit—to the extent that they do so in their actual behavior—not as a self-purpose (that is, in order to keep increasing the living standards and reserve funds of their families) but as a symbol of other goals, at least after reaching a rather moderate level of income and assets. Ever since Thorstein Veblen there has been frequent discussion of the real motives behind profit, a discussion which has now become rather common in business literature, too. To quote one example, *Fortune* magazine some years back arrived at the conclusion that

money is no longer a prime incentive in getting a good day's work out of the boss. . . . What is happening today is that the bosses of business (i.e., those high-class hired hands like presidents, vice-presidents, treasurers, and division heads) are in the confused process of discovering for themselves what the experimental psychologists and a number of sages have known for a long time: money isn't everything. . . . The executive is now more of a trapped man than a free one. He is trapped by a sense of duty to his job and loyalty to his associates. But he is also trapped by his own feelings of insecurity, for curiously enough he is one of the most vulnerable of the beasts in the corporate zoo.

What he really wants these days along with his employees, *Fortune* concludes on the basis of surveys by Elmo Roper, is security, and he believes that it is to be had out of the following ingredients:

1. recognition of achievement, 2. dignity of position, 3. autonomy of management, 4. rewards paid in leisure. Nothing is said here about money *at all*.[23]

It is doubtful whether the competitive profit drive of business enterprise ever expressed a gambling impulse chiefly, as has been asserted. If any such impulse existed, it has been outpaced in our contemporary economy by other motives. It would be foolish, we repeat, to deny the potency of profit orientation, especially in owner-management, as the *first* line of incentive on the conscious level. Evidence, however, has been increasing that profit, for an individual or for a company, is actually sought for two interrelated reasons: first, as an intervening or indirect expression of the various forms of personal assertion, such as prestige, power, and status; and, second, as a path to expected financial security, which, in turn, often symbolizes personal security. In other words, if the needs of the persons concerned for status and security were taken care of in some other way, much of the supposed profit drive would promptly disappear once a certain minimum level of income and assets had been reached.

Both friends and foes of private business have often overrated or misinterpreted the role of profit maximization, especially in the short run. "Both apologists and critics of capitalism have assumed the political genius of the businessman. A Marxist or perhaps pseudo-Marxist myth, indeed, glorifies the capitalist with particular assiduity, portraying a demonic figure of infinite calculation and ruthlessness, committed to the pitiless destruction of every obstacle to the maximization of profits." [24] Veblen, on the other hand, discerned some "sentimental factors in business" but regarded them as aberrations which no enterprise could afford very long, and which in any case were unlikely to happen among industry captains of the first class.[25] What is pictured in one camp as the mortal sin of the businessman is considered his great historic contribution in the other; but although some examples of reckless profit drive and, indeed, the spirit of a whole period could be quoted from history in support of such theories, any generalization or uncritical application of these cases to our own period would be unrealistic.

Why then do people go into business and what do they expect from it? To begin with, for some of those who went into business—either as owner-managers or as executives—this was not a decision of their own volition. Sometimes the decision was largely made for them by parents or circumstances; an unemployed person, for example, may see no other way out but to start a business of his own with his last savings or on credit, although he would much prefer to be employed by someone else. Even in these cases, it is true, personality factors enter into the picture: any number of young men and women did not let their parents or anyone else make the occupational decision for them, and many an unemployed would never think of starting a business of his own under any circumstances.

If we count out for the purpose of this discussion, however, all those whose decision to enter business was not entirely their own, the underlying motives of persons who enter into it and stay in it might be summarized as follows: status desires including considerations of power, prestige, and emulation; personal assertion in a more direct sense including creative urge and security needs; group identification, loyalty, and service. Generally speaking, personal success in business appears to be of far greater importance to the executive group than immediate rewards in money. The only people who are directly and chiefly motivated by short-run profit expectation are the stockholders. For them profit is ordinarily neither a measure of personal self-assertion nor one of group cohesion and usefulness in any considerable degree. It is true that management endeavors to organize shareholders into a well-knit body of opinion and policy as indicated by corporation letters and publicity materials.

At any rate, the widespread and quasi-official assumption among businessmen that it is profit that really makes themselves and the national economy tick need not be taken at its face value. The very emotion that, in North America, is often attached to the profit concept and, with it, to the idea of free enterprise is suggestive of more powerful driving forces that such concepts conceal. In particular, corporate business policy can only be understood in terms of identification on the part of executives with "the company," rather than with the stockholders. Success of the company—its solvency, its profitability and, especially, its expansion almost for its own sake—becomes a measure of the success of its management. "Fear of loss, not profit, dominates the business complex," according to Chester I. Barnard, former president of the Rockefeller Foundation and of the New Jersey Bell Telephone Company, who also contributes the following conclusion from his long business experience:

My observation in several different well-managed businesses convinces me that business decisions are constantly being made that are not based upon economic motives. This is something that businessmen seldom admit, and of which they are frequently unaware. Prestige, competitive reputation, social philosophy, social standing, philanthropic interests, combativeness, love of intrigue, dislike of friction, technical interest, Napoleonic dreams, love of accomplishing useful things, desire for regard of employees, love of publicity, fear of publicity—a long catalogue of non-economic motives actually condition the management of business and nothing but the balance sheet keeps these non-economic motives from running wild.[26]

Others, however, have attempted to formulate a related proposition in terms of a profit orientation of companies, which is claimed to be quite independent from the very different motives of the individuals who run them. It is argued that corporations are profit-guided even if individuals are not and that this improves the case for corporations as the most rational form of business.[27] But even assuming strong identification of managers with the company, do individuals necessarily behave more "rationally" in an executive role than they do in other situations? Does the organizational setup of a corporation always provide strong mutual checks against nonrational behavior, however defined specifically; or might it not bring in new emotional elements, such as status fights within the corporate hierarchy or intracompany rivalry among departments, with strong subgroup identifications? On the other hand, while identification either with a department or with the company as such may be strong at a given moment, such group membership is voluntary on the whole and may sometime be exchanged for another.

In general, can we really take it for granted that business corporations do not keep their wheels running unless it is for short-run profit, even while owner-managed companies next door may undergo distracting nonprofit influences? In an interview, Henry Ford II pointed out that turning over 95 per cent of the nonvoting stock of the Ford Motor Company to the Ford Foundation had not brought any change in incentives either for him or for his executive staff. "I don't think we ever consider that we are working directly for the Foundation. We consider we are working against our competition in the industry. . . . There isn't a great deal of difference, I suppose, in the fact that we work 90 percent for an institution and somebody else works for a million or two stockholders." [28] *

What such evidence boils down to is this: companies, in the last analysis, are run by individuals, and individuals cannot and do not change their personality completely even when they join other functionally related individuals in an executive group after 9:00 A.M. Only during a short period of Western economic history, when profit making dominated the thinking and emotions of some individuals day and night, was the conduct of firms sometimes guided by profit expectations of a direct, short-run type on the part of the owner-manager; profit making was then almost uninhibited by public restrictions, but this fact did not necessarily make for realism in those expectations.

* Reprinted from copyrighted material in the *U.S. News and World Report,* an independent weekly news magazine published at Washington.

In the modern large corporation, an interesting dichotomy takes place. On the one hand, company profit becomes a matter of quasi-scientific calculation which occupies the executive during office hours in a professional way as a functional assignment for which he is paid a salary; on the other hand, this same company profit tends to lose for him all personal meaning and involvement but one—as an indirect yardstick of personal performance, assertion, and group status. Even in this capacity it is often displaced by the yardstick of production and sales volume in comparison with other companies during prosperous times, and by the yardstick of successful entrenchment and survival in times of crisis.[29]

The reactions of consumers, employees, and stockholders have also increased in their importance as a standard of company success, and the special goals and yardsticks of company departments have come to provide intervening measures of success and satisfaction. Sometimes, of course, it is not easy to draw the exact line between advertising devices, rationalizations, and genuine standards of production, consumer satisfaction, and public service.[30]

It is interesting to note that in the judgment of some anthropologists this whole mechanism and symbolism of material success in our present-day economy, while unique in some respects, has certain parallels in other forms of society. "Most societies have a dual economy, one for the satisfaction of material needs, and one that is directed toward satisfying the desire for prestige. The *prestige economy* can only operate where the mechanisms of production provide more than is needed for the fulfillment of the requirements of living." [31]

The distinguishing trait of our economy appears to lie in a degree of productive power that has removed to the background the physical problem of satisfying the basic material needs; our economic arrangements have thus opened up competition for social status as symbolized by further material success. To put it in another way, material success has been rationalized into social values. In the judgment of a British student of American ways, "what the American admires in wealth is achievement, success in a game in which all are playing and whose rules are reasonably fair. . . . Americans admire their rich for the energies that made them rich." [32] In a somewhat similar vein, the Lynds wrote thirty-odd years ago, "This whole complexity of doing day after day fortuitously assigned things, chiefly at the behest of other people, has in the main to be strained through a pecuniary sieve before it assumes vital meaning." [33]

All this, however, is undoubtedly far more true of some people than of others. Is it then emphatic ability and urge to translate personal needs into money standards that make for success in business? Or what other factors of personality, if any in particular, are conducive to the entry of an individual into business followed by successful performance in it?

Personality and Business Success

It is, of course, quite possible to assert that initially, at least, people get into business activities by accident, as one way among many to provide the necessities of life for themselves and their families, or by some sort of external circumstance such as economic pressure without any other way out. This assertion implies that business as a social group represents a cross section of nearly all the conceivable types of personality. In the absence of any conclusive sampling of the group of persons concerned, it is impossible to disprove this assumption or to prove the opposite one. In the light of available studies of personality, however, any such cross-section hypothesis would seem rather improbable and deficient.

The next question then is whether we should assume certain innate or inherited qualities that make a person go into business and succeed. Sombart appears to assume such an effect of *Veranlagung*, a capitalist disposition which varies in incidence from nation to nation (*Bourgeoisnaturen*). Similarly Taussig and Joslyn, unimpressed by their own finding in the early thirties that "the proportion of respondents having fathers who were businessmen of one kind or another (owners or executives) is no less than 56.7 per cent" concluded that business showed no strong tendency toward castelike inbreeding as no specific positions were handed down typically from father to son, and that fundamental inequality of native endowment, rather than privilege, accounted for the fact that 10 per cent of the population produced 70 per cent of business leaders.[34]

Such theories, however, look rather outmoded today. To begin with, personality formation is now in large part attributed to developmental factors, especially family influences during early childhood, which affect, in particular, the future level of aspiration. Further, in order to be illuminating any explanation of successful business personalities would have to consider the total personality structure concerned.

No potential capacity or trait of an individual operates in isolation. They function in interaction with the environment (physical and cultural) during the process of the individual's strivings to adapt himself successfully to the life conditions around him. Under the specific requirements of his environment, certain of his capacities and traits are sharpened to the fullest, certain others are barely called on to function, still others remain untapped.[35]

If we assume that the decisive standards in evaluating a personality are supplied, not by behavioral but by character traits, Erich Fromm's categories would seem to be of considerable help in this discussion. He sees the fundamental basis of character in the specific ways in which a person relates himself to the world in the process of living—first, by acquiring and assimilating things and, second, by relating himself to people (and himself). On this basis, productive orientations in the broadest sense are differentiated from nonproductive ones. The latter include the purely receptive, the exploitative, the hoarding, and the marketing orientations. This last concept implicitly includes putting your own personality on sale too. The productive orientations, on the other hand, are characterized by a man's ability to realize the potentialities that are inherent in him and to be guided by responsibility and reason as distinguished from mere intelligence.[36]

Even if these categories, or some of them, should not be considered completely distinctive, they would seem to have wide applications to the relation between personality traits and business success. According to the specific phase of capitalist development, different requirements or opportunities for an exploitative, hoarding, marketing, or productive character come to the fore in each country and period. These psychological orientations are not identical with strictly economic ones; they overlap them. Roughly speaking, however, the period of initial accumulation offers great opportunities to a combination of exploitative and hoarding traits; the period of commercial capitalism supplies a wide field for the marketing personality; and the rise of industrialism offers new opportunities for some kinds of productive orientation. In our own period, with its greatly developed mechanisms of finance, capital formation, marketing, and production, there is room, in varying and constantly changing degrees, for several of these orientations.

The incidence of these various types in a given period is, however, not purely accidental. In some degree the cultural, institutional, and motivational setting of a given society fosters the appearance of specific kinds of personality. Sometimes the incidence of the kinds that a society helps to create may be out of tune with its personality requirements; for example, the frequency of exploitative characters may be in excess of the objective opportunities offered to them. In any such case the society concerned is likely to incur serious trouble sooner or later.

To come back to the more specific problem of business personality in our period, the requirements have been changing with the institutional setup and have also become more diversified historically than they used to be. In earlier stages of capitalism unqualified optimism, as a general attitude, was necessary in order to induce a person to enter venturesome enterprises; and almost any enterprise was venturesome at first. Today a flexible attitude that emphasizes optimism at some times and pessimism at others is of far greater economic promise. Under early capitalism an authoritarian disposition was required in order effectively to run a shop with illiterate semislaves; today a democratic, conciliatory, or matter-of-fact character is often far more conducive to success. Similarly, the thrifty type was favored at one time, the easy-spending type at another, and today a flexible attitude toward saving and investment may promise the best results. Incidentally, it is up to the orthodox Freudians to express related personality problems in terms of oral and anal types if they wish; certainly, however, the opinion I have heard expressed that capitalist business breeds or, at least, rewards narcissism is a gross overstatement in the absence of many historical and other qualifications.

The American economy today, we repeat, offers varying opportunities to more than one kind of personality. Since conclusive data are lacking thus far, we can only raise the question whether new business fields such as electronics or nuclear power tend to attract persons with high-aspiration tensions and the restless initiative that goes with them; on the other hand, railroads, banks, and established family businesses of all kinds may lure the conservative, low-aspiration, or conformist types to the extent that somebody (or something) has pushed them into business activities in general. Some kinds of positions in corporate management hold special attractions or rewards for people with organizational gifts and interests. Still other business roles attract or reward independence, ambition, capacity for adaptation, keen time perception, calculation and combination gifts, consistency, capacity for planning or decision making, or else conformity and routine. In many cases, the relation between the type of activity or position and the degree of authoritarian attitude would be very illuminating to explore. What really matters today, at any rate, is not so much who goes into business in general but what kind of business he goes into, what role he assumes or achieves, and how he carries it out.

More particularly, the exact meaning of business success in our society needs some further discussion. Assuming that business success is characterized by some combination of large income and high-ranking position or status, allowance must, of course, be made for external circumstances that may have had a causative or, at least, a conditioning effect upon it. We do not mean the famous "accidents" or "luck" which some people deem so decisive in personal achievement. Accidents are not lucky unless the personality concerned lends itself to the best use of opportunities offered. Even so, such objective conditions as business fluctuations, wars, or natural events obviously are of great importance; in a prolonged, structural depression, for example, chances for successful innovations are very slim no matter how much ingenuity and initiative a person shows. Further, the degree of appreciation that ingenuity and initiative receive varies greatly according to the culture and institutions concerned. The fellow who wants to introduce sweeping innovations—no matter how useful from any "objective" point of view—in an essentially conservative society will fail disastrously. So will a man who is driven by a reckless urge for self-assertion which was socially rewarded yesterday but no longer is today.

If allowance is made for such qualifications, a variety of personal traits, though by no means a cross section, appears to be conducive to business success in our period whenever the personality concerned is channeled into the right type of business activity.[37] On the level of corporate management, it appears that an organized, rather than a reckless, drive for self-assertion, in combination with rather compulsive work attitudes and work concentration, has led to success in many cases, though this was sometimes achieved at a high cost in terms of personal and family happiness. In recent years, there has been a growing demand for prolonged executive training, expressed in the statement of a student of business administration "You can't afford to work for money." The standardizing effect of business schools and clubs is likewise affecting the personality requirements for a successful business career.

Family influences in shaping the choice and management of a business career on the part of a given person have been studied in many individual cases, but sufficient data for foolproof generalizations appear to be lacking. There is clearly an unusual, though often overstated, degree of social mobility in American society. The frequent desire of parents for their children to be better off than they are is likely to have a considerable effect upon the aspiration tensions of children. To some extent such parental attitudes reflect either fear of economic instability or family ambition for higher status. Depending upon other formative factors, they may lead either to objectively unwarranted identification of the children with upper classes, along with a frantic desire for business success, or else to idle emulation of upperclass habits.

Such attitudes may sometimes result in an association of outward success with a reward from above for being a good boy, or else, where the parental influence is emotionally upsetting, in a nonconscious fear of success which may result in business failure. The question has been raised whether (or in what sense) an individual must have braved full socialization during the crucial childhood years in order to qualify for success and leadership in business, and perhaps in other spheres of social life.

All this, of course, is not easily compatible with the folklore, à la Horatio Alger, of the diligent, smart, thrifty newsboy (almost any such newsboy) rising to a corporation presidency. It is precisely this decision to be a good boy and the ability to carry it out, which conceal some basic factors of personality that are involved. A good many people who had made the same decision, or who on the conscious level thought they had, failed miserably even when objective economic conditions were favorable. There is also considerable evidence of a self-perpetuation of business-elite families, not only through a financial push but through "inheritance" of aspiration levels.[38] At the same time, the *formation* of families in the business-leadership group—and thus, indirectly, the aspiration level of children—have been influenced by the social valuation given to business success. What the Germans call *Einheirat* (marrying "into") has been widely practiced not only in their country (in the Krupp family, for instance) but in England and in the United States. Successful or promising executives may thus hope to be "adopted" by patrician business families, though this hope may be disappointed in many individual cases.

An ample supply of life stories of successful businessmen offers a wealth of information on this subject—admittedly in a very uneven and inconclusive way as the stories represent different periods, opportunity situations, and personality requirements, quite aside from differences in presentation. So much is certain—the concept of and path to business success have greatly changed. Bernard Baruch, the philanthropist, at the age of eighty summarized his life experience by saying that it is tougher today to make a million than when he was twenty. "I think that today a man has to be more exceptional to make a fortune. . . . You've got to make up your mind what you want to do. If you want to make money, you've got to go into the money-making business. You can't make money and do something else, too." [39]

Andrew Carnegie offers another outstanding example of a successful businessman who gave much of his money away. Here is some of the explanation in his own words: "When you ask me what business really means, I would begin by saying that the root of business must always be service to the community. . . . Dollar making is not necessarily business." "A man must get money before he can give it—isn't that self-evident? He must be egoistic before he is altruistic." Business to him personally has been "the means to an end—nothing more." A businessman, Carnegie adds, must have an all-around judgment based upon knowledge of many subjects; he must be an excellent judge of men, must know how to bring the best out of various characters, must have the gift of organization, and must be able to decide promptly and wisely. "The dividend which the businessman seeks and receives today is not alone in dollars. He receives with the dollars something better—a dividend in the shape of satisfaction in being instrumental in carrying forward to higher stages of development the business which he makes his life work." He defines "the business career as one in which there is abundant room for the exercise of man's highest power and of every good quality in human nature. . . . No man ever saw a foolish businessman successful. . . . If a young man does not find romance in his business it is not the fault of his business, but the fault of the young man." [40] Allowing for rationalizations and wishful thinking, these are revealing passages regarding the motivation of one of the most successful money-makers of all times.

Pierpont Morgan stood as a symbol of personal power through money, economic royalism, reticent aloofness, and perhaps megalomania, combined with an orderly, tidy mind, a passion for organization —he was the great private planner of his period—traditionalism, and a conspicuous lack of intellectual interest or understanding. His value system emphasized "character," by which he meant reliability, loyalty, and personal responsibility.[41] We know little about the influences that shaped his personality, but it is unlikely that his traits would have been conducive to any comparable success a hundred years earlier or, for that matter, fifty years later.

The literature about Henry Ford fills several library shelves. It ranges all the way from slick uncritical glorification to the great-villain approach. His famulus, Harry Bennett, pictures him as an entirely authoritarian, conceited, touchy, and superstitious person with some psychopathic traits; but Bennett's story is primarily designed to exculpate its author. The picture of Ford that emerges from the various sources of evidence is very complex and contradictory. A very friendly biographer passes this judgment on him and his son Edsel: "The elder Ford was an industrial autocrat, the younger a democrat. One was gentle and liked people, made friends and held them; the other could be as hard as his forgings and distrusted friendship as a general proposition. He allowed himself few." [42]

Henry Ford's autobiography is a very revealing document, which rambles over the whole range of human experience and problems and offers saintly homespun prescriptions for nearly everything. The record of his life shows that, while he lived up to many of the industrial principles he preached, this applied in a far lesser degree to other spheres of life. He despised money as the goal of business; it was service that mattered. However, "a man ought to be able to live on a scale commensurate with the service he renders" (p. 11). "Money comes naturally as the result of service. And it is absolutely necessary to have money. But we do not want to forget that the end of money is not ease but the opportunity to perform more service" (p. 13). Such service is to be guided by an absence of fear of the future and an absence of veneration for the past; a disregard of competition—"Whoever does a thing best ought to be the one to do it"; the putting of service before profit; and a ban on gambling, speculation, and sharp dealing.

In shaping his personality, the experience of a country boy in the sixties was very important; he felt strongly that "there was too much hard hand labor on our own and all other farms of the time" (p. 22). From the beginning he preferred tinkering with any kind of machinery to becoming a farmer as his father wanted him to. The creative urge in a direct, tangible sense was certainly an important trait of his personality; he remained full of an empirical, nonintellectual kind of curiosity throughout his life. Other traits which his friends, enemies, and biographers have often emphasized were daring, ambition, energy, capacity to concentrate on one production problem at a time along with a dilettante involvement in all sorts of nonindustrial problems, an iron will, and last, but not least, a keen sense for the needs and likings of consumers in his period.

His strong authoritarian power-drive was accompanied by a certain shyness and awkwardness in social affairs. His rigidly paternal attitude toward labor, which led him to a ruthless (and at times quite costly) drive against unions, was part of the same picture. So was his propensity for picking a scapegoat, which affected at different times the Jews, the newspapers, Wall Street, the politicians, and various individuals. His frequent appeals to folksy simplicity and sentimental traditionalism have a phoney air about them, especially in the light of his own life practice. They reflect an attempt to flee from a social reality which had brought him much success and yet did not really satisfy him.

This escapism is confirmed by various eccentric attempts such as the famous Peace Ship in 1915. His pacifism did not prevent him from engaging in a profitable production of arms, for the popular claim that he had renounced all profit on such production was apparently a myth. A deep guilt feeling must have disturbed his enjoyment of the new industrial civilization that he had helped to establish and of his own creative achievement and personal success in this process. That basic insecurity also led him to surprisingly unrealistic and inconsistent attitudes, of which his affinity for criminals was not the least. How could a moral preacher of his type reconcile such policies with his principles unless he was capable of rationalization in a near-pathological degree?

The question whether these mental qualities were conducive to outstanding business success in the early part of this century or whether we are faced with a mere coincidence cannot be decided here. Certainly these personality traits did not prevent his success and his becoming something of a folk hero. We have noted already the enormous difference in personality between Ford and his only child Edsel, whom Henry kept subdued all his life.

In the last two generations of Fords the choice of a business career has occurred in a way entirely different from that of Ford, Senior. It was, in fact, made by the family setting and the overwhelming authority of the founder of the dynasty, neither presumably meeting any great resistance. The second and third generations, moreover, grew up in a period which no longer encouraged the great individualistic innovator with strong elbows and which came to endorse social insurance, labor legislation, and public policy designed to cushion economic fluctuations. Business requirements favor different personality types today from those of sixty years ago, and persons who embark on a business career simply because they have no other predilections and because the family situation seems to point to such a course, are likely to react, behave, and succeed differently from the way in which they would have in that earlier period.

These few examples of outstanding business careers do not, of course, permit any generalizations on the personality factors that are involved in achieving business leadership. The examples are merely designed to emphasize the differences in the personality traits that are required or, at least, tolerated by each phase of business practice, institutional framework, and socioeconomic philosophy. In a period of increasing demand for expert executive training and streamlined efficiency, the whims of great captains of industry or finance, no matter how ingenious they may be, appear to promise far more rarely "success" in terms of money or status than they did around the turn of the century; for at that time America had just undergone its classic wave of industrialization and the frontier was just being changed from a geographic to an economic concept.

Although all the opportunities for young Carnegies, Morgans, or Fords may not have disappeared today, they have become scarce and are subject to greatly increased restraints from public regulation and changed mores alike. It is the executive type that now commands the greatest market. Its personal traits usually include organizational ability and interest; the kind and amount of security needs that make for ambition and somewhat compulsive work without involving neurotic tension; a propensity to feel and, in a way, to seek pressure (for "being busy" is to represent a *raison d'être* both for the man and for his company); recognition of profit as the standard of achievement without any great *personal* drive for profit, all the business energies thus being channeled into company profit; conservatism in the sense of single-mindedness on the job and of social conformity, but not in a technological or administrative sense; ability to make other people work effectively, either by persuasion or by genuine authority; the gift to avoid unnecessary antagonism as a result of domineering, avaricious, unfair, or immature behavior; and the ability to believe that he always performs a service of social utility, or to rationalize himself into such belief if necessary.

Quite often executive functions, including top-level jobs, emphasize or require some special talent in engineering, marketing, financial, or administrative performance even though such specialization may have been achieved at the expense of other fields. The real business leader, on the other hand, is characterized by generalized ability even though his chief training may have been in a special field. Such over-all ability of the leadership type, however, is much rarer than many people assume, and it is more rarely a result of business activity as such. Most people who have achieved an outstanding performance both as business leaders and then as government servants or community leaders have been persons of high intelligence, integration, and responsibility who probably would have done just as well on their various jobs in the opposite sequence. This, in fact, has also occurred repeatedly. We are, of course, speaking here of genuine personal endowment and not of contacts and pulls resulting from an earlier career in a different field.[43] Some variety of such endowment is essential for business success even when the objective situation favors such success.

Creative Urge, Salesmanship, and Personal Needs

Within the range of personal propensity for business success in general, however, an important distinction should be drawn between basic creativeness and salesmanship, which represent different structures and needs of personality. Hitler's famous if demagogic distinction between *schaffendes und raffendes Kapital* (creative versus acquisitive capital) has somewhat discredited the many attempts, both before and after, to distinguish among various types of business according to the motivational and personality factors involved. Many years ago, when psychology was dominated by instinct concepts, F. W. Taussig discussed an "instinct of contrivance," a distant relative of Veblen's instinct of workmanship.[44] The instinct of contrivance was thought to be present in everybody, but it was assumed to be developed in an exceptional degree in some persons in whom it far outdid any considerations of pecuniary success. It was thought of as paralleled by an "instinct of construction" that sometimes led to a "building mania." "The wish for additional wealth," said Taussig, "so far as it appears at all, is a most complex psychological phenomenon, the resultant of a number of instincts or dispositions, of which the possessor himself is only half conscious." "The business man whose competitor has been ruined will subscribe most willingly and liberally for the support and comfort of a bankrupt rival."

Although we have become quite wary today regarding inborn human instincts, there remains the problem of just what personality traits are conducive to a person's going either into the producing and organizing end, or into the marketing and financing end, of business activities. Chester I. Barnard claims that the main difference is in the comparative amount of logical and nonlogical processes required,[45] but this does not sound like a full explanation.

We are more likely to approach the solution if we realize the impact of a creative urge in certain kinds of personality: activity frustrations manage to avoid outlets of destructive aggression either toward others or toward the self; instead they are channeled into a continuous desire to create, thus making up for what is felt (consciously or not) to have been missed. Such a creative urge, of course, occurs frequently, but it does not always lead to business activities of a productive type. The latter channel is used only when the creative urge is accompanied by a strong desire for independence in addition to some of the executive abilities that were discussed earlier. External influences and circumstances, while obviously very important otherwise, need not be taken into account for the purpose of this particular discussion.

The salesman type, on the other hand, appears to be characterized by an urge for acceptance, almost regardless of whether he happens to peddle suspenders or edifying tracts. An underlying frustration, again often below the conscious level, may have fostered a feeling of rejection which must be made up continuously by being accepted by people, either personally or symbolically through his merchandise. Here again, personal needs have been channeled into activities of potential social utility (depending on the product offered in relation to genuine consumer needs and on the organizational effort that goes into such marketing) even though they may be nonproductive in a strictly physical sense. Failure in selling, with its effect on personal frustration, is depicted in Arthur Miller's play *Death of a Salesman*.[46]

In both producing and marketing activities the personal needs of the individual may sometimes get into conflict with those of his family—a conflict which is manifested in, rather than explained by, a choice between the interests of the company and those of the family, especially in case of compulsive work at the expense of home life. In our society the quest for financial security for one's family is often justified in objective terms; in many cases jobs and incomes *are* threatened by competition and business fluctuations. In other cases, however, such a quest may cover up exaggerated aspirations or else a general psychic unrest.

Complaints have been numerous about the human wear and tear from competitive pressure in executive management, the health disturbances involved, and the effects both on industrial efficiency and on family life. One observer of business practice claims that he has often seen businessmen "make the most wrong moves—based on wrong decisions—when they have tried hardest to be rational and logical," and he asks for a six-hour day for executives as a remedy. Another one blames for these overwork habits the continued influence of certain religious phrases in management—"In the sweat of thy face thou shalt eat bread"—along with psychic inability to delegate work or to trust people; he claims that "common observation of the business world yields a melancholy record of duodenal trouble at forty, of nervous breakdown at fifty, of premature senility at sixty." [47] Without attempting any undue generalization, we may note the incidence of such statements in business literature.

Such personal pressures upon executives have apparently been accentuated in recent years by certain company policies and, especially, by conformity requirements that reach right into the home of the executive unless he is at the very top and perhaps even then. A recent study by *Fortune* magazine of "the wives of management" conveys a picture which is uncomfortably reminiscent of George Orwell's *1984,* the supertotalitarian integration of the individual into a collective concept. According to this study, the kind of wife that top management wants its executive personnel to have these days is to be, first, highly adaptable; second, highly gregarious; and, third, fully cognizant that her husband belongs to the corporation. Her conformity with the corporation has to be of the internalized type, not merely imposed from the outside. The children, too, must be integrated into this system: they must not "bother" their overworked father. One can only guess what effects this may have on their personalities. Wife screening is a regular practice with one-half of the companies canvassed by *Fortune;* and if an executive has "outgrown" his wife, he is quite free either to divorce her and get one who more nearly meets the specifications or to get out of the corporation. Various top executives are quoted as follows, "We consider the home an integral part of this corporation. . . . If a man's first interest is his wife and family, more power to him—but we don't want him."

We must leave the responsibility for these findings to the magazine concerned—which is not likely to be accused by anybody of antibusiness attitudes—but if this picture is anywhere near the truth, the incidence of nervous strain among this social group must be very considerable. Some aspects of this problem will be discussed in the following chapter. In a separate study of the New Rich who have made their fortunes since the end of the second World War, the same magazine interestingly finds a tendency to avoid any great change in living habits in accordance with gain in income and status and a general disposition to continue the previous pattern of home life—not because of any profound philosophy of values but as a device to keep the confidence of customers and business associates. Even so this new attitude sounds like a kind of antidote—if it is of any general significance and if it concerns comparable groups of businessmen, which is uncertain.[48]

At any rate, business activity and family factors appear far more closely interconnected than they were thought to be in the past. These indications are further reinforced as soon as we allow for the range of paternal attitudes in the business process.

The Paternal Attitude

Paternal attitudes in economic relations generally go back to the very beginnings of capitalism, and in some respects to much earlier phases of society. Some recent forms of such attitudes, however, may more definitely represent a displacement of personal functions or needs from the home to the shop. To the extent that authority on the job simply expresses the inevitable hierarchy of functions in a complex enterprise, it can be classified as objective or "rational," although the manner in which it is implemented varies greatly. The moment, however, that power for its own sake (or that of hidden personal needs) is exerted in shop relations, Lord Acton's famous and much misused statement on the corrupting influence of power, especially absolute power, applies no less to industry than to government.

Such power drives of individuals in key positions may affect any part of a corporation structure, not only the ordinary worker but also stockholders and high-ranking executives. One of the most widely quoted examples was the regime of Sewell Avery as chairman of the board of Montgomery Ward. In the spring of 1950, for example, the newspapers reported that neither the president nor a single one of the nine vice-presidents who had been in office at the beginning of 1948 were any longer with the company, and that the chairman of one of the largest institutional stockholders in the company had characterized Avery's managerial methods as dictatorial and had declined to vote the 95,000 shares involved.[49] In other cases the stockholders willingly recognized the "paternal" superiority of management. In the judgment of a writer with long experience in top management, "there is a strong tendency to support management blindly. The exception is provided by the case of a few professional obstructionists or reformers. . . . The degree of success that management must produce to remain in office is surprisingly small"; it enjoys "relative immunity to criticism and accountability."[50]

The main field of paternal attitudes in business, of course, is that of personnel relations. Neither the early nor the more recent history can be fully understood without realization of the implied intrinsic superiority of the businessman—especially the owner-manager but also to some extent the corporate manager—over those groups of the population which cannot be classified as business. The question, "Have you ever met a pay roll?" thus becomes the great yardstick of the social contribution of an individual and of his claim to social leadership. Some laissez-faire diehards are then unpleasantly surprised to discover that Adam Smith never met a pay roll while Friedrich Engels and Lord Keynes did.

The concept of business, which on so many other occasions is perceived as a purely rational process of money-making, often acquires missionary (or intolerant) traits and an implied charismatic claim when this question of social leadership is at stake. Yet the very essence of an economic leadership group, especially one based on the pedestrian process of business bargaining, does not easily lend itself to the maintenance of a charismatic role, particularly in the long run. What Max Weber calls *die Veralltaeglichung des Charisma* ("the routinization or profanation of charisma") [51] constitutes the real weakness of business neopaternalism toward other population groups, especially toward labor.

This is not the place to appraise the enormous literature on human relations in industry and on the actual competition between management and labor unions for prestige, affection, and identification on the part of employees in what so often looks to the superficial observer like a clean-cut brutal fight over money. There are good reasons to believe that the rejection by labor of a quasi-paternal authority on the part of management is a powerful emotional factor which has been growing in importance. It now challenges the value system and self-appraisal of management to such an extent that management has come to struggle for recognition of its social role by the unions much as the latter had to fight for such recognition throughout most of their history.

Apparently the paternal attitudes of business are often appreciated by the workers in an early phase of capitalism or in other cases where the workers come from a rural background with strong family ties. This, at least, has been the case in some parts of Europe. Urban industrial workers, on the other hand, tend to reject such attitudes with growing emphasis. In other words, the sociocultural (and subcultural) scale of values concerned determines the degree of acceptance or rejection of father images in management.

Specifically, the blame or praise of subordinates in public and, conversely, the overt or implied questioning of a superior's authority or competence have tended to arouse strong emotions because of the father-child images involved. Apparently this also applies in some degree to the managerial functions of foremen and even stewards in decisions on "bumping" workers off to a lower-grade job, for example. Destructive blame and hollow praise in contrast with the actual performance or personality concerned both symbolize a power to give and a power to withhold. Conversely, suggested improvements may imply criticism of the superior authority. "One just does not imply that the boss doesn't know his job. The boss knows all the answers; and if I were to make an issue of it, he would think that I wanted his job." [52]

The appearance of strict cost-efficiency-profit logic on the part of management along with emotional if not "irrational" attitudes of employees is deceptive or it offers, at least, a grossly oversimplified picture. To some extent, however, the difference of the two group approaches to industrial problems reflects the difference between the value system of formal organization and that of informal relations. The formal organization was set up for the normative goal of rational logic; the informal relations inevitably are full of emotions, often below the conscious level.

In summary, paternal attitudes of business, whether conscious or not, are often connected with a claim for leadership not only within the shop but in society. On the company scale this claim potentially concerns the workers, the stockholders, and various business contacts including consumers. On the social scale this claim has led some groups to aspirations for national leadership by business alone. Finally, such leadership claims tend to encourage various kinds of rationalizations concerning either competitive practices or those of a monopolistic or oligopolistic character. For once the paternal authority of business over society has been firmly established in everybody's mind, no longer will it be considered respectable to raise prying questions concerning the actual extent and forms of competition in our economic life as compared with conventional images of that competition.

Motives of Competition

The traditional conception of competition assumes that a general drive for profit and wealth makes each individual or firm attempt to undersell the others in order to capture the largest possible proportion of the market; the general aim of underselling the others leads to ever-increasing efficiency of each company, thus making competition an instrument of social progress. According to this assumption societies which are not competitive in the sense of having a private profit orientation cannot be efficient in their economic procedures.

Contemporary thinking has thrown new light on the personal meaning and impact of competition and, more generally, of rivalry as contrasted with co-operation. To begin with, the old belief that it is natural for human beings of any kind or social background to fight with the pack for the bones has been replaced by a recognition of the very complex and malleable traits of the human mind under different social circumstances. It now appears rather unnatural (in the sense of exceptional) for a human being to be an economic man. Further, evidence from anthropological sources indicates that, while competitive attitudes in a very broad sense are widespread, they are not universal. More than that, the object and method of competition show extremely great variations; the "negotiational psychology," to use John R. Commons' term,[53] varies likewise; monopoly is no less frequent than competition and actually resembles it closely in the underlying motive force of self-assertion at the expense of others.

Some societies recognize this assertive function of competition as valid but exempt from it the area of basic individual needs, thus centering competition on the display of personal capacities without harm to others. "In Comanche the competition is of the very keenest; but the competition does not involve security in the form of subsistence or social regard. With security of subsistence guaranteed and the freedom to display and develop abilities unobstructed, competition is accepted and the best man becomes leader."[54] In various societies, such as Fiji and Kwakiutl, people compete in giving things away rather than in acquiring them, in the interest of the same status desires.

Generally, personal drives for either competition or monopoly are now widely recognized as stemming from the same basic need under different conditions of social and individual upbringing. In both cases it is a need for self-assertion—in the case of competition through proving one's superiority over other persons in a comparable situation, and in the case of monopoly through elimination of any outside threat to one's security. Either competition or monopoly may thus become a self-purpose from the viewpoint of personal needs—often nonconscious ones—rather than a mere device for money-making and the living comfort that goes with it.

In our own culture and society, economic competition has long been adopted as the main standard of personal success, though there are some subsidiary standards such as sports competition. Even there, however, financial success has often been assumed to be the ultimate aim of athletic competition. In Bertrand Russell's words, "What people fear when they engage in the struggle is not that they will fail to get their breakfast next morning, but that they will fail to outshine their neighbors." [55] It is *relative* income that measures success—relative to the prevailing social standard as well as to that of the specific group concerned. Dollars assume somewhat the role of comparative school grades, with graduation into the next-higher class expected as a regular occurrence. Financial promotion, even without functional advancement, thus means a continuous process of graduation, sometimes at the expense of alienation from the preferred activity or location. Above a modest minimum level, making money begins to matter more than having it. Once it has been made, it loses some of its interest, and much of it may be given away through generosity, gambling, or waste depending on other personal and social factors.

It is as if a whole cultural value scale had got stuck in an autistic phase of personality development, in constantly emphasizing a selfish type of competition which it really does not take quite seriously. Successful businessmen have stated on more than one occasion that competitive business means fun to them more than anything else, fun representing here largely one kind of self-assertion. Most of us have experienced the psychology of that especially clean-cut case of competition, the auction place; many people who are not really interested in the wares participate in the bidding just for the elements of excitement, emulation, prestige, and self-assertion that are involved.

In other competitive situations, relative size and recent growth of a business unit are widely accepted as measures of success and status for the persons who are credited with such company development. Superficially, bigness thus becomes a self-purpose almost regardless of other economic and noneconomic factors. In still other situations, the decisive area of competition may be a fight for status *within* a corporation, or rivalry among companies for "fixing things" most effectively in Washington or the state capital, for the best purchases on the "personality market," or for the most efficient use of such business services as research, consultants, public relations, or mass communications.

This is not the place to discuss the conceptual and institutional aspects of competition and monopoly in general. It is important, however, to point out the fallacy of any assumption that competition is uninhibited whenever there is no explicit or tacit agreement to restrict it. The cultural background and, with it, the perceptive propensities and group standards involved have some unifying effect upon the businessmen within the same population and industry. Their mutual guesses about each other's reactions are sometimes no worse than would be information due to a clean-cut conspiracy.[56] Where the actual degree of economic concentration is high, competition may even become a kind of fixed game with prearranged parts: weaker companies are allowed to survive as long as they remain reasonable in order to show that there *is* competition. At times, the American practice allows some leeway among competitors in letting each regular player take his turn as monopolist in some respect—for a while, at least.

In other cases, however, intricate processes of rationalization take place. In the judgment of two social psychologists,

the official ideology of "private enterprise and competition" has had a valuable integrating function for many business people over a period of many years. It is a well-developed, satisfying belief system, which gives desirable status and meaning to many different kinds of discrete business activities. . . . It is an ideology that integrates the strivings for personal wealth and power, with the culturally accepted ideals of democracy, freedom, and service to one's fellow men. . . . Business groups, and especially big business, have yet to develop an integrated belief system that can be substituted for the old one.[57] *

The challenge to this belief system comes not merely from enemies of its underlying institutions, who attack either the competitive principle as such or its counterpart in actual economic life. An additional challenge comes from a frequent clash of this belief system—sometimes in the soul of those who profess it most ardently—with religious or other norms that make competitive bargaining appear immoral, unaesthetic, embarrassing, or at least cumbersome. Worse than that, if the social norms emphasize successful economic competition as the legitimate outlet for the discharge of tension, failure in competition

---

* By permission from *Theory and Problems of Social Psychology*, by D. Krech and R. S. Crutchfield. Copyright, 1948. McGraw-Hill Book Company, Inc., New York.

easily turns into additional tension and may find such outlets as group prejudice. Karl Mannheim commented on the basic problem by saying that competition among unequals always has a demoralizing effect.[58]

In summary, competition may serve an assertive function that is quite different from the economic one which the actor himself perceives. Competition and monopoly alike represent specific manifestations of rivalry; and these may be in conflict with values of cooperation that the same society may also try to convey, especially through its educational, ethical, and religious norms.

Competition and Gambling

The surprising conclusion that money cannot be the sole purpose of competition, professed or practiced, in the American culture has been reached by a number of Americans and Europeans. Shall we go to the other extreme in concluding that competition is mainly the application of a gambling drive to the industrial or commercial scene? Such a conclusion would be very lopsided.

To begin with, gambling in some ways competes with business in absorbing the financial resources and human energies of nations. Further, gambling is far more widespread among cultures—ranging all the way from the most primitive to the most sophisticated with only a few exceptions—than is business in the specific sense that was defined at the beginning of this chapter. In contemporary America, where gambling is mostly outlawed by the Puritan tradition, the annual gross revenue of the gambling "industry" was estimated at $15,000,000,000 by the *New York Times* in 1950; between $6,800,000,000 and $21,500,-000,000 by the Citizens Committee of Massachusetts, Inc., also in 1950; and at $20,000,000,000 by the Kefauver Committee in 1951, but these are all guesses. In the course of these studies it has been claimed that Americans spend more money on gambling than they do for medicine, housing, or private education and research, even in a period of high taxes.

The *New York Times*, in its worldwide investigation of gambling operations in late 1951, came to the conclusion that "all mankind except the Eskimo has a weakness for gambling, but nowhere on earth today does gambling breed as much concern, confusion and corruption as in the United States." [59] The reason is in the links between gambling, organized crime, and civic corruption in this country compared with the legalized, regulated, and "reasonable" forms of gambling in such countries as France or Britain. A British government survey in May 1951 showed that three out of four Britons over the age of sixteen bet—usually modest sums—on horses, dogs, soccer pools, or lotteries.

To come back to the American scene, a Gallup poll on gambling found that 57 per cent of the population gamble at one time or another, however mildly; that the average race-track customer is apt to be a church member who goes to the tracks about once a year; that 87 per cent are 26 to 55 years old; that 44 per cent are businessmen, executives, or professional men; that 42 per cent own homes and 76 per cent own cars; and that 49 per cent earn $5,000 a year or more. We must leave the responsibility for these data to the polling agency, but there is little doubt that gambling, either casual or regular, is very widespread.

Now at first glance gambling, which has been described as an organized rejection of reason, seems to be the very contradiction of the clocklike reasoning which has traditionally been associated with the successful conduct of competitive business. It is true that one kind of gambling, that based on exact calculation of the chances, could be interpreted as extreme expression of "rationality." The essence of the real gambling mind, however, is precisely in the refusal to recognize the weight of adverse odds in spite of mathematical evidence or even the individual's own experiences. A French proverb says, "One rarely finds a rich gambler," and a Chinese proverb states, "If you must play set three things first: the rules of the game, the stakes, the quitting time." The essential trait of the real gambler is precisely that he does not quit at the "right" time; he does not quit until he has lost everything he could lose.

Gambling thrives in social or personal situations where any calculating or "rational" action appears to offer little hope. To assert one's "luck," *corriger la fortune*, then helps to preserve one's self-esteem, and the drive to do so becomes more powerful as the gambler wins and irresistible as he loses. At the same time, gambling also reflects perplexity about social happenings and renunciation of any attempt to understand them. In this sense gambling represents a form of protest against the social process, transformed into a kind of superstitious ritual. It is especially stimulated by social disorganization or anomy,[60] or else by the extreme rigidity of social institutions or hierarchies. In some societies gambling is legalized in order to serve as a safety valve for social frustrations; in others it is outlawed and, on this value basis, easily becomes the province of criminals and neurotics. One psychiatrist describes the latter type of gambling as "the prime example of misusing money for the solution of inner conflicts completely unrelated to money," for most of the real gamblers unconsciously want to lose.[61]

Competitive business, on the other hand, is based on the assumption of calculated risk, not a blind challenge to fate—at least on the conscious level. This is opposed to the risk-reducing function of cooperation. To the extent that competition is a game it is ordinarily one of the strategic type, where every player tries to outguess the other players, rather than a mere game of chance. Moreover, some kinds of gambling are noncompetitive. Yet there is clearly an *element* of gambling in competition and business or, at least, in some types of them. The most widely discussed example is the stock market.

In the days of the bucket shops, the connection was clear, for stock-exchange happenings were made an object of clean-cut gambling there. But this is an extreme case, and is frowned upon today. On the other hand, any picture of the stock exchange as just another market, the one which confronts the objective capital requirements of corporations with cold-blooded calculation of revenue and appreciation on the part of investors, would also be unrealistic. In his weekly advertisements, a much-publicized investment adviser promises to "explain why so many of the crowd are nearly always wrong; why orthodox opinion is often dangerous; why the public so often loses; why the majority tends to make itself wrong automatically; and how you cannot cut profit-taking slices out of an inflationary cake or bubble without making the paper profits (the bubble) shrink or disappear." The "behavior" of stocks, psychological chain reactions of bearishness or bullishness with their possible traits of self-fulfilling prophecy, the fluctuations of "confidence," the roots and spread of market panics, the various "systems" of forecasting—which usually assume constant behavior patterns—all this has been the object of endless guesswork, with very few foolproof data to support the various generalizations in circulation.

Actually reliable data on the typology, motivations, and behavior patterns of the stock-market public thus far are rather scanty. Apparently a sizable proportion of the public consists of investors in a strict sense who buy securities in the expectation of reasonably safe capital values and yields; some others are driven by a desire to get rich quick; still others are of the speculating type and enjoy the gambling element in the stock market as such. In other words, while the stock market is a glorified and legal gamble for some, it is something quite different for others. It would be very illuminating to secure more concrete data than are available about the types of people who use the stock market and the various ways in which they do it; about such personality factors as are involved in speculation, in safety-first attitudes, in profit taking, in bearish or bullish disposition; about ethical codes and superstitious or ritualistic practices; about the exact connotation of the term "security" in stock-market terminology; and about historical and geographical variations in the respective degrees of venture and caution that prevail on stock markets.

Attitudes toward Money

The broader problem involved in understanding the emotional role both of gambling and competition is that of attitudes toward money insofar as the latter represents the traditional measure of business success. The psychological meaning of money to various cultures, societies, groups, and individuals is an extensive subject in itself. It will be discussed here only to the extent that it is relevant for studies of business motivation. The basic question is to what extent attitudes toward money represent timeless traits of human nature with personality variations only or else social types which vary with the culture, institutional setting, and class situation.

The best available answer is that *all* of these factors are effective in some degree and that they overlap in various ways. The comparative incidence of personality traits that make for various attitudes toward money depends in part on social influences upon the child—through the family and otherwise—during the years of personality formation. In other words, thrifty, generous, venturous, greedy, stingy, hoarding, and acquisitive people exist in most societies; but their frequency distribution and the valuation given to these traits vary greatly.

In our own society the basic dichotomy is offered by the wide acceptance of money as an overt standard of success, on the one hand, and the more or less hidden guilt charge of money, on the other hand. For example, making a cash present to friends is usually frowned upon, chiefly because money is impersonal; giving money does not involve the "opportunity cost" connected with spending time and effort on selecting a gift in kind. In clinical cases such associations may develop into a general aversion to receiving gifts that represent any potential money value.

Another example of the emotional meaning of money is supplied by the changing evaluation of tipping, which has in many cases been replaced by a fixed or proportionate fee; tipping affects the social status and involves such feelings as contempt, hostility, guilt, and even parental images. The success-guilt connotation of money is exemplified by the fact that insolvency, far from being a purely financial failure, also tends to have a stigma attached to it. In *The Madwoman of Chaillot* the author makes the Rag-Picker say that money means honesty and that a businessman without money must be a shady character.[62] For comparable reasons of moral impact it has been said that an empty purse is much emptier than a full purse is full. Yet the example of monks and ascetics, who shun any contact with money except through their collective, or else retire individually from the money-ridden world, shows that the status implication and self-assertion symbolism of money can potentially be replaced by a different value system on an individual or group scale.

Some remnants of the old usury connotation of lending for interest apparently have survived from the Middle Ages. Conversely debt, in many people's feelings, has a certain stigma attached to it unless it is a socially accepted and general condition. In our business civilization this condition by and large applies to private company transactions. At the same time government debt (or deficit spending) often meets an emotional—not merely economic—resistance which can only be explained from displaced childhood fears in combination with an anthropomorphic misinterpretation of government.

Both the magic exerted by and the mistrust paid to that time-honored symbol of money wealth, gold, can also be attributed to the emotional impact of its symbolism; the psychological significance of gold in both domestic and international finance has come to exceed greatly its economic role. Similarly, inflation not only means objective harm to the purchasing power of various population groups; it also symbolizes a break with the past and a perceived threat which have a general unsettling effect on many people in nearly every group.[63] The popularity of tinkering with money in all sorts of quack social programs has comparable reasons of emotional character.

Turning to the symbolic meaning of money in a business civilization, wealthy people are often known to be negligent in paying private bills even though they may be meticulously correct in their business payments. This has been explained from a desire to show that they enjoy credit and can afford to keep others waiting, thus symbolizing a claim for special privileges; but it may also indicate a basic contempt for money once it has been made, occasionally combined with "conspicuous nonconsumption." Apparently money-making is often conceived of as a kind of creative art in contrast to money spending.

The symbolic and emotional meaning of money in the middle of a business civilization assumed to be rational is exemplified by the frequency of enormous damage suits and their acceptance by juries. Despite all legal advice, juries in accident cases tend to feel that a person is "entitled" to money compensation just because he has suffered pain, regardless of the guilt question—somewhat in the nature of candy offered by mother for consolation to a child crying because he hurt himself.

In other words, contemporary attitudes toward money and, correspondingly, toward profit and business are strikingly ambivalent. On the one hand, selfishness, not generosity, is considered normal and necessary; on the other hand, the emotional nonbusiness appeal of generosity is quite strong. Psychotherapists are familiar with emotional conflicts which center or crystallize around money even though their real roots may be in personal or social factors of a different nature. The Freudian school tends to ascribe specific money attitudes to personal traits that were acquired in early childhood; for example, the parsimonious-orderly-obstinate type is interpreted as a sublimation of anal erotism. Such theories mean little to the social scientist, for they explain neither why the incidence of the various attitudes varies according to the society or group concerned nor why the character traits in question manifest themselves most conspicuously in attitudes toward money, rather than toward, say, music or athletics.[64]

There is, however, plenty of evidence that some people are emotionally unable to work for money, especially if such work means competition, thus giving up the protected status of a child and his privilege of "getting something for nothing." Conversely, work compulsions (sometimes leading to economic "success") may have resulted from guilt feelings and anxieties that were instilled into a person at an early age by parents or others who themselves were driven by specific socio-cultural norms of their period. It is true that the miser, the spendthrift, the gambler, the success hunter, the embezzler, the dependee, the sucker, the recluse occur in a great many cultures and societies. Some of the latter, however, have institutional sanctions against this or that kind of behavior; some are more conducive than others to a frequent occurrence of certain kinds of personality; and some offer greater appreciation than others to specific character traits, with great differences in the definition of normality or deviation. The miser and even the recluse may be heroes in a society that values thrift highly, while they may be considered mental patients in a society that emphasizes spending as a socially useful device.

This, indeed, brings up the broader question of what constitutes normal and abnormal behavior in contemporary economic life and especially in business activities, and, in particular, of what kinds of aggressive attitudes are conducive to a successful drive for the acquisition of money profit through the medium of such activities, even allowing for deeper needs that may underlie this drive.

The Meanings of Aggressiveness

The term aggressive has two rather different connotations. It may refer to the kind of attitude and behavior that is characterized by anger, rage, attacks, violence; or else it may mean great activity, initiative, and ingenuity. Most of us speak favorably, even admiringly of an aggressive promoter, while we usually regret or fear an aggressive person. Has the business connotation of the term anything to do with its psychological meaning, or is semantics playing a trick on us?

In order to answer this question, we need agreement on the psychological meaning of aggression. By and large it is explained from frustrations, especially those that are deeply embedded in personality, often as a result of crucial childhood experiences. Such frustrations produce a need for emotional outlets with a tension-reducing function. If no such outlets are found, continuous tension along with free-floating aggressiveness and a state of restlessness and unhappiness will result.

Certain cultures which typically produce great frustration in their individuals appear to fail in organizing aggression patterns of a socially acceptable kind. Abram Kardiner explains the behavior pattern of the Alorese in financial and other affairs on the basis of such a failure.[65] At the same time, purely adaptive behavior based on outward conformity with repression of the underlying frustrations does not solve the problem; an example of such a pseudo-solution is offered by the culture of the Saultaux, a tribe of Canadian Indians with a long reputation of being mild-mannered and overtly unaggressive.[66] Similarly withdrawal, rationalization, and autism offer no outlets that meet individual needs and social requirements alike. Sublimation of aggression or its channeling into various identification processes sometimes yields better results but still leaves many problems. Regression, that is, unresolved aggression leading to a setback in maturity, or a projection of aggression to targets that are unrelated to the causes of the frustration likewise is full of dangers for individual and society alike. Especially is this true when both the frustration and the reaction to it are of a lasting type.

Now the various cultures and societies differ significantly in the amount and kind of frustrations (either real or anticipated) they tend to foster in their individuals, in the definition of aggression, and in the types of organized outlets they allow for such frustrations through socially accepted patterns of aggression. In particular, the channeling of aggression into a productive orientation is more appreciated and encouraged in some societies than in others. Certain societies put a premium on "realism" in the sense of a keen perception of surface phenomena and adaptation to them, without any attempt to achieve perspective in depth or even an awareness of its possibility and value.

Our own society tries to channel aggressive propensities largely into competitive activities in business, though there are some additional outlets such as sports. Actually, our society has encouraged and rewarded the aggressive personality to the extent that it went into the production or promotion of marketable goods and services. Aggressiveness in the commercial sense is considered one of the main requirements for business success; and the latter, in turn, has been a leading factor of self-assertion and social prestige, as has been shown earlier.

Yet there is considerable evidence from psychotherapists and related sources that this outlet has not always been adequate. It would be

foolish to succumb to any unwarranted generalizations about personal
dissatisfaction with business success, but apparently such dissatisfaction does occur in a number of cases. Neurotic patients who have been
"successful" by prevailing social standards are a fairly regular occurrence in psychotherapeutic practice, and the familiar saying "I am
not in business for my health" sometimes assumes quite a different
meaning from the ordinary one. A leading psychiatrist formulated his
experience with competitive attitudes as follows:

The ambition-ridden person comes to the psychiatrist to get what he can
in the way of aid in his career. He may be willing to pay for this. He may
be most determined in his efforts to achieve it. But he lives in a world of
competitive violence and necessary compromise, and he will have none of
the psychiatrist's skepticism about the finality of his formula. He cannot
escape the competitive attitude, even in this regard, and all too frequently
by dint of competing with the physician at every step, reduces the potentially therapeutic situation to a struggle about who is doctor and who is
patient.[67]

Apparently the conflict which affects a number of persons in business life expresses in part actual feelings of uneasiness and insecurity
that underlie the accepted attitude of overt confidence. In many cases
the conflict stems from the double life which the requirements of business rivalry and competition impose upon the persons concerned as
contrasted to the consideration, co-operation, and altruism that home
and church require. The switchover for evenings and weekends appears to be hard on those people, at least, who are already under some
strain for other reasons.

Moreover, aggressions may not only be channeled into business activities but may sometimes be aroused by them as well. A recent study
in comparative anthropology claims that "our economy is a prestige
economy to a pathological extent. . . . To some considerable degree,
frontier virtues are the intolerable vices of contemporary America.
. . . Egoistic individualism remains long after the economic place for
it has passed." [68]

Regardless of whether or not this is generally true, there are indications that the personal strains mentioned, if anything, tend to increase
under managerial enterprise. In Knauth's experience, such a setup is
both more complex and more difficult to operate than either free enterprise or monopoly, and it produces wearing tensions and anxieties

which are not compensated by immediate tangible achievement. "The joy of attaining a definite goal has been submerged in the vastness of space and time. Management must learn to get its satisfaction vicariously, trusting that its contribution will sometime fructify to the benefit of the community as well as to the enterprise." Further strains result from the necessity of combining an impersonal character of enterprise with great requirements of co-operative loyalty.[69]

Additional tension comes from the accepted, though not always conscious, status device of "being busy," with its compulsive implications; the atmosphere of "action" for its own sake; and the emotional strain of modern industrial conflicts. If we add up these influences, we begin to understand why the business outlet that is offered to aggressive needs does not always fill this function today and why it sometimes generates new tension instead of relieving the existing one, both in North America and in Western Europe. Here again a warning against unwarranted generalizations is necessary, but the medical evidence of physical, psychosomatic, and nervous disturbances among businessmen (whatever the exact relationship of such disorders may be) is considerable. Whether the real stakes are worth such tension, whether some other population groups are not similarly affected, and whether the age composition of the business group has something to do with the incidence of health disorders—all these are questions that can only be hinted at here.[70]

Among those relatively few cases that reach the clinical stage, a psychiatrist lists the following traits he has found in the typical "success hunter": (1) contempt for moderate earnings, high-pitched ambitions, and exaggerated ideas of success, combined with a drive to overwork; (2) constant inner tension, stemming from inner passivity, regardless of the importance of the stakes; (3) a propelling impetus toward more and more success; (4) dissatisfaction and boredom if deprived of new business excitement and resulting opportunities to show off; (5) cynical outlook, hypersensitivity, and hypersuspiciousness; (6) contempt for and ruthlessness toward the unsuccessful; (7) onesided and opinionated I-know-better attitude in general; (8) hypochondriacal worries: doubts concerning continuous flow of ideas and luck; (9) inability to enjoy the simple pleasures of life; (10) hidden depression, warded off with tempered megalomania and extensive air of importance.[71]

This list is not altogether convincing. We should, at least, be careful in keeping the purely individual traits of this extreme personality type apart from the objective economic requirements of a more or less competitive system of enterprise. Such objective requirements involve considerable aggressiveness in the sense of initiative and ingenuity. The degree sometimes depends on the specific assignment an individual receives within a corporate hierarchy; but aggressive action on his part can seldom be dispensed with completely if the enterprise concerned is to survive. To that extent an individual, once involved in doing business, has to follow the objective requirements of the market.

The clinical problem begins if and when the personal drive for success exceeds such objective requirements, though the exact point is not always easy to determine. The insatiable success hunter in business may have succumbed to work compulsions due to unresolved guilt feelings far below the conscious level. He may suffer from an obsessive need for self-assertion and may wish, without necessarily realizing it, to prove to himself and to others through constant success that Providence does love him. He may be desperately fighting in this way against a hidden self-hate. He may seek new competitive ventures all the time in an unwitting guilt-ridden urge to fail and be penitent sometime; or else he may, more harmlessly, lose interest in doing business once he has asserted himself by establishing his success.

In extreme pathological cases, he may join the constant array of recluses or miserly characters who are regularly reported by the newspapers under such headlines as "Recluse Had $150,000 But Lived in a $4 Room," "Recluse's $400,000 Estate Found after He Is Buried in Potter's Field"; "Recluse Widow, 73, Loses $52,500 in a Zipper Bag Left in Cafeteria"; "Theft Victim Rues Fortune in Closet: Had a 'Reason' for Reno Cache Looted of 2½ Million"; "Wilks Estate Is Put at 95 Millions, Third of It in One Checking Account"; "3 Live in Squalor But Own $100,000"; "Recluse Dies at 78; $52,000 In His Shack"; or "65,000 Life Hoard Found Amid Refuse." [72]

To sum up this section, specific factors of personality are of great importance in determining the various patterns of business or financial behavior, whether normal or abnormal. These factors are for applied psychology to define in each case. What the social scientist is mainly interested in is the *incidence* of those personality-forming influences that tend to produce the specific kinds of emotional detachment, assertive drive, or aggressiveness that are conducive to business success later in life. The social scientist is also interested in the status rewards, through the medium of money, that society may confer upon the manifestations of such personality traits. At the same time, the psychological standards of individual success, sometimes for lack of a better term summarized as fulfillment of all personal potentialities, are by no means identical with the economic criteria of business success, though they often overlap in some degree.

The discussion which follows will apply the motivational factors mentioned to a number of specific business situations and will then offer joint conclusions for both chapters.

Chapter II

How Is Business Done?

EVEN in persons who are free of any excessive drive for self-assertion or of other major problems of personality, temporary influences which affect their perception sometimes lead to fluctuations or errors in judgment or in decision making. Such errors may be inexplicable to the individual concerned and may appear as irrational to his business associates later on regardless of whether or not the company suffers any serious harm. Even if profit maximization were a more general business aim than it actually is, it still would have to be carried through by frail human minds. We are not, of course, referring here to purely hypothetical or normative concepts of profit maximization that are designed to serve as tools of economic analysis without any necessary relation to actual business behavior.

John M. Clark has expressed the issue that underlies business behavior as follows, "To report that a given employer seeks maximum profits, as so determined, may miss the most important things about his conduct of his business." [1] Generally speaking, doing business represents an intricate interaction of incentives, expectations, forecasts, uncertainty, risk, confidence, and decisions on location, investment, production, employment, pricing, and so forth. At each step of this

54

ladder—and the steps are not always arranged neatly, logically, consistently, or permanently—influences of far greater complexity than the term profit maximization expresses will come into the picture. An explicit aim of profit maximization, it is true, usually serves as channel, catalyzer, or symbol for the underlying factors of personality, self-assertion needs, or group standards.

The much-misused term incentive may apply to a stimulus in persons or groups to do business in general, or to go into a specific field and enterprise, or to carry out a concrete transaction. In each case, the financial incentive symbolizes and quantifies the underlying motives, which may or may not center around profit maximization in any objective or accounting sense. At the very least, a clear distinction should be drawn between the motive to make profit (*some* degree of profit) and the single-minded drive for real maximization of profit. Such single-mindedness, in any respect, is a very rare occurrence. Moreover, short-range profit aims may be at odds or compete with those of a long-range character, with security goals, or with direct desires of prestige, power, or work satisfaction—especially under the impact of cultural or group norms.

In practice, therefore, the incentive for John Doe to start digging for gold in the wilderness of northern Canada may be influenced not only by desire for profit maximization but by the gambling impulses that were discussed earlier, by a deeply rooted desire to get away from it all and to be in a lonesome wilderness, or by a symbolic meaning that gold may have assumed for him during his formative period. All these motives may merge into or be rationalized in, an overt incentive to make huge profits by digging gold. Actually those indirect influences may be so powerful, especially below the conscious level, that they may blind him to the objective risks (that is, the handicaps to actual profit maximization) that may be involved in the enterprise concerned, and he may fail even though all the objective information was available to him all the time.

In case gold digging should look like too extreme an example, less dramatic applications to everyday business can easily be found. The history of business—railroads, electronics, or local grocery stores— shows numerous instances of what to an outsider looks like a fixed idea. The idea may lead to either success or failure depending on the general situation but it cannot be explained in either case from incentives or maximization principles in the purely financial sense alone. In a good many cases ample allowance is required for distorted perception of the objective situation even with adequate information available.

Expectations, Confidence, and Decision Making

In order to be translated into action a general incentive must crystallize in specific expectations. From the viewpoint of business practice the expectation concept of economic theory usually requires far-reaching adjustment or amplification in order to be meaningful. To begin with, any static assumption that expectations are always realized must be eliminated. This also applies to any preconception that business expectations simply reflect the actual business conditions. We approach business practice more nearly in J. R. Hicks' concept of "elasticity of expectations," which places the emphasis on expectations concerning general market conditions rather than on specific prices; moreover, expectations are not expressed in terms of a precise figure but in terms of a probable range of figures, with considerable allowance for noneconomic factors that influence expectations, such as weather, politics, health, superstitions, or "psychology." Even so, the concept mentioned remains closely tied to either past experiences or past expectations.[2]

Whatever evidence is available on expectation patterns as determinants of business behavior indicates that these patterns are subject to cultural, institutional, group, and individual variations of great import. Both the degree of definiteness and the time perspective involved vary considerably. Certain sociocultural norms or situations, as well as certain individual traits, favor habitual behavior in which the term expectation has a purely formal meaning; in other cases expectations are more diversified or more definite. In any case the concept of expectation, in order to be helpful in explaining actual business behavior, should not be confined to objective market trends that can be seen by *any* businessman who cares to obtain the necessary information. It should also refer to socioeconomic factors, such as a war danger or a recent depression, that set the general framework for individual expectations and to personal characteristics, such as the perception pattern, that shape it in each case, thus helping to explain inconsistencies of expectations in particular.

Psychological findings indicate that expectations tend to change infrequently, radically, and simultaneously. The strong motivational forces that are required to arouse the need for genuine decisions and, with them, definite expectations are quite likely to act upon many businessmen in about the same direction at any given time. The idea that expectations of businessmen tend to cancel each other out is thus seldom realistic, not to mention the impact of leadership in causing like decisions.

At this point that important factor of "organized expectation" called forecasting requires some emphasis. We cannot realistically speak of business expectations today as if they were arrived at through purely individual contemplation. The pattern of expectations at any given time is significantly influenced by the various forecasting services of a public or private nature. This is true regardless of the comparative value of these various services and of any self-fulfilling prophecy or band-wagon action they may produce. We cannot go here into the question of why businessmen, to judge from some available polls, may tend to be more optimistic than economists in forecasting the general trend, and more optimistic in evaluating the future prospects of their own businesses than in forecasting the general economic trend. The special biases to which stock-market forecasters are exposed have also been an object of discussion ever since their sad experiences during the Great Depression.[3]

The real questions here are, first, whether the whole idea of organized, generally available forecasting is not at odds with the basic assumptions of a competitive economy, and whether—even in the absence of a band-wagon effect—organized forecasting does not tend to replace individual estimates and decisions by group-oriented behavior and decision making; second, whether economic forecasting based on individual estimates of investment (which are notoriously incorrect in small businesses, at least) can hope to offer a realistic picture of the trend; and, third, whether in the absence of motivational data on the reasons *why* businessmen, rightly or wrongly, expect to do certain things, formal forecasts may not foster more errors than they remove. It is quite legitimate for public or private research agencies to attempt an estimate of concrete economic needs, especially with a view to possible action of a compensatory type; it is another question whether social forecasts based on unanalyzed individual expectations are of any real value.

With or without the help of organized forecasting the businessman is up against the impact of uncertainty. Here again the term can have very different meanings. In economic theory it is mainly used to characterize either lack of information concerning the circumstances under which an economic action will be carried through or the indeterminate nature of the effects of such action even under known or foreseeable circumstances. F. H. Knight has more specifically restricted the concept of uncertainty to nonmeasurable cases, as distinguished from risk. In this sense uncertainty, under dynamic assumptions, has been interpreted as the chief barrier to perfect competition and, at the same time, as the ultimate cause of profit.[4]

The term uncertainty may, however, assume quite a different meaning in business life. It may refer to unsettled and insecure conditions in economic society, which put the very basis of consistent expectations and decisions into question. A danger of war and attack, social upheaval, political upsets, or steep rise in taxes may expose business action to surprises and uncontrollable new influences. The term uncertainty may also refer to a personal state of mind which may grip an individual or group at certain times or may even affect them during their whole lifetime, thus preventing them from perceiving in any clear way the situation in which they are involved. Last but not least, creeping uncertainty about the merits and the future of the socioeconomic order has shaken in many quarters what little was left of the original belief in a calling or permanent mission of business as a social group. Attempts to cover up such uncertainty by periodic self-glorification have had little real effect upon the actual self-assurance of this group. What it is striving for is constant social approval. It has become quite sensitive to any criticism which it perceives as implying an alternative to its own social leadership.

Uncertainty in the three substantive meanings just mentioned may affect, either periodically or chronically, the whole process of doing business whenever the personal or social situation concerned is felt to be unsettled. Instead of representing a normal condition of doing business, if not the very root of profit, uncertainty then becomes an impediment for the persons, firms, and social groups concerned.

Comparable considerations apply to the risk concept. Here again the concept may refer to the probability that certain events, especially those of an adverse character, might happen in the course of a business transaction though not necessarily as its result—a probability which may ordinarily be considered measurable on the basis of comparable happenings in the past. Or else the risk concept may be concerned with possible dangers, to a company or to the individuals who make it up, either from socioeconomic events beyond its control, such as war or depression, or from personal characteristics of its managers, employees, suppliers, customers, or creditors. In the former case raw materials, for example, might be cut off suddenly or be subject to wild price fluctuations, while in the latter case one or more erratic or negligent persons might sometime cause unexpected spoilage or waste despite a perfect record in the past.

Ordinarily major risks are knowingly incurred only if and when there is enough "confidence." Some fundamental issues that underlie this concept will be discussed in the next chapter. At this point it suffices to say that confidence in business may simply mean an affirmative evaluation of the risk situation, leading to the conclusion that the probability outlook for favorable results from an action is good. In this sense confidence means a prevalence of favorable expectations in facing a given business situation or a concrete decision such as investment. This still leaves the question of whether business fluctuations represent accidental clusters of individual confidence reactions (or diffidence reactions) which lead to widespread capital replacements at a certain time, for instance; for "objective" economic trends still have to pass through human minds in some way in order to influence actual business behavior.

We can count out both antipsychological objectivism and the opposite extreme. The presence or absence of confidence, whether it occurs in an individual or in a community, *is* of prime importance in shaping the business behavior concerned; but in producing a certain state of mind objective economic factors, such as the inventory situation or the credit supply, ordinarily have considerable effect. This does not mean, however, that they constitute the only influences; noneconomic factors on both the social and the individual levels may, at certain times at least, be more powerful.

On the social level such factors may comprise the political outlook at home or abroad as perceived by the people concerned, regardless of whether this perception is accurate, including dangers of war, destruction, revolution, reaction, hunger, epidemics. On the individual level the effective noneconomic factors may comprise the frequency of either confident or diffident personalities in a given period, due to influences that prevailed during the formative period or to the spread of personal insecurity in a more short-run sense. In both cases the patterns of perception, expectation, confidence, and risk taking will be affected, thus leading to a social aggregation of certain types of business decisions at a given time. The specific arrangement of factors within such interaction, and even the direction of its flow, will vary according to the specific constellation in each case.

If we apply the preceding considerations to the actual process of decision making in business, the following picture emerges. To begin with, the range of genuine decisions is much smaller than has often been implied in the past. Habitual behavior is widespread in many areas of business conduct and can in these cases be shaken only by profound "traumatic" changes in attitude, such as those resulting from the loss or failure of a reference group. Such habitual behavior is greatly influenced by the sociocultural scale of values. For example, the habit in some retail lines of getting rid of the inventory at the end of the season almost regardless of loss can easily be explained in a country where the pioneer idea, the spirit of innovation, and quick changes in all sorts of fashions are taken for granted. Such a practice, however, would be hopeless in an essentially tradition-bound, conservative, and parsimonious population with comparable levels of income and wealth. Aside from habitual business behavior, there is also a wide and historically growing area of involuntary "decisions" through institutional and social action. Such action replaces individual decisions by collective ones, at least in a conditioning sense, such as zoning regulations, the tax structure, or patent laws.

Allowing for such influences, the area of decision making required remains considerable. Generally speaking it includes the following main types of decisions: entrance into an industry, location, expansion, reduction, liquidation; capital supply, profit allocation, and liquidity; technological and managerial organization; production types and quantities; manpower supply and labor relations; pricing and marketing; relations to other firms, associations, and public agencies. Some of these decision types obviously overlap.

Among the factors that influence decision making in each of these cases, both the objective intrafirm situation and its socioeconomic setting will be supplemented by the inevitable effect of the personalities and interpersonal relations involved. Family background, status aspirations, creative urge, desire for independence or authority are all of considerable importance in shaping the initial decisions and many of the following ones. Deeply rooted attitudes toward money and debt, which may precede by many years the business activity of the person concerned, may influence later decisions on credit or liquidity. Father images may be back of decisions affecting the labor force. Pricing or marketing decisions may be subject to the impact of moral norms or competitive attitudes in the persons concerned. In every case the degree of rigidity, conformity, or security feeling will be of great importance in determining the threshold of decisions and the general ability to make up one's mind at the right moment, to reach a decision promptly when the objective situation requires one.

It might be argued with some justification that such problems affect the old-fashioned owner-manager far more than the streamlined corporation executive; that the latter is subjected to a network of intracompany checks and balances designed to encourage decisions that are less personally colored than they used to be; that the business schools and the growth of industrial research have had an equalizing effect upon the patterns of decision making and that this latter process has become more nearly objective than it used to be. There is a good deal of truth in such statements, but they overlook the fact that the rise of corporate management—which has not affected the entire economy in any case—has brought some new emotional problems, such as competition within a company hierarchy, along with mitigating some of the older ones. There is plenty of evidence from top management itself that its decision making remains far from being completely impersonal.[5] This applies both to long-range decisions such as industrial location and to short-range decisions such as current pricing.

Price Determination

Determination of prices is an especially frequent instance of decision making in business. The traditional assumption has been more or less in line with the statement that sums up for many people all they ever picked up of economics—namely, that prices are determined by supply and demand or, in a slightly modified form, by competition on the market. We are not concerned here with the institutional factors, such as administered pricing, private price fixing, price discrimination, public price controls, or intrinsic imperfections of competition, that have always impeded this supposed rule in a varying degree on the level of business practice. Our interest centers on those modifying influences that have resulted from sociocultural and personality factors.

Now here again a warning against any overstatement of the case is necessary; in some areas of the American economy, at least, a certain approximation of the supply-demand, market-competition principle can be discerned. Yet the evidence of a wide disregard of this principle is no less impressive. To begin with British experiences, R. L. Hall, C. J. Hitch, and R. F. Harrod found before the second World War—on the basis of an admittedly small sample—that pricing followed either *long-run* profit considerations or, far more frequently, a rule of thumb. Prices were usually based on full average cost including a conventional—or, in its absence, an arbitrary—allowance for profit; they were "reached directly through the community of outlook of businessmen, rather than indirectly through each firm working at what its most profitable output would be if competitors' reactions are neglected, and if the play of competition then varied the number of firms." Once fixed, prices tended to be stable in the absence of significant changes in costs. However, moral considerations such as the "right" price were also part of the picture, and so were the history of the industry and the possible presence of an element of oligopoly.[6]

Evidence from American sources on the actual process of price making differs in details but not in the general range of influences other than competitive profit maximization. There are considerable differences according to the type of market—especially between production goods and consumer goods, and between wholesale and retail pricing—but in general the evidence of habitual or conventional pricing is widespread. This also applies to the observance of unwritten trade codes, price leadership, the priority of production needs and capacity considerations over short-run profit maximization, crude inventory rules, and, last but not least, intuitive or rule-of-thumb pricing.[7]

Security needs appear to be of particular importance in determining the pricing patterns in various types of business. Profit maximization sometimes yields to safety as the decisive factor. Uncertainty may be so repulsive to businessmen that they assume the same of their customers regardless of the exact gain or loss involved. The case of the whisky industry is especially interesting because of the double security desire involved, not counting that of the drinker. Bonded whisky tends to be far more expensive than unbonded, in excess of the cost difference, for a smaller but certain profit is usually preferred to a larger one two to four years later. Moreover, the continuing impact of the prohibition experience makes the industry unusually anxious to be respectable both in its profit drive and in its moderation campaigns.

On the basis of long experience, Oswald W. Knauth summarizes the pricing process as follows, "A change of price is a nervous affair. The perfect price cannot be reasoned out. The only guide is public reaction which is discovered by trial and error. . . . The price is arrived at by obscure methods of reckoning having an historical rather than a factual background." It often has little relation to the costs of manufacture; sometimes it is vaguely connected with whatever is considered a fair price. Personal rivalries may be a determining factor of great effect as the history of price wars in the rubber and carbon-black industries shows.[8] Price wars rest in part on the assumption that one can guess the reactions of the other fellow on the basis of one's own reactions, an assumption which also underlies nonformalized collusion.

Moralistic aversion to open price competition, even while competitive practice may continue on the nonprice level, appears to have a substantial part in the phenomenon of price leadership. Such a role may originate in a power position but is derived more often from a reputation for sound judgment and initiative. It is usually followed more easily upward than downward. Sometimes price leadership develops from bitter initial competition; the person or firm that asserts itself in this contest assumes a reference role for the entire trade group. In this process, the function of the price leader may become either a dominant or a barometric one. Unwritten group norms and personal propensities to conform are also important in explaining, at least in part, the phenomenon of tacit parallelism in pricing practices.

There are definite signs that changing sociocultural values or economic philosophies influence pricing practices no less than other types of decision making in business. This applies especially to the connection between wage level and price level. In a survey of Michigan industries, the Survey Research Center found that although companies representing 51 per cent of employees listed "labor (largely labor costs)" among the disadvantages of Michigan, a sizable proportion of these companies also considered the high wage level an advantage as it reflected high productivity. This was exemplified by such statements as "You get more from your labor here although you pay for it" or "We pay high labor rates but we get high labor production." [9] In Spain, Egypt, or Bolivia it would be most unusual for a businessman to make any such statement; perhaps it would still be in some areas of the United States today and it certainly would have been anywhere fifty years ago. The old philosophy of high prices with low wages has been exposed to amazing attitudinal changes in a sizable sector of American business. In national policy, it is true, the concepts of depreciation of people (not merely plant) and of the necessity of human conservation have lagged behind.

The impact of value scales upon pricing is also exemplified, in quite a different cultural environment, by the following statement from an innkeeper in a remote Alpine valley in southern Austria with a very conservative population. The writer heard her say, in the summer of 1950, that she was anxious to keep her prices low because high prices might attract all sorts of people, whereas with low prices she could afford to take recommended guests only. Money power was thus associated with low personal quality, and downward pricing decisions in this case were meant to be an instrument of status policy, rather than profit maximization. In a different cultural setting comparable status goals might be aimed at through upward-pricing decisions.

A great variety of psychological factors goes into price determination depending on cultural and institutional conditions. It is doubtful, for this reason, whether marginal analysis in a psychological vacuum can hope to make any decisive contribution to the understanding of actual business pricing. In particular, great practical limitations are implicit in any price analysis that explicitly or implicitly assumes preestablished full production, complete information, purely objective and standardized rules of accounting, or "rational" conduct in the sense of an undiluted drive for profit maximization. This is not an argument against the use of marginal analysis for purely normative purposes. On the level of actual business behavior, however, such analysis would have to reintroduce a forbidding number of factors previously omitted before it could hope to be a guide for the understanding of economic reality. One alternative in using such analysis practically would be an assumption that businessmen follow marginal pricing rules unconsciously and instinctively in practice while rationalizing them away in interviews and other public statements—somewhat like Molière's Monsieur Jourdain who had talked prose all his life without realizing it. Such an assumption of pre-established harmony would be very unrealistic indeed. Another alternative would be to adopt marginalism as a strictly *normative* yardstick without any claim to explanation of past or present business behavior.[10]

Industrial Location and Investment Decisions

While pricing, on the whole, represents the short-range type of decision making, other kinds of business decisions tend to be of a long-range character. This is especially true of industrial investment and location. Traditional location theory usually emphasizes considerations of expected profit maximization, expressed in a varying combination of natural resources and power, labor supply, and marketing factors.

These assumptions were borne out only in part by the Michigan survey of the Survey Research Center.[11] In this survey, executives representing 64 per cent of employees emphasized proximity to markets among the general advantages of a Michigan location; favorable labor situation, proximity to materials, and favorable transportation facilities followed far behind, in this order. Among the general disadvantages of this location, labor in general (largely labor cost) was emphasized by executives representing 51 per cent of the employment; pressures from organized labor (overlapping with the former factor), distance from materials (especially steel), distance from markets, taxes, and utility rates followed in this order.

When it came to the actual history of the company location, however, executives representing 51 per cent of employees listed personal reasons of one kind or another, while only 33 per cent mentioned market proximity and even fewer listed enabling factors such as plant availability, proximity of materials, or manpower supply. Neither the sample nor the replies offered an entirely conclusive picture; but apparently executives tended to answer questions of a more or less general kind by giving "economic" reasons for the choice of the region concerned, while they emphasized personal factors when they explained the actual location history of their own company in that particular town or state. Especially was this true of small firms. Possibly these data indicate that personal reasons either were perceived as an "exception" or did not quite reach the conscious level; or that the respondents felt a bit ashamed at being somewhat less than economic men in their general philosophy. We have to allow, however, for possible rationalizations in both directions: personal reasons may conceal economic ones, and vice versa. For example, when "labor conditions" are mentioned, this seemingly economic factor may conceal a deep personal resentment on the part of a paternalistic respondent. Conversely, reference to grandfather's pioneering in a given location may spread a cover of sentimentalism over the fact that transportation facilities there are excellent. Inertia often is quite important as a factor that deters industrial movement from an established location. A number of individual answers which stress personal factors in the location of industries will be found in Appendix I.

The same survey also yielded some factual information on investment decisions. This information indicated that investment was not necessarily driven by a spontaneous desire to grow and often followed behind an increase in sales. In some cases a subjective feeling of compulsion to invest for competitive reasons led to semiautomatic responses or habitual action with regard to investment. There was a moderate correlation, but by no means a perfect one, between expected business trends and investment plans; quite a few of those who anticipated better business conditions had no plans to invest, and vice versa. In some cases expected deterioration, not improvement, of business conditions encouraged decisions to invest. Genuine investment decisions appeared to require strong motivational forces.

Other studies confirm the impression that there are great variations in the degrees of planning and centralization that are involved in an investment decision, in the accuracy of anticipation of capital outlays, and in the differentiation between current profitability and long-range outlook. Apparently the reliability of such judgments is somewhat related to the size of the firm, the amount of total investment, the age of existing assets, and other economic factors. There is some tendency to understate the investment plans, and for small enterprises to be less accurate in anticipation than larger ones.[12] Some factors of inaccuracy, such as business fluctuations, can be classified as economic, but two major kinds of psychological variables are also involved: first, the personalities, reaction patterns, and interpersonal relations of the decision-making individuals; and second, the general atmosphere of security or insecurity which prevails at a given time in the population and, especially, in the business community.

Similarly, regular procedures for reappraisal of the remaining life of equipment and for revision of the depreciation rates appear to be none too frequent. In a good many firms the decisions involved are made on the basis of personal reactions rather than objective criteria. Especially is this the procedure in many small enterprises and, most of all, in family-based companies where there is no strict dividing line between business and household. In this type of business, about which little quantitative evidence is available, the business role and the consumer role of the persons concerned merge into one pattern of behavior—a pattern which may seem uneconomic to the outside analyst or to the management of larger enterprises but which potentially has its own intrinsic logic.

In these units, savings have alternative uses for either investment or consumption. The choice between self-financing and credit as the source of investment may involve crucial decisions affecting personal or family life; the liquidity preference may be excessive because of great personal insecurity, or else liquidity may be reduced below business requirements so that the family cannot draw on the assets for consumption purposes too easily. High interest rates which handicap business expansion may be welcome if they also mean higher income during an imminent period of retirement, for many people habitually hate to eat up assets during that period—even if they were accumulated for this very purpose—and count on income from interest or dividends.

In other words, the less definite the dividing line between business and household, the greater the likelihood that investment decisions will be colored by personal factors. It would be wrong, however, to count out such factors entirely even in very large corporations. In fact, the latter may be exposed to different kinds of hidden motivational influences which do not affect smaller enterprises in any comparable degree. This applies especially to long-range attitudes toward expansion and innovation, which may become a self-purpose here.

In a related study of the way in which business looks at banks, the Survey Research Center found that the stability of banking connections of larger American business firms is due largely to inertia and tradition. More generally, the attitudes of business executives toward banks, and the financial policies of many business firms, are colored by a variety of personal factors. These factors often modify the financial considerations of firms concerning the choice, continuance, and specific use of a banking connection, and include essentially three types. One personal factor is the individual variation in the personality traits of business executives themselves, or of bank executives as perceived by their customers. Another personal factor centers on ideological preferences and the perception of the economic and political system. A third factor consists of interpersonal relations and contacts between business executives and bank management.

Traditional assumptions, other than purely hypothetical, that investment is determined entirely by financial incentives in the specific sense of expected profit maximization in a rather short run, are increasingly subjected to important qualifications. Drives for high profit frequently serve as a symbol (or rationalization) of deeper urges that are rooted in personality needs or group norms. At a time when monetary measures and incentive taxation receive great attention as tools of public policy, their effectiveness is threatened by the same mechanistic interpretation of practical market behavior that has plagued the older, more conventional approaches to economic policy. Credit and taxation undoubtedly are powerful tools in influencing the course of economic life, but any notion that investment, or managerial and other work for that matter, depend on monetary and tax incentives alone is psychologically unrealistic.[13] Actually many "economic" factors in investment—especially the degree of asset liquidity and, indirectly, the reserve requirements within the credit network that are considered necessary—depend in a high degree on the perception of investors, managers, and consumers concerning war, slump, or inflation threats; on social or group norms; and on the prevailing kinds of personal needs including the state of security feelings.

To sum up, important influences of a noneconomic type—if we follow the conventional terminology—are not an exception but a rule in determining the ways in which business is started, expanded, and currently done. Ordinarily such influences replace, supplement, or (most important of all) underlie those factors that are usually classified as economic. Decision making in business, as in other spheres of life, does not follow inflexible incentives or motives that are derived from human nature as such. Decision making depends in a large degree on the institutional setting, which determines the area of decisions open to individual or company action in the first place; on the cultural value system, especially in its impact upon perception and norms; and on the group loyalties, personalities, and individual needs of the persons concerned. The pattern of decision making in business thus changes with the sociocultural, institutional, group, and personal variables, and it may vary enormously according to the given combination of these factors. Under certain conditions it may, in fact, deviate in an almost incredible degree from what is ordinarily classified as economic determination of business decisions.

Folklore, Myth, and Symbolism in Business Life

Once it has been "discovered" that businessmen are people, at the company offices no less than at home, in church, or in a club, nobody will expect them (save for purposes of theoretical abstraction) to behave like standardized automatons, or to be ashamed of actions and attitudes in business life which cannot be associated with profit maximization in any objective sense. In the following paragraphs some of the more conspicuous manifestations of such attitudes will be discussed. It should be emphasized that we are not concerned here with neurotic or other deviations of clinical interest chiefly. This discussion deals with normal practices which fall outside the kind of behavior usually associated with rationality, whatever the exact meaning of this term may be.

Astrologists and palmists are known to have a wide clientele from business no less than from other groups, but how many business decisions have actually been influenced by them is anybody's guess. In December 1949 the Securities and Exchange Commission revoked the registration of an investment adviser in New York mainly because he based his recommendations to clients on his interpretation of what he believed to be a code contained in the daily comic strips.

However, such conspicuous examples of myths in business may not be the most important ones. The range of superstition in some areas of business behavior must be considerable, if we may judge from various experiences of the stock exchanges, for instance. If superstition is a widely shared belief which is at odds with demonstrable facts and which stresses supernatural influences, there also are widespread manifestations of superstition in certain appeals to consumers. It is not always easy to decide, indeed, to what extent commercialized "charms," dream books for lottery games, or hotels with missing thirteenth floors represent intentional playing on consumers' superstitions and to what extent they are manifestations of businessmen's own attitudes.

The desire to get rich quick with the aid of magic played an important role in the early history of capitalism,[14] and some vestiges of this desire have survived. According to Bronislaw Malinowski, magic fulfills a definite function in coping with needs which are not satisfied by any other factors in the society concerned, especially in overcoming uncertainties in practical decisions, in strengthening confidence, and sometimes in providing an established aggressive outlet for anxieties.[15] It is not too surprising to find its partial survival in an economic environment which is characterized by widespread insecurity both on the social and on the personal level.

In modern business practice such magical survivals are expressed, for example, in various patterns of etiquette and ritualism in business life including those governing club activities and conventions. Semimagical rituals serve, in particular, as symbols of the hierarchic structure of the business community itself, or else as a kind of incantation designed to ward off such sorcery as government intervention. On the marketing level, the symbolism that is often implicit in brand names and their advertising often represents a semiconscious appeal either to habitual reactions or to magical needs of customers. Unfortunately the magical or, at least, strongly emotional connotations to potential customers of such goods as liquor lend themselves easily to misuse by pseudo-business enterprises, as the failure of prohibition, for instance, demonstrates.[16] The general impact of nonrational factors, including magic and superstition, upon consumer preferences and product differentiation, and the active part which business may play in encouraging or discouraging such consumer behavior, represent in themselves a special area of studies. This area, which has undergone wide development since Veblen's pioneering essays, can only be mentioned generally in this context.[17]

In industrial plants, paternal symbolism toward employees (and sometimes toward suppliers, customers, or competitors) and the rationalizations that go with it have often been observed. This is one of the reasons why the logical arrangements in a plant or company that industrial theory requires are often disregarded in industrial practice. Few of us will go as far as certain Freudians who claim that even the choice of names for tools, fittings, or processes is often determined by paternal or sexual symbolism.[18] Business life does show, however, more aggressions, defensive reactions, and inconsistencies than a detached observer would at first suspect in a group that has so long been associated with cold logical calculation.

Within the business process itself—both in its intrinsic aspects and in its social position—folklore, myth, rationalizations, and quasi-incantations are fairly widespread. To begin with, professed support for competition in general is seldom matched by equal enthusiasm for it where a man's own position in business is affected. It has long been a pattern of a good many businessmen to support and demand tariffs or subsidies in their own specific line while theoretically advocating free competition. As a rule businessmen are perfectly sincere in these recommendations. What matters here is their inability to perceive the contradiction involved. To present price-fixing agreements as fair-trade practices and to classify freedom to form monopolies as free enterprise is too common an occurrence to need much discussion. Although there have been some attitudinal changes in recent decades, we might apply to some of our contemporaries what Knauth says of J. Ogden Armour, who "wanted free competition for the people who dealt with him, and . . . wanted unrestricted power to do away with competition when he dealt with them." [19]

Here we step on some very sensitive toes, for the intensity of rationalizations and myths increases as we touch upon the problem of competitive institutions as such. Few people like to be told by others about their real motives or attitudes, or to be disturbed in their established patterns of rationalization. This is one reason why intellectuals are seldom popular among businessmen (or farmers and workers, for that matter), although recent years have brought a new type of intellectually trained businessman. It is part of the function of a teacher or research worker to interfere with other people's rationalizations even if he may tend to replace them by his own.

The semantic lag between reality and lingo in business life is too great to be neglected in any discussion of the subject before us. The self-glorification ritual of business, which is performed regularly at conventions and on other occasions, has a meaning that transcends a mere defensive need for constant self-assertion, although this, too, is of considerable importance. The continuing identification of the business community with free enterprise even while business thrives on defense orders, government credit, subsidies, tariffs, and other types of public action can only be understood in a normative sense: many hard-boiled men of practice *want* to live in their ideal world without government, and in the absence of any such world, and of any hope for it, they indulge in wishful images which they then identify with reality. Thus they manage to contrast "the American system of free enterprise" with the interventionism of other nations while, at the same time, bitterly criticizing their government for its "socialistic" practices of the last twenty-five years.[20]

The underlying myth of origin perceives government as the natural enemy of business. This myth implies that America was born as a free-enterprise nation but that in recent decades it has succumbed to a socialistic statism due to sinister villains. Any serious student of economic history knows that this myth is at odds with historical reality; actually capitalist institutions and many specific branches of business were everywhere created or, at least, greatly encouraged by the governments concerned. What Malinowski says of the role of myth in primitive societies continues to apply in a considerable degree to sophisticated ones:

It is not an explanation in satisfaction of a scientific interest, but a narrative resurrection of a primeval reality, told in satisfaction of deep religious wants, moral cravings, social submissions, assertions, even practical requirements. . . . It expresses, enhances, and codifies belief; it safeguards and enforces morality; it vouches for the efficiency of ritual and contains practical rules for the guidance of man.[21]

The free-enterprise myth thus tends to become a quasi-religious belief with some magical traits that promise a cure for all evils. At the same time it is endowed with a symbolic meaning to which the paternalistic attitude that was mentioned earlier may provide a clue: the way in which free enterprise is contrasted with government often resembles a fight for independence from "father" by someone who now wants to be the head of the family himself and who feels that he has a moral right to this role.

Free Enterprise and the Government: Emotional Factors

The semantic confusion surrounding the term free enterprise has been discussed elsewhere.[22] In some people's minds this term simply refers to private property; to others it means freedom of individual initiative regardless of whether or not any specific property relations are involved. For some the connotation concerned is absence of legal or actual impediments to entry into business; to others it means freedom to engage in restrictive practices as long as they are private. In this study we are mainly concerned with the myths and emotions involved in recent use of the term by a wide sector of the business community, led by some of its national associations—a use which has entered political life, too, with rather serious implications.

If the term free enterprise means what the words would seem to indicate in any strict sense, it can only refer to a virtual laissez-faire situation regarding unimpeded entry into business, undistorted competition, and general absence of any artificial twisting of the market process regardless of whether such twisting is of a legal or an actual, a public or a private, nature. One need not be an economist in order to see that any application of such requirements to the contemporary scene, either in North America or elsewhere, has little relation with reality.

Common observation shows that while privately owned enterprise prevails in the United States, it has long been modified, influenced, and at times guided by extensive public policies on top of organization or restriction of competition through business action. We have long had an intricate network of public grants to private enterprise, ranging all the way from railroad and shipping subsidies to tariffs, mail-rate support of newspapers, and the very elaborate farm program of the last few decades. We have put a floor under the wage rates and working conditions through social-security legislation. We have had an extensive system of financial controls including an enormous tax structure, the reserve, discount, and open-market policies of the Federal Reserve System, government insurance of bank deposits, and so forth. We have had elaborate programs of trade promotion, patent laws, soil conservation, and research carried out by government agencies of a federal, state, or local character. We have had the Tennessee Valley Authority and other public programs of power supply. Last but not least, we have had a defense establishment ranging from the Veterans Administration to the foreign-aid program and the Atomic Energy Commission—an enterprise which far exceeds in size anything that private business could be expected to build or operate even under the most favorable conditions.

In addition, there has been plenty of private action designed to modify or eliminate competition. Despite the long, uphill fight of the antitrust authorities, price fixing has been frequent and often legal over extensive periods—for instance, under the Miller-Tydings amendment or the basing-point system. Further, the requirements of modern technology and organization have raised the initial capital needs for entry into many industries to such levels that entry and survival have become extremely difficult for newcomers in these fields.

Yet the historical myth of free enterprise is still effective and strong emotions remain attached to it. A whole series of identification processes is involved here with the help of semantic links. These processes provide a connection between private property of the family-store type (or the consumer's type) and corporate stockholding, between private ownership of industrial or commercial property and the general freedom of individual action in life, between financial business interests and the personal values of a farmer or workingman.

More than that, one connotation of free enterprise tends to involve an atmosphere of confidence on individual and social levels alike, a feeling of independence and optimism. In this sense the concept meets a deep emotional need of many people, including the underprivileged, and assumes a moral, quasi-religious meaning: it helps them to build up an image, a normative ideal of opportunity, hope, or at least escape, quite regardless of the institutional features of business enterprise in economic reality. Apparently the term capitalism—which is usually associated with money gain rather than with personal hope—does not produce the same ego-involvement effect as the term free enterprise.

"Do you believe in free enterprise?" This economically meaningless phrase has been asked by investigating committees in the same psychological atmosphere in which earlier generations subjected religious beliefs to inquisition and in which they prosecuted any deviation from the one approved creed. The existence of any doubts with regard to free enterprise is in this case associated with giving up the hope and security which this pseudo-religious belief promises to the faithful. This is more than investigating crusaders can take; their emotion-laden belief in free enterprise ends rapidly when it comes to free enterprise in ideas.

Business as a group should not be associated excessively with such attitudes. Many individual businessmen have reacted to such emotional intolerance in the same adverse way as would any person who is familiar with the real American heritage of intellectual freedom. But positive action on the part of leading business organizations against attacks on freedom of thought has been rare, and so has any clean-cut disassociation from the totalitarian image of a world with only the absolutes of "free enterprise" and "communism"—with nothing else to choose from. Standardized individualism, with every individual expected to arrive on his own at the same social attitude and philosophy, is expected by many, and the explanation is in a single word, fear. Under its blows free enterprise ceases to have any economic meaning and becomes a kind of incantation designed to ward off personal threats; no one can be tolerated who fails to share in this ritual.

Yet a strong case for the present economic setup could be made on the basis of a factual and realistic picture of contemporary American society. Its greatest asset, the cultural propensity to develop individual initiative and ingenuity without the burden of outmoded traditions, could only gain from encouragement of constructive dissent and innovation. Its greatest productivity has been achieved at a time when public intervention and government participation in economic life have also reached a peak. In other words, the productive performance of the American economy impresses the world through the weight of facts, and the nation does not need the rotten crutches of an unrealistic image of itself; but a sizable sector of the business group hangs on to them fearfully. This is one of many cases in which emotional blocks prevent a social learning process from taking place on a reality level.[23]

Nowhere is the contradiction more conspicuous than in the usual attitude of business toward government. The fact that business mistrust has apparently been far more intensive toward the federal government than toward state or local governments cannot be explained entirely from the complexion of American political power during a prolonged period. Public intervention on the national level symbolizes a challenge to the social leadership claim of business as a group, to its identification of the perceived interests of business with those of the nation. Hence the frantic attempts to persuade the general population that such challenge, and the institutional alternatives to free enterprise that it implies, are bound to bring dire consequences to everybody's freedoms and way of life. Sometimes such attempts operate with the assumption that no rational or objective yardstick of ends in public economic action and, especially, in welfare policy and public budgeting is possible.

This approach applies especially to attitudes toward taxation—attitudes which cannot be explained entirely from objective financial interests or even from the discomfort involved. It is infringement of the claim of social leadership that really matters here; private "taxation" through a price squeeze, for instance, may meet about as much economic resistance but will seldom arouse the same emotional reaction. Corporate taxes appear to meet even greater opposition than taxes on individual high incomes; the exposure of a detailed balance sheet to the prying eyes of a tax collector appears to many to be an almost immoral act.

Such emotional resistance is usually rationalized into financial theories concerning the devastating effect of taxes upon incentives. Actually taxation designed to encourage incentives is a commendable policy, but its practical effects are often overrated. In a survey by the Brookings Institution of one thousand manufacturing corporations (of which, however, only about 20 per cent answered) 94.7 per cent of the respondents believed that the incentives to work and save were affected by high tax rates; but only 41.3 per cent thought that high taxes affected the availability of managerial personnel. The conclusions of the author were as follows:

The establishment of new businesses is not greatly affected by taxes. . . . Decisions relating to business expansion are influenced by taxes, especially income taxes. . . . Small and moderate-sized firms hoping to expand from earnings are seriously affected by the corporate income tax. . . . The volume of money savings available for investors is profoundly influenced by personal income taxes. Work incentives of wage earners are not materially influenced by taxes. . . . Industrial incentives are not much affected by property taxes. . . . Capital expansion and the level of business operations have not been appreciably affected by payroll taxes at recent [1947] rates.

These conclusions, we repeat, were derived from a survey of corporate opinion, but if they showed anything it was the fact that even executives were not quite convinced about the impact of taxation schedules on business incentives.[24]

Similar evidence applies to the actual effect of taxation on executives. In the light of a Harvard study of interviews with 160 executives, no substantial reduction of their work or effort occurred as a result of taxes; in large companies and in most smaller corporations the importance of nonfinancial incentives and of the compulsions of administrative organization and discipline was far greater than that of taxes. The exception was men who were on their own in all essential respects, especially owner-managers in noncontinuous activities. Otherwise the effect of taxes was mainly a refusal of promotion or of employment offers when acceptance would have involved a greatly increased burden with little increase in net compensation; sometimes retirement was postponed because of tax commitments. "What all history goes to show is again confirmed by a great deal of evidence in this study, that difficulty, danger, and strenuous effort are themselves incentives to many men."[25] Yet the emotions that are involved in business reactions to taxation either of companies or of executive incomes are usually quite strong.

An ambivalent attitude also prevails toward the antitrust laws and their administration. On the one hand, this legislation finds much acclaim because it is designed to preserve and encourage competition in general. At the very least it arouses a respectful fear of potential government intervention in case an undue proportion of the market should be conquered by any one corporation. On the other hand, nearly every company which finds that it has run afoul of these laws complains bitterly about bureaucratic meddling. Sometimes free enterprise is practically interpreted as freedom from any public restriction of attempts at monopoly. And the courts—often faced by government attorneys with a limited interest in prosecution and by laws of doubtful meaning —have not always been consistent, especially with regard to such factors as the motives of the defendants, their formal "meeting of minds," and the "rule of reason."[26]

The basic paradox is in the fact that capitalistic United States prosecutes private companies under its antitrust laws while European nations, which have all been exposed to some degree of socialist influence, have no effective antitrust legislation and have sometimes encouraged if not sponsored cartels through public action. The traditional reasons for this difference have been: first, the widespread belief outside North America in an inevitable concentration of capital, more or less along the lines of Marx's prediction; second, the fact that monopoly has widely been interpreted outside North America as a logical outgrowth of competition, not its opposite; third, the basic intention of the American government to protect private business against itself, while many European governments have no particular objection to its digging its own grave. In other words, the American government, under the influence of a national philosophy which associated business with leadership in society, was not at all antibusiness insofar as the *system* of private enterprise was concerned. On the contrary, the government desired nothing more ardently than to preserve the system, even if this meant action against a number of *individual* businesses. The latter, however, often misinterpreted such action as an attack upon private enterprise as such and were unable to perceive their own long-run interests as a group.

Similar considerations apply to frequent business attitudes toward contracyclical measures, full-employment policies, and most types of economic planning. A manipulation of interest rates, often a psychological warning rather than an effective challenge to a real slump, will usually find only mild opposition from those directly affected. Full-employment programs, on the other hand, have unloosed bitter attacks, and long-range planning is apt to be associated with subversion. Yet there is no objective reason why business should be opposed to a public employment policy of a compensatory, insurance type or to a concerted plan for the development of water, land, and power resources in an entire river valley. On purely economic grounds there is much evidence that such measures help business as a whole; moreover, they have actually been carried out on a considerable scale and have found wide *ex post facto* approval.

The attitudes of businessmen toward the Tennessee Valley Authority offer an illustration of this point. Some years ago I spent a most interesting morning at the office of the secretary of the Chamber of Commerce in a northern Alabama town. Nobody could have delivered a more efficient sales talk for the T.V.A. than he did; he showed me photos of the ghost town which this community was before the T.V.A. period in contrast to its booming prosperity at the time of the interview; he pointed out the many new industries which the availability of cheap power and the digging of a deep navigation channel had brought to his town. Yet, he added, he had fought the T.V.A. program tooth and nail at first, and so had the bulk of the business community. When I asked why, the real reason emerged immediately. They had been emotionally incapable of perceiving that anything good could possibly come out of government intervention. Several years of T.V.A. in action on their local level, however, succeeded in shaking and changing their initial attitude.

The attitudinal factor involved here is essentially a nonrational resistance or emotional inability to admit that the business system and the actual degree of competition are less than fully automatic, and that they might require public correctives or protection. Sometimes this basic attitude is shaken by important new developments or a quasi-traumatic experience such as the T.V.A., a major depression, or a war, but in other cases the underlying resentment against that "rival father," the government, is so intensive that those affected would rather cut their own throats, individually or collectively, than admit that their premises might be wrong.

Pressure Groups and Social Utility

Similar emotional blocks to the perception of economic reality result from the frequent failure of businessmen and, especially, of associations to acknowledge the simple fact that the government in America, regardless of party complexion, is greatly influenced by business and quite often staffed by business people. Their image of government is that of bungling, unpractical bureaucrats or academic misfits who have never met a payroll. When acknowledgment of the business experience and group association of government servants like Bernard M. Baruch, the two Charles E. Wilsons, Averell Harriman, or John Foster Dulles becomes inevitable, further theories are sometimes adduced concerning the confusing influence of government service even upon former businessmen. The institution of dollar-a-year men who perform public functions while remaining on the payroll of private corporations has seldom stirred up any criticism among business.

Other emotional barriers to a realistic perception of economic life impede the general acknowledgment of the fact that many public controls have been instituted at the insistence of business groups, though usually not the ones who fight those particular controls subsequently. Perhaps the most important case is the group that is so dissatisfied with the effects of an unregulated market that it mobilizes political support in order to modify these effects through legal or administrative action. Jean Marchal has suggested that an entirely new theory of profit be developed on the basis of collective business action upon the market structure, the consumers, and the public authorities—an action designed to modify some essential factors of production and cost.[27]

Inability to perceive social needs that might outrank specific short-run desires of the group or company, or even to see its own long-run interests, is one important feature of pressure-group mentality. It was exemplified by local resistance in some prosperous communities to the channeling of federal purchases into unemployment areas during short recessions. Another example was the indifference, if not hostility, of a sizable sector of the New York garment trade toward municipal attempts to relieve the traffic congestion in its area through decentralization of operations or staggering of deliveries; this occurred even though the constant traffic jams had substantially increased the cost factor in this trade.

Another feature of pressure-group mentality consists in the presentation of perceived group interests in terms of social utility, if not of essential importance for society. We are not concerned here with conscious overstatements made by group members against their better judgment. Such overstatements undoubtedly occur in professional lobbying. Rather are we interested in the range of rationalizations in the mind of group members, which manage to transform a narrow group interest or program into an absolute necessity for society. The most effective actor is always the one who really identifies himself with his part.

In a strictly individualistic society it is theoretically conceivable that a given trade group, no matter how narrow or peripheral, might mobilize sufficient political influence to push through a subsidy or tariff purely on the basis of power relations; it might then boast of this success openly, perhaps triumphantly, as evidence that it is smarter than others. This may have been fairly frequent in the past, but it is far less likely to happen in our period. Today every pressure group appears to need social-utility rationalizations for its own peace of mind.

This applies in varying forms and degrees to large and small, recognized and informal groups. The public appeal of the farm bloc is still partly based on a feeling that farm products are basic to survival while most other goods are not and that farming is a healthy way of life compared with the parasitic character of big cities. Direct or indirect contributions to employment, to tax revenues, and especially to national defense are used as arguments by almost any group, not only in order to solicit public recognition but, above all, to persuade its own members that their pursuits are worth while. The old philosophy that every economic activity, if not human life in general, is a racket anyway and that everybody should try to make the best of his own, is still fairly widespread on the verbal level; but usually it suffices to scratch the surface in order to be faced promptly with social-utility rationalizations (claiming, say, service to consumers) even in fields where considerable ingenuity is required to work them out.

Such rationalizations, however, easily lead to personal conflicts of an open or hidden nature, and these contribute to insecurity feelings. Every person inevitably belongs to more than one group, and there is frequent doubt either on or below the conscious level concerning the priority of loyalties. There are also variations in the importance of the various groups to the individual according to the specific situation involved. Conflicts are thus apt to occur among his occupational, income, religious, educational, and family identifications. They occur, in particular, between reckless advocacy of group interests, with all the rationalizations involved, and any social needs that are felt, especially below the conscious level, to transcend these group interests.

Advertising and Security Needs

Such conflicts of identifications and group norms tend to affect some fields of business more than others. They appear in an especially interesting form in an activity which easily lends itself to rationalizations if indeed it is not engaged in them professionally. We are referring to advertising. At first glance advertising means announcement or public information, especially with respect to goods or services available. Any such definition, of course, does not cover the essence of advertising in contemporary economic life. Today advertising means an application of the communications disciplines to a skilled appeal for the acceptance of products, services, or aims, usually on a commercial basis of operation. It is the ground-level neighbor of public relations upstairs and propaganda in the basement. The principle of the Middle Ages and of early capitalism that "good wine needs no bush" has long since been discarded with only a few notable exceptions. Advertising is now widely assumed to be a self-propelling agent in arousing or awakening wishes, hopes, fears, and other emotions on the part of the prospective customer, either on the conscious level or below it. Only a fraction of the advertising appeal is directed at his power of reasoning, though logic or pseudo-logic are often invoked in order to rationalize the emotions that are the real target.[28]

In skillful advertising, especially if it is of a long-range character, psychology may aim at influencing the prevailing patterns of ego involvement in a degree sufficient to alter or form specific attitudes in the population. Appeals to certain sectors of memory, attempts to bring subconscious elements to the surface (even ones affecting psychosomatic factors at times) are quite common. One of the limitations of such techniques is the fact that they inevitably mirror in some degree the mentality of the advertisers themselves and perhaps that of their clients—*their* personal involvements and power and prestige needs— a fact which may color their selection of stimuli designed to influence the audience. Only the naïve fringe still believes that the mere presence of an audience suffices to assure the effectiveness of a stimulus and that every band wagon actually reaches a public which is just waiting to jump on it.

It is very difficult to estimate the exact proportion of advertising that goes into attempts to arouse certain emotional responses on the part of an audience, into factual or neutral information, and into a fight against other people's advertising. On the basis of publicized budgets, however, there is little doubt that the rise of big corporations which cater to nationwide markets has tended to increase all of these advertising types and also to add a new driving force, advertising as a status device. A nationally advertised product, especially in the field of consumer goods, is something that a self-respecting corporation is assumed to owe to itself, that is, to its management, employees, stockholders, and customers. Even the annual corporation reports have in many cases become a glorified advertising device.[29]

The effectiveness of advertising has seldom been measured in a foolproof way. Success may impute to advertising certain developments which are actually due to different though simultaneous factors. The ill will or suspicions which are sometimes aroused by aggressive advertising may affect beyond repair the basic attitude of customers toward the product concerned. I know a person who wrote to the advertising manager of a cosmetics company that, although he had been using the product advertised for years, he was going to give it up because he was deeply annoyed by the daily singing commercial (which came with his favorite radio program at breakfast). Hard-boiled advertising men who do not believe in psychological subtleties may interject that they do not mind if consumers feel annoyed; consumers who are actually exposed to an aggressive advertisement will sooner or later start buying.

Yet suspicion and resentment are poison to the effect of advertising. Even the medicine-man approach of hiring "scientific experts" to prove the superiority of this or that brand through a modern equivalent of incantation has lost much of its persuasive appeal.

In its survey of industrial mobility in Michigan, the Survey Research Center asked manufacturers what they thought of various methods that had been used by several states in order to attract industry. Measured in percentages of employment represented, the reaction of 40 per cent to advertising was favorable, of 13 per cent mixed, and of 19 per cent unfavorable; 19 per cent did not know or their answers were not ascertained, and 9 per cent had not seen any advertising. Among the reactions listed as favorable were: "I think the advertising put out by the southern states has been excellent and I judge the results for them have been good," and "Oh, I think advertising is good. We've never really been sold by any of it but it does make interesting reading!" Another respondent stated more skeptically, "Well, it's not 100 per cent effective; it's about 10 per cent effective." Others had distinctly unfavorable reactions: "The fellow who is going to buy has to look for the flaws in the picture," or, "I believe that industries gravitate to places where it's best for them to go and where they want to go without help of advertising." Significantly there was a certain inverse correlation between the number of employees and the reaction to advertising; large companies showed lesser frequency in favorable and higher frequency in unfavorable reactions than small companies.

This sample, of course, does not permit sweeping generalizations.

However, resistance to advertising appears to be a more serious factor than business practice has often assumed. It is true that a person may be unwittingly influenced in a certain direction despite unfavorable reaction on the conscious level. It is also true that demand behavior on a market, for example, is subject to change during the marketing process as a result of new stimuli. Yet any notion that supply can always create its own demand faces no lesser limitations in advertising psychology than it does on the level of economic theory in Jean Baptiste Say's famous Law of the Markets. Advertising creates or stimulates effective demand when it activates an underlying ego involvement of large groups or else when it manages to change basic attitudes through long-range effort. The latter is probably quite rare. In either case the positive or negative results of advertising do not necessarily depend on the intrinsic merits of the product.

One of the most effective approaches in a society that is plagued by widespread personal insecurities is the appeal to the security needs of prospective customers. Such an appeal occurs most obviously in the advertising of tobacco, chewing gum, drugs, vitamins, tonics, liquor, laxatives, and similar products which are claimed to provide tension release in one way or another. Appeals to childhood eating experiences as symbols of a past security setting are not infrequent: "Pie crust just like Mom used to make it." In other cases either sex appeal or mail-order religion is offered as a means to obtain security.[30]

More frequently, brand names appeal to security needs either directly (by reducing the area of genuine decisions, promoting the formation of habits, and offering the customer assurance as to what he buys) or indirectly (by encouraging his identification with groups he admires or, at least, approves). Status needs are appealed to by encouraging the identification of the customer with Clark Gable, who smokes the same cigarettes, with Betty Grable, who uses the same lipstick, or simply with an imaginary upper-class person who feeds his or her guests with the same mayonnaise or whisky. Identification with patriotic, religious, or successful persons or groups in general is often promoted in similar ways. Such appeals are frequently beamed to women on the basis both of their economic role as household managers and of their assumed emotional characteristics. This, of course, is especially true of the fashion industry.

A special appeal to American consumers has been based on the

changing meaning of luxury. No longer is the average consumer allowed to be overawed by inaccessible luxuries of the rich, even though
the actual differences between consumption patterns of socioeconomic
groups remain substantial. The aspiration for a growing "standard
package" of consumption, to use David Riesman's term, has been
consciously fostered by advertising. A constant attempt has been made
to reduce the range of those goods and services that are perceived
as unnecessary.

Perhaps the greatest reinterpretation of luxury has been based on
the expansion of leisure. For the great majority of the world's population, leisure—not to be confounded with apathetic indolence—is still
the greatest luxury of all. Yet our society is worrying now about a
sensible way in which people could spend all the leisure time available. A do-it-yourself campaign could not easily be explained to an
Indian peasant who must toil incessantly in order to survive precar-
iously. In the West, however, the lengthening span of vacations and
the travel that often goes with them are seldom thought of as luxury
any longer. With ingenious help from the advertising industry, the
perception by the rank and file of what constitutes luxury has been
changing constantly.

Along with the equalizing influence of mass advertising, it is true,
there has also been an appeal to the "unusual" expenditure that is to
generate excitement and a high intensity of demand in the buyer,
quite contrary to the conventional assumption that he always looks for
a bargain. Shopping is often an emotional experience, especially for
women, in endowing them momentarily with a sense of power. High-
priced goods may stimulate this sensation; the term "cheap" carries
not only the connotation of inexpensive but that of common, not
respectable, and not desirable. Advertising often strives to point out
that the specific expenditure concerned will contribute to a feeling of
higher status without, indeed, running afoul of the prevailing requirements for conformity in general.

Advertising carries forward the desire for constant material innovation through the use of group influences, friendship patterns, word of
mouth and, last but not least, that real power in America, the children.
They see to it that any "luxury" which the neighbors have acquired is
soon converted into a "necessity" for their own family. The "child
market" itself has become an important aspect of American consump-

tion and production with the help of skillful advertising. It has, for example, had a considerable share in the rapid spread of the once luxurious television.

The conscious use of psychological methods—some of them less up to date than others—in the field of advertising has produced a huge literature, which can only be mentioned here.[31] Symbolism in establishing connections between the product advertised and personal needs, especially security desires, is attempted through certain combinations of layout and color or through personalized appeals of a visual or acoustic type, which address themselves to such associations as health, appetite, comfort, personal appearance, efficiency, ambition, vanity, sex, children, fear, safety, or altruism.

The development of radio broadcasting and, especially, of television has brought about some new approaches to psychological advertising which are still in flux. Certainly broadcasting lends itself very well to emotional and personalized appeals; since it relies on momentary sense impressions, it has to work in a highly concentrated and almost traumatic way. It often attempts to reach the latter effect through a constant switching of attention, for example, from politics or music to product advertising; but instead of making listeners more susceptible this method sometimes leads to confusion and rejection.

A detailed comparison of actual responses to commercial broadcasting with the responses to noncommercial stations in the United States, and also with the effects of publicly owned networks in European nations, would be very illuminating. Certainly the usefulness of this advertising medium has been impeded by such practices as the child-appeal campaign of television some time ago. In this campaign was used a newspaper advertisement which, under the heading "There Are Some Things a Son or Daughter Won't Tell You," depicted a child crying for a television set. One of the advertisements read in part, "You can tell someone about a bruised finger. How can a little girl describe a bruise deep inside? No, your daughter won't ever tell you the humiliation she's felt in begging those precious hours of television from a neighbor." [32] Quite an array of concepts and devices of psychology is here put to a perverted use: parents are to be driven to fear that the personality of the child may be warped by repression of its suffering; the aspiration level of the child and, indirectly, of the parents is to be measured by and oriented toward ownership of a television set; and social status needs are to be expressed and channeled in a similar way. Basically this method is meant to assure the use of children as unsalaried salesmen regardless of the emotional and family conflicts it may entail.

Other misuses of psychological advertising that have attracted the attention of the Federal Trade Commission or the Better Business Bureaus have included excessive claims for antihistaminic drugs and sharp practices in promoting the sale of various household goods through alleged special discounts or consumer bonuses. In the former case, an appeal to the personal security needs of the customer used the medium of health association; in the latter case, a similar kind of appeal emphasized a supposed opportunity to outsmart other consumers and perhaps even the sellers.

Now it does not take a skilled psychologist to realize that annoyance, mistrust, or ill will on the part of the prospective customer is very detrimental to the advertising process. The socializing effect of advertising—through its help in overcoming the isolation of the individual consumer—can be ruined by practices which annoy him, such as the mixing of reading matter and advertisements; and once this has happened, the physical fact of putting the advertisement before the eyes of the reader will have either no effect or an adverse one. Since it is pretty much a matter of common sense to realize this rule, the question remains why it is violated so frequently just the same.

The only plausible answer is that advertising is often unwittingly addressed, not to the personal needs or security desires of the customer but to those of the advertiser, and occasionally to those of the professional agent who serves him. In view of the antagonizing effect of certain advertisements, the question suggests itself as to who really likes them unless it is the advertiser himself. To some extent they may reflect his own prestige needs; unless he advertises extensively he may not meet the role requirements that are implicitly assigned or ascribed to him by the rest of the industry including his chief competitors. Usually he will defer to the group standard no matter what his feelings may be on the conscious level. Sometimes the advertiser, who stands here potentially for an entire corporation hierarchy, feels that he owes it to himself to create his own brand of an identical product (say, aspirin or antifreeze) and to advertise it widely and expensively. Conversely, artificial product differentiation with the advertising involved may serve similar prestige purposes. Knauth, who has had wide experience in this field, describes the underlying attitude of advertisers as follows,

Fear that their products would be forgotten explains their feverish extortions to keep their names before the public. . . . Advertising policy is dominated by fear. Hope creeps in just sufficiently to emphasize the dominant role of fear. . . . Professionalized, it has become a psychological pressure, backed by all the tricks of repetition, analogy, and association that may make a product a national institution.[33]

The good-will appeal of effective advertising is of decisive importance even though it may sometimes lead to paradoxical situations. It is probably sound advertising policy for a newspaper to carry announcements such as the following, "In order to continue the complete presentation of the news THE NEW YORK TIMES was obliged to decline 130 columns of advertising for this issue." The advertising of charitable or educational causes at no cost or at greatly reduced rates helps create good will toward newspapers or radio stations, and thus a predisposition for effective commercial advertising.

It is much more doubtful whether the peculiar self-advertising campaign of Free Enterprise—sometimes disguised as "economic education"—which has almost become an industry in itself, has been psychologically sound, quite aside from the doubts mentioned earlier concerning the realism of that concept as such. This campaign reminds one of a man who keeps looking at himself in a cracked mirror while talking to himself. We are here concerned, not with the orthodoxy and conformity aims of this campaign but only with its advertising features, which *Fortune* has summarized as follows: "Why the failure? This brings us to a riddle: how are democracy and free enterprise like toothpaste and frozen food? Or, rather, are they? Can you merchandize a concept as you do a concrete article?"[34] The cleavage between the product advertised and socioeconomic reality is too great to promise much of a missionary success. This, however, is not the actual purpose of the campaign, psychologically speaking; what it really represents is a kind of continuous revival meeting for the advertisers themselves designed to reassure them of their own values and to heal their own insecurities.

Advertising thus reflects, more conspicuously perhaps than most other lines of business, the emotional and symbolic factors that in social reality are inseparable from the conduct of business in an "economic" sense. These factors, may we emphasize once more, in turn reflect the cultural and historical setting in which business is actually conducted in a given period.

Changing Codes of Business Conduct

This brings up the crucial problem of the historical changes and sociocultural variations that occur in the basic values at the root of business activity. It was pointed out earlier that the term business has historically been associated with very different types of motivation and behavior. The saying "business is business," interestingly enough, is not true from any comparative point of view, whether historical or geographical. Within the United States the defensive needs of business, as a group, for constant self-justification—especially in terms of social utility—are much stronger in our period than they were half a century back. In many parts of the world today, such as most of the Arab or Latin American countries, there are few signs of a defensive business attitude. Fantastic profits are made and tremendous wealth is accumulated there by a very small minority, which feels no great need to justify this accumulation to the millions who live in squalor under its eyes, to their clergy, or to anyone else. On the other hand, business in most parts of Europe is far more defensive and less self-confident or optimistic than it is in the United States; it has a tendency to lie low or else to claim social welfare functions no less than private material purposes.

Actually the motivation of business activity has been changing ever since the beginning of capitalism, in North America and elsewhere. It has been a long way from the early phase when making money was considered a kind of transcendental calling—a Calvinist influence quite evident in the ideas of Benjamin Franklin, for example—to the period of rugged individualism when playing rough-and-tumble was regarded as something of a social as well as an individual virtue; and from there on to our time, in which either a genuine sense of responsibility on the part of business toward society or, at least, the appearance of such a sense is widely recognized as indispensable. The Better Business Bureaus mark an organized attempt to subject the conduct of business to social norms of its own devising in order to maintain public faith in private enterprise as a system. In some cases a flight from the ranks of corporate management into small independent business or, less conspicuously, into early retirement has occurred for comparable reasons.[35]

A more important outlet for social responsibility needs is presented by philanthropy, especially since the partial change in emphasis from religious charity to general welfare goals. In the United States a great structure of private philanthropy has been built up with widespread acclaim, while some suspicion regarding public welfare policies has persisted despite their actual expansion. In her Christmas, 1949, column in the *New York Times*, Anne O'Hare McCormick wrote, "It's a funny thing about Santa Claus. At Christmas time everybody loves the jolly and benevolent old gentleman who delights the heart of childhood. . . . But when a government is called Santa Claus it is a term of opprobrium. . . . Generosity, in short, is regarded as a noble attribute in individuals but as a vice and weakness in nations." The movie "Miracle on 34th Street" had a somewhat related theme.

There is little doubt that philanthropic giving by successful businessmen has often been motivated by feelings of responsibility, guilt, or frustration either on or below the conscious level. The story of Alfred Nobel is well known: his early experiments with explosives resulted in a nitroglycerin blast that killed his younger brother and gave his father a stroke; throughout the rest of his life Alfred remained a lonely and melancholic person without friends, who sought escape in writing fiction both before and after establishing the Nobel Prizes. More recently the newspapers reported the deathbed order in 1922 of George Robert White, a soap manufacturer in Massachusetts, which instructed his company to contribute to charity "forever" two dollars out of every three dollars of net profits and not to inform the public until the thirtieth anniversary of his death. It is asserted that he had given away two-thirds of his own earnings during his lifetime—also that the order mentioned has not prevented his company from doing very well during the decades since White died.

In still another case which the newspapers reported, a man who inherited a fortune from the industrial earnings of his grandfather gave all of it but a few dollars away years ago with the following explanation: "I had a shell of money about me, like a mollusk. I was spineless, as the shelled creatures of nature are. . . . I wanted to experience the reality of being poor. . . . I've found a great peace. Extreme wealth is certain to distort one's point of view. I never knew what living was before." The story was revealed when, twenty years later, he inherited another $650,000, which he intended to keep! [36]

It should of course be emphasized that any generalization of such cases would be quite naïve. Some of them may represent manifestations of "abnormal economic behavior." Yet their occurrence illustrates certain feelings and needs which, in a less extreme or dramatic form, may guide the behavior of a good many persons and agencies.

Neither should we overlook the fact that the field of philanthropy has often been a happy hunting ground for charity racketeers and busybodies, or an outlet for various queer mentalities. Self-assertion by making yourself feel important or generous, regardless of the objective merits of the contribution, is not infrequent. The incidence of those who give only for very specific purposes (for example, for readily seen school buildings to which one can "hold on" but not for less tangible scholarships or educational improvements) is still considerable, as every academic money raiser knows. Money raising has become an industry and, at the same time, a field for the kind of competitive self-assertion and status desires that philanthropy seeks to modify; benevolence of aim does not always seem to assure an atmosphere of kindliness and co-operation.

Contributions from individuals still account for the bulk of the total, but corporation gifts have also become a sizable item. Undoubtedly the fact that the tax structure made Uncle Sam contribute a large part of many corporation gifts has influenced this trend; philanthropy in these cases is simply an inexpensive way to buy good will. Apparently, however, there is also somewhat less resistance than there was in the past to "giving away the stockholders' money," especially in those lines which feel subjected to explicit or implicit pressures from consumers.

Such corporate giving thus far appears to favor community agencies or research institutes that are of definite interest to the company, but a gradual broadening of the horizon is indicated. This new pattern of giving, sometimes through company foundations, is more hard-boiled and businesslike than were some earlier patterns of philanthropy. It may not always mark a good heart, but it does point to an increased awareness on the part of business either of social responsibilities or of moral defense needs.

A very real conflict, however, has been in existence between the materialistic profit drive for its own sake—in which business supposedly has always been engaged if we are to accept its own traditional assumptions as well as those of most other people—and various ethico-religious norms which either have survived from earlier periods or have newly been created in the course of social development. Attempts to resolve this conflict in some way have far exceeded philanthropy even of the most genuine kind. The conflict has assumed various forms. One of the most important ones has been the contrast between the norms to which a person is subject in church on Sunday and those which govern the executive office on Monday; genuine piety and hard-boiled profit maximization, assuming the person concerned subjectively believes in both, are not easy to reconcile unless either complex rationalizations or reckless cynicism prevail.

The latter is illustrated in the novel *The Naked and the Dead*, by Norman Mailer, in this statement of General Cummings' father: "He's right and I'm right, and it's just in religion you act one way, and in business, which is a lesser thing, well, you go about things in another way. It's still Christian." If we assume that extreme cynicism is rare, a successful reconciliation of two contradictory codes would presuppose a combination of two entirely separated systems of involvement in each individual concerned, a psychological task of great difficulty.[37]

Aside from religious norms, certain secular values from the feudal or early capitalist periods continue to have some effect upon business standards in our time, especially in Europe. These values, too, frequently conflict with contemporary economic norms, as will be shown in the next chapter. Material success is sometimes achieved at a sacrifice of ethical standards of a precapitalist, capitalist, or postcapitalist character, either on or below the conscious level; and this, too, may lead to nervous tensions involving fear of more success, for example, or else to an interpretation of economic failure of either an individual or of society as punishment for improvidence, laziness, or luxury.

In a society where money gain and assets measure status, the lure of an indifferent attitude toward the source of gain is likely to be considerable. Money greed, it is true, may also occur in totalitarian or collectivistic societies, for somewhat different reasons. Since strict rules of the game are not always available in our society—and, where available, do not necessarily produce readiness to abide by them—someone has to step in in order to ensure observance of assumed standards and

perhaps to protect the moneymaker against himself. When the authority of religious norms and groups is weakened, either self-policing of
the business community is invoked or public agencies step in. The
codes of fair competition of the defunct National Recovery Administration, the Federal Trade Commission, the Securities and Exchange
Commission, and the antitrust agencies all came into existence when
the self-policing method failed to work. In the case of the professional
ethics of physicians, lawyers, and accountants the self-policing approach has been more successful without always eliminating the conflicts of codes between professional ethics and business incentives or
between group self-regulation and the public interest at large.

The familiar saying, "We are not in business for charity," illustrates
the practical problems involved in reconciling opposing norm systems.
In March 1950, for example, the newspapers reported that a country
banker in Westphalia, Michigan, got into financial difficulties by allowing substantial overdrafts because he could not bear to see his
friends in trouble. This case was somewhat reminiscent of the movie
"Mr. Deeds Goes to Town," in which a small-town fellow distributes
to poor farmers a million dollars that were handed to him and is cleared
of insanity charges by a judge with the words, "You are the sanest man
I have ever known."

The personal impact of conflicts between norm systems in contemporary society will be discussed in the next chapter. In the present
context we merely wish to point out that such conflicts are real in
practical business life as well as in other social processes. Individual
doubts and collective guilt feelings on or below the conscious level
affect top business groups no less than other people, thus contributing
to the constant and far-reaching re-examination of values and standards
in the course of business history.

It is a matter of opinion whether such historical re-examination is
to be interpreted as a sign of strength or a symptom of weakness, and
whether the pattern of business that has thus far emerged from it will
display less or more vitality than did the older one. In a rather unhappy
mood Joseph A. Schumpeter attempted to show that capitalism was
doomed because it tended to undermine its own values and to remove
its own incentives in the course of history.[38]

Certainly the self-confidence of business as a group has suffered
severely from the blows of history in Europe. It has not been spared

all damage in North America either, despite outward exuberance and productive success. Some wealthy "angels" of the Communist Party have tried to rid themselves, in this hopeless way, of the guilt that they feel adheres to their money. More important than that, there is ample evidence of a defensive group attitude on the part of business in our period. This attitude is manifested by the extreme sensitivity of this group toward public opinion.

There is little objective evidence, however, of any widespread resentment on the part of the American people toward business in general or even toward big business. A survey of public attitudes toward big business indicated that there were no decisive differences between the business groups themselves and most other occupational groups in their evaluation of the economic and social role of big business.[39] It is true that the businessman has often been pictured as a villain in American literature—by Jack London, Sinclair Lewis, Booth Tarkington, Frederic Wakeman, Marcia Davenport, John P. Marquand, and others—but as long as business could lean back on its self-confidence these novelists were regarded as approved court jesters. Apparently the sensitivity of business and its need for affection have greatly increased since the Great Depression.

Under the cover of defensive and largely self-deceptive incantations business has been undergoing another major shift in values and motivation on top of the important changes experienced since the beginning of modern capitalism. In its perception and accepted norms of behavior American business has changed considerably, assuming more social responsibility. It still claims the role of social leadership, but this claim is now increasingly raised in reference to a past or promised contribution to social welfare; it is no longer asserted on the basis of rugged individualism as a transcendental privilege. Hence the actual acceptance of a wide measure of social-security policies despite vigorous rear-guard action on the verbal level, and also the frequent attempts to ascertain and possibly to influence the climate of opinion among consumers and citizens at large.

Perhaps business has simply become the prisoner of its own advertising line—the recent emphasis on social values and social contribution —but the net result is the same. Profit maximization, which business on the whole still perceives as its main yardstick or *raison d'être,* is now presented as an economic function that involves many obligations toward society. It is a matter of opinion whether one chooses to interpret this shift in values and motivation as a historical process of group learning, or else as a sign of aging of the business system. There is little doubt about the far-reaching nature of the change itself, even allowing for rationalizations and public-relations stunts.

This brings up our final question. How durable can business be expected to be, not merely as an institutional setup but as a state of mind? Since it came out of somewhere in the past, it might conceivably disappear again at some future date. This, however, is not the most meaningful way to put the basic question involved. What really matters is what is to replace or supplement profit as the great economic yardstick once we realize that profit is not the all-embracing or durable standard that it has long been assumed to be. The answer is that to the extent that profit actually represents other, more ultimate, motives it might sometime be replaced by other, more direct yardsticks and rewards of achievement, as it actually has in sizable areas of economic life. In other words, to the extent that profit really symbolizes self-assertion or social status, other measures of either need might increasingly come to the fore without any loss in economic efficiency or managerial performance.

Conclusion

The first of the questions raised in the Introduction can now be answered as follows: Far from being a universal single-minded drive for profit maximization, the underlying motivation of business activity represents a complex and varying structure of financial, institutional, cultural, and personality factors. Accordingly, this motivation varies with the locale concerned; the type, size, and history of the enterprise; and the personal background of the individuals who manage it. It is subject to strong influences from such extraneous factors as the world situation, political trends, community affairs, and the pattern of family life. It is of a somewhat more impersonal character in the executive management of large corporations than it is in small owner-manager units, without ever eliminating completely the impact of the businessman's personality.

The perception of a business situation and the pattern of expectations and decisions, such as those affecting pricing, location, and investment, are strongly influenced by the prevailing sociocultural scale of values. This fact in large part explains the variations in business behavior from country to country as well as the historical changes in American business behavior.

The business mentality and the successful business activity of individuals thus depend on a varying combination of, first, objective economic factors such as the institutional setting, the aggregate income, the monetary and fiscal policy, population trends, and the state of technology; second, personality factors such as the degree and type of aggressiveness, anxiety, or conformity in an individual; and, third, the sociocultural and group scales of value such as ethicoreligious standards, group norms for personal ambition, or social appraisal of material success. Business activity, therefore, is guided by a wide and varying array of motives, among which those ordinarily classified as economic represent a fraction of changing importance depending on the locale and period.

Aside from being subject to such historical and geographical variations, the conduct of business in our society is based on a far more complex motivation than many businessmen realize. Not only are there many kinds and levels of doing business, but on each of these levels the actual meaning of profit orientation is different. Various types of business practice coexist and are interconnected through the market, but this does not mean that everybody does business for the same reasons or that the actual reasons are always revealed on a conscious level.

Profit maximization is important as a normative standard or general financial principle but it does not explain very much with regard to actual business behavior. Many business actions contradict this principle in practice. Even where it is most influential the fact remains that in any given period and locale some people are driven by a strong desire to make profit (not necessarily to maximize it) while others are not, that the comparative incidence of these types fluctuates, and that various people try to achieve such an aim by widely different methods. The drive for profit, such as it is, often reflects or symbolizes deeper needs of a social or individual character—needs for personal assertion, prestige, power, security—which could potentially be satisfied (perhaps better satisfied) through other means. Human beings and groups are complex, fallible, and changeable, no less so in business processes than in other life situations.

Business as an institutional setup and as a state of mind has been undergoing great changes in America and elsewhere, changes which affect its attitude toward profit maximization and social responsibility. Business conduct inevitably reflects sociocultural conditions in their impact upon prevailing values and patterns of personality. Any attempt to remake business abroad in the image of American business (especially in an unrealistic image) would, therefore, be quite hopeless, but there is undoubtedly a wide field everywhere for technical improvements in productive or organizational efficiency.

Although business in the sense of an exclusive, fundamental, and unqualified orientation toward profit has become rare in this part of the world, if indeed it ever existed in any strict sense, many great ventures and achievements have been carried out in the name of profit. As long as no other, more direct, standard of personal self-assertion and social status receives wider recognition, society will presumably continue to give those who think they carry out their productive pursuits for profit an opportunity to do so. Adequate social checks, however, are necessary in order to prevent them from taking their own assumed motives too literally, in terms of the prevailing values of ethics and welfare.

A realistic picture of world society with its great variety of value systems and motivations could save American business many frustrations; it could contribute to greater clarity about its own motives; and it could help in preventing a defensive-aggressive oversensitivity toward analysis of historical, cultural, and psychological differences. This, indeed, brings up the crucial question of interaction between instability in economic and social life and the wide incidence of personal insecurities in our period.

Chapter III

Socioeconomic Instability and Personal Insecurity

THE dynamic effects of a competitive business economy have traditionally been associated with lack of economic security for anyone under the system. The absence of financial guarantees for the individual or firm has been assumed to act as a powerful stimulus for efficiency in working and in doing business.

At the same time, *economic* insecurity and *personal* insecurity have usually been considered occurrences or problems on two entirely different levels of human experience, which might coincide occasionally but should not be confounded simply by virtue of a semantic pseudo-identity. As far back as 1914, it is true, a well-known psychologist attempted, somewhat casually, "to show that our social difficulties are ultimately dependent upon mental conditions which ought to be cleared up with the methods of modern psychology"; [1] but most of the time psychology and the social sciences proceeded quite separately. More recently the question has been raised whether there might not be a causal connection in the opposite direction, i.e., from socioeconomic problems to psychic problems; or perhaps there is some other relationship to be defined. In order to avoid any semantic misunderstanding, we shall apply the term insecurity to personality factors and use the term instability to characterize happenings or conditions on the socio-economic level.

To assure a meaningful discussion of the problem raised here, in line with Question 2 of the Introduction, it is essential, first, to point out the specific types and manifestations of socioeconomic instability in a business economy as compared with other types of economic society; and, secondly, to specify also those kinds of personal insecurity whose occurrence and incidence may be rooted in socioeconomic conditions. The question then to be determined will be whether there are any impressive indications of correlation between socioeconomic instability and the incidence of personal insecurities; and if so, in which direction any causal connections would seem to work. We use the term indications because we cannot hope at this point for any unassailable evidence of a quantitative type. We must confine ourselves to a number of promising hypotheses which may lend themselves to empirical verification sooner or later.

Socioeconomic Instability: Types and Impact

Strictly speaking, the term instability refers to extensive and uncontrolled fluctuations in economic and social life which face either individuals or groups (especially, firms or families). It should be emphasized that stability in this sense is clearly to be distinguished from either stagnation or absence of change. Likewise, stability is not the same thing as predictability. Sometimes instability can be predicted no less than stability. Yet the prediction of a rise in prices, inventory reduction, or unemployment does not necessarily mean that everybody will hedge against it. Even in the absence of disagreement among forecasters, blocks to perception and unconscious influences will prevent many people from hedging, a fact which need not discourage continuing endeavor to predict objectively.

For the time being, this discussion will generally refer to socioeconomic instability as it affects the individual, even though the group situation may be the real trouble. The first major question to be determined concerns the ways in which such instability in our contemporary society differs from comparable conditions in other societies. In most phases and periods of culture and society, it is the constant struggle with nature that makes for uncertainty and instability. In primitive, as in ancient and mediaeval societies, the threat of hunger seldom disappears for a lengthy period. Even when it does, the threat of natural disasters, such as floods or droughts, usually lingers on. Epidemics or the memory of them contribute to instability. The danger of war is usually present and war means both hunger and epidemics.

Although much of the recurrent instability in such societies is thus due to deficient control of natural forces, the kind of instability that is man-made or imagined, according to our standards, is usually of even greater impact. Even when the objective dangers from natural events or external aggression are moderate, a constant threat of dark forces often disturbs economic society, sometimes leading to an all-pervasive fear such as the one that plagues the people of Dobu. Malignant spirits may place a curse on someone, or on the whole population as the Alorese, for instance, assume. These spirits may have to be appeased by costly feasts, making wealth a requirement for security. Men, therefore, spend practically all of their time on a fearful pursuit of finance, while women work in the rice fields to the neglect of their babies. In other societies, such as the Comanche, strength is achieved in an economically labile society, by robbing other societies. Anxieties may result from reduced stability in the wake of a far-reaching change in economic methods, such as the shift from dry to wet-rice cultivation (due to land depletion) among the Tanala of Madagascar, with resulting changes in property relations.

In some of these cases, the social prevalence of man-made anxieties —owing to imaginary threats which, in turn, can often be traced to inadequate understanding or control of nature—encourages more socioeconomic instability among primitive populations. Similar trends can be observed among other precapitalist types of society, as, for example, the feudal. They are by no means absent in Western societies; Carlo Levi, for instance, in his remarkable book *Christ Stopped at Eboli*, describes the common belief in witchcraft in southern Italy, with its disastrous contribution to poverty and instability of economic life.[2]

The lasting stability of an economic society depends in part on whether it succeeds in creating a basic personality that performs effectively, at least in terms of that society, or whether a fundamental conflict arises between basic personality and socioeconomic requirements. A change in objective conditions, such as the exhaustion of good land, may result in such a conflict where none existed originally. We must beware, however, of evaluating such socioeconomic requirements or conflicts in terms of our own culture, which often assumes quite different thinking patterns, emotional responses, and values.

Even if allowance is made for the frequency of man-made or imagined instability in earlier forms of society, the direct or indirect impact upon them of inadequate control over nature remains overwhelming. Socioeconomic instability, it is true, is by no means universal. Some economically or technologically primitive societies show a high degree of stability over prolonged periods as long as no natural disaster or interference from the outside world occurs. At any rate, the pronounced lack of stability in the Western competitive societies of the nineteenth and twentieth centuries should not be confounded with the kind of problems facing noncapitalist societies. Our own period and phase of society is characterized by rapid progress in mastering the traditional threats from nature, by the elimination of much belief in magic and many superstitions of the past, though by no means all, by widening markets, central banking, and old-age pensions; but also by the introduction of some *new* factors of socioeconomic instability in the short as well as the long run.

This discussion is not meant to imply that every aspect of economic stability is good or that every aspect of instability is bad. Similarly, the question of whether or not the contemporary factors of instability represent either necessary or desirable incentives to industrial efficiency requires a separate discussion (see Chapter IV). With these qualifications the main types or sources of economic instability in our society are the following:

1. The competitive process as such. Even in the assumed absence of large-scale economic fluctuations and with full allowance for productive or other advantages that may result from competition, a competitive economy inevitably means continuous turnover in the business population and ever-present threats to every business firm, to every established type of production or commerce, and at times to whole industries. In the absence of extensive regulation, competition means a continuous fight for survival against bankruptcy, against underselling, and against monopolistic practices of others in formal or informal ways. The very argument for unfettered competition, namely, its propensity to keep everybody on his toes, implies a high

degree of economic instability both on the individual and on social levels.

2. Business fluctuations. Opinions are divided on whether or not there is any real rhythm or regularity in the periodic fluctuations that have been observed since the beginning of the capitalist system, and on whether or not we are justified in speaking of a business cycle as such, rather than various types of special cycles. There is no doubt, however, about the general impact in our period of recurrent swings in economic activity. The mere anticipation of a probable or possible repetition of slumps, an anticipation which has been widespread since the great depression of the thirties, is bound to have a far-reaching psychological effect. At times people feel that "things are just too good to continue," somewhat on the theme of Schiller's poem *Der Ring des Polykrates.*

3. Deflation and inflation. The question of whether the fluctuations in money and credit circulation and in price levels are primarily a cause or an effect of the cyclical swing need not concern us here; in either case they are a characteristic of our economy. This is not the place to enter into a controversy on monetary policy, but in the public mind deflation is usually associated with bankruptcy and unemployment while inflation means a loss in savings, consumer purchasing power, and money value in general. It could, of course, be argued that such fluctuations are a necessary part of a self-adjusting mechanism, or that deflation means lower prices for the buyer while inflation mirrors a boom—at least as long as the swings are moderate—but even this argument would not deny the contribution of oscillations in credit supply and money value to economic instability in general.

4. Unemployment. The most important effect of cyclical fluctuations upon an industrial population is, of course, the periodic occurrence of unemployment, though the business cycle is by no means the only cause of unemployment. The latter is also potentially influenced by seasonal and technological factors, the special problems of age, sex, minority, or substandard groups, unstable occupations, lags of industrial or agrarian development behind population trends, and so forth. In nearly all of its forms—excepting only that which results from relative underdevelopment of resources, often concealed by socially wasteful employment—mass unemployment represents a periodic or chronic form of socioeconomic instability that is peculiar to industrial

or semi-industrial market economies. It is supplemented by a relatively high (and sometimes excessive) degree of geographic and occupational mobility, which is likewise peculiar to market economies. Various plans for guaranteed annual wages aim at increasing the security feeling of workers as well as the stability of their incomes, but thus far such plans have found very limited applications.

5. Housing shortage. The inadequacy of the housing supply has by now become so universal that it must be listed among the typical forms of economic instability in contemporary society. The two World Wars, of course, have greatly influenced this situation, but the roots of the problem are deeper. Housing is a field where the market principle has rarely functioned properly insofar as facilities for the lower and middle income groups have been concerned. The shortage has become chronic or endemic nearly everywhere. The resulting lack of privacy, the social morbidities, and the individual difficulties in following up favorable job openings, in long-range family planning, and so forth are a powerful factor in socioeconomic instability in many countries.[3] Slum clearance, it is true, has not always avoided the disruption of communities, of deeply rooted habits, and of informal social organizations.

6. The old-age problem. The challenge of high infant mortality and periodic epidemics, which faces so many societies, has largely been met in America only to be replaced by other population problems. New sources of disability, such as industrial hazards and traffic accidents, have now appeared on a mass scale, and medical care has become a great financial problem. At the same time, the average life span has been extended so greatly that social and, very often, individual provisions for a long period of retirement have turned out to be inadequate both economically and psychologically. The worry about obtaining an old age that is carefree yet socially useful and personally fruitful contributes, for an increasing proportion of our population, to an atmosphere of socioeconomic instability.[4]

7. The socioeconomic impact of science and technology. The rapidity of scientific discovery and its technological application, exemplified by the development of aviation, electronics, space rocketry, and nuclear energy during the last few decades, has outpaced completely the adjustment of socioeconomic institutions, policies, and attitudes to the requirements of an industrial era. This cleavage has been added

to the general human problems of an industrial economy, such as fatigue, monotony, and "morale" in a narrow sense. These problems have persisted regardless of whether or not one believes that such effects of industrial technology would be with mankind under any socioeconomic system.[5]

The innovations referred to have been great enough to have traumatic effects upon social attitudes, although their manifestation may be temporarily retarded by the escapist use of modern mass media, another product of the scientific and technological revolution. Actually these same means of rapid communication tend at other times to spread a sense of impending hostile and threatening events everywhere.

Individuals and governments alike face rapid changes in the basic facts of economic life: consumer goods, standards of living, energy sources, modes of production, cost factors, military needs, and manpower requirements are in a process of hectic change toward unknown goals. The discovery of the almost unlimited yet uncertain possibilities of either progress or destruction, including the transformation of matter itself, has contributed in a high degree to the instability of our socioeconomic arrangements even where the hope for mainly peaceful applications of the new technology still prevails. Apparently a sizable minority would rather do without atomic energy altogether if they had the choice. Opinion surveys have also shown the receptiveness of a sizable minority of the population toward rumors about the odd or unusual effects of atomic energy, even if allowance is made for the spread of factual misinformation.[6]

More recently, space exploration has aroused various new expectations, hopes, and fears, the socioeconomic impact of which can be only dimly discerned at this time. We do know that the fiscal burden of space exploration, which has been a few hundred millions of dollars a year thus far, will skyrocket long before space stations or manned moon-bound vehicles do. We also know that the boundaries between the various industries that work on space equipment—propulsion, chemistry, fuel, airframes, electronics, photography, even rubber and textiles—are increasingly and inevitably blurred. Civil defense, on the other hand, has hardly begun to catch on to the consequences of the space age.

High-powered rockets will soon change the entire economics of transcontinental and transoceanic travel, of mail services, and perhaps of industrial location and business opportunities. The research required for rocket purposes on high-temperature metals and ceramics, on new methods of cooling, and on resistance to friction and heat may lead to sweeping changes in daily consumer goods and employment as well. Satellites serving as relay stations for telegraph, telephone, radio, and television may also affect profoundly consumer preferences and business methods.

Weather forecasting and, later on, weather control with the help of satellites may bring a real socioeconomic revolution. Storms, freezes, floods, droughts, even coming changes in climate will become predictable. The weather hazards of agriculture will greatly diminish, but the farm surplus problem may well increase. Construction, vacation industries, and health services will be up against entirely new situations and challenges. Unfortunately the possibilities of destructive misuse of such innovations by aggressor nations will increase equally.

We can barely guess how much the biological, physiological, and psychological segments of space research may contribute to our knowledge of man, but here again coming changes may well be revolutionary. Perhaps the most crucial question of all is whether socioeconomic motives and attitudes will change as rapidly as space technology, or whether each nation will attempt to go on with price wars, price fixing, labor racketeering, tariffs, and war preparations in the middle of a space-oriented world.

8. The new warfare. A sequence of World Wars, interrupted by periods, not of assured peace but of uneasy truce or cold war, would ever be a cause of socioeconomic instability. Coupled with the fast changes in the meaning of warfare, the constant necessity to adjust the economy to the possible requirements of a future war long before it is definitely known whether, when, and how one will actually occur has upset many traditional assumptions of a competitive economy. The constant struggle of two entirely different sets of principles and value systems in economic policy—one based on competitive markets and the other on a potentially total planning for all-out warfare—could not possibly help socioeconomic stability. On top of this predicament, the anticipation of the probable destruction of big cities, and perhaps many other population groups and facilities, in the course of nuclear warfare would make any assumption of long-range stability in the

countries concerned quite hopeless. Some groups also loathe the socioeconomic equalization which is implicit in the threat of whole-sale indiscriminate destruction.

"Confidence" in Economic Life: Meaning and Range

Socioeconomic instability in our period tends to create a general atmosphere of doubt and anxiety even when the individual or group concerned is in a relatively safe position objectively speaking. Time-honored concepts of economic thought such as expectation, uncer-tainty, and risk assume an entirely new meaning when the social atmosphere in general, instead of purely company-wide reactions and decisions, becomes the central factor. Morale and confidence, two other concepts on the fringe of economics, likewise refer increasingly, not to specific company attitudes and market situations, but to the socioeconomic outlook in general, to the social "field" in which busi-ness decisions take place. Specifically, fluctuations in saving, spending, and investment today appear to depend in a large degree on people's ideas of the general outlook, rather than on past experiences or the objective situation of the individual business or household unit.

Confidence has often been declared to be the main variable in business fluctuations without any specific explanation either of the reasons for its oscillations or of its exact frame of reference. At best, confidence in business life has been interpreted as reflecting, in the minds of individual businessmen, such objective data as the inventory situation, consumers' incomes, the interest rate, or the labor supply —always from the specific viewpoint of the firm and market situation concerned. However, the difference between an individual mood of optimism and a socioeconomic atmosphere of confidence is very important. In particular, it is only the simultaneous occurrence of many capital investments or replacements (that is, of specific confi-dence reactions) that may help in explaining economic fluctuations.

Similarly, confidence factors may have an important impact upon population trends. People's ideas or practices in planning their families may be influenced by the prevailing level of confidence, especially in countries with widespread birth control. It would be very illuminating to know whether Western populations intentionally have more chil-dren when prolonged prosperity has had a reassuring effect on indi-viduals, or whether the incidence of unintended procreation increases whenever social frustrations and insecurities are unconsciously translated into compensatory creative urges on either the individual or the national level. In either case the state of confidence in the population is likely to be of great importance.

At the same time, such an expansion of the confidence concept to include the general atmosphere in society should not be done to the neglect of the specific personality factors involved. A specific person may either be confident in general or he may develop a confident attitude in certain phases of his life (or certain situations) even though the objective conditions of the moment may not warrant it. The opposite, of course, may occur just as easily. This distinction might be restated by keeping apart the confidence in future stability or in improvement of external factors from confidence in one's own ability to tackle whatever instabilities or adversities may occur.

The incidence of individual confidence attitudes in economic life is thus determined by a varying combination of the following factors: (a) past experiences or objective data that influence the decision maker in the business or household unit concerned; (b) the general social atmosphere; (c) long-range personality factors, that is, the incidence of certain kinds of personality among businessmen and consumers; (d) the effect either of immediate happenings in the business experience of the individuals concerned or of the general atmosphere in bringing out into the open certain personal traits and reaction patterns which otherwise might have remained under the surface of their personalities, for good or bad.[7]

Although a general atmosphere of socioeconomic instability is bound to affect nearly everybody, its specific effects upon the various social groups are likely to differ considerably, and so do the objective factors that typically engender frustration in the members of each group. For the worker the big bogey is still unemployment, with the resulting loss of income, status, and self-respect, which eventually may lead to "thinking on relief." For the businessman the threat is primarily in a failure to achieve surpluses or even in a failure to expand. Success in this case, in the very specific sense of growth in profit and total investment, is the medium or yardstick of personal self-assertion. For the farmer the land tenure, the creative activity, the function of feeding others, and the constant if increasingly hopeful fight against the challenge of nature are typically at stake. The white-collar group is especially vulnerable to inflationary losses and at the same time is not immune to the threat of unemployment; it occupies an uneasy middle position between business and labor.

The personal impact of socioeconomic instability also differs according to social groupings other than occupational. The big-city dweller often suffers from frustrating handicaps due to the housing situation; he is also in the front line in case of war, especially nuclear attack. The young generation is particularly exposed to the threat of unemployment whenever there is a slump in business, and that at an age when satisfying activity and family planning are of special importance. The expanding old-age group suffers, not only from lack of adequate financial provisions in many cases but from the difficulty of finding satisfactory outlets for its remaining energies; it is especially exposed to the leisure frustrations that are characteristic of modern society. Special problems of racial or rank groups also come into the picture here.

In each case the personality structure—and the incidence, in each group, of personalities that are especially sensitive toward frustrating outside events—determines the actual effect of instability factors that have an objective propensity to shatter confidence. In each case, however, the degree of group coherence, organization, and solidarity has an important impact upon the actual state of confidence. Objective socioeconomic instability may be outweighed, in its psychological effects, by the feelings of confidence and security that result from sharing a predicament with a well-defined group of one's own kind. Moreover, the sharing of insecurities or fears may strengthen the coherence of a group. In some cases such sharing may even be the real origin of the group. To belong to and be accepted by an organization—which may be a trade association, a gang, an exclusive club, a labor union, a neighborhood association, or a church—means feeling that others are in the same boat and perhaps that they will protect you.

Group loyalty thus has the important function of overcoming some of the frustrating effects of socioeconomic instability. The psychic roots of nationalism, incidentally, are similar. Group belonging may, however, involve some dangers to the economic stability and personal security of an individual, for it exposes him to the codes and sanctions of the group concerned. To be expelled from or ostracized by his club, union, or church may leave the individual in a far worse position, both economically and personally, than if he had never been a member.

Group acceptance and belonging thus are of very great importance in economic life, first, in securing a definite setting for business contacts and transactions; second, in supplying standards of behavior; and, third, in potentially offering to the individual a feeling of protection and confidence which makes it far easier for him to survive in a general atmosphere of instability. Much depends for him on whether he is able and willing to adjust himself to the setting which he chose or into which he was put. The trouble is that such an adjustment, with adequate success in acceptance and belonging, often occurs only at the price of conformity; and conformity requirements tend to bring into the picture a new element of objective instability and personal insecurity alike. The consumer who fails to purchase a new luxury car when he is expected to and the businessman who fails to spend as much on advertising as he is supposed to risk unwritten sanctions from the group, and constant fear of a *faux pas* does not encourage confidence.

In short, the protection from socioeconomic instability offered by the group economically and morally is usually far from perfect. Two alternatives that are sometimes presented are even less satisfactory. One is the positive argument for unmitigated socioeconomic instability in the alleged interest of initiative and progress. This argument has lost much of its influence in consequence of the period of extreme instability that the present generation has undergone. The other is the quest for a totalitarian "escape from freedom," which for most people in a society with democratic traditions is quite unacceptable on the conscious level, though many people may be groping for it in an indirect way.

A host of "insecurity industries" thrive on this general atmosphere, although most of them also fulfill a real economic function as far as their roots are concerned. Real-estate trading profits from the desire of many people to build up self-confidence by owning something tangible and lasting, as well as from the status element that is implicit in property ownership according to a traditional scale of values recognized by many people. Insurance corporations have experienced an amazing growth in business, which again can be explained in part by a widespread desire for safeguards, both economic and psychological, in a period of widely felt instability. Especially is this true of life insurance which, contrary to widespread opinion, is not perceived by the average citizen as a savings outlet but as an emergency protection for the family.

For many the function of the movie industry is that of a dream factory, which enables the individual to escape for a few hours from an unsteady and frightening environment into a world where a happy end is guaranteed. The liquor industry thrives similarly on the desire of people to get drunk, that is, to forget. Tobacco consumption likewise varies with the incidence of worries. The fashion industry, today no less than in Thorstein Veblen's time, is based on group emulation and a drive for conformity in the frantic desire of the individual to be accepted by his group and thus to build up self-confidence. The advertising business profits from the turnover of the industries mentioned and also, more generally, from needs for self-assertion and status assurance in a period of instability. The emphasis upon brand names and the standardization involved, as well as the boastful self-glorification in high-pressure advertising, reflect the general quest for confidence.

Personal Insecurity: Forms, Incidence, Roots

In what ways and to what extent can an interaction be traced between this social atmosphere of fluctuating "confidence" and the frequent occurrence of personal insecurity? Has the latter anything at all to do with socioeconomic trends, either in the short or in the long run? Can it be traced entirely, as some psychoanalytical authors insist, to personality factors which, in turn, depend on early childhood experiences rather than on later socioeconomic developments? Has mankind perhaps been chasing a phantom in trying, off and on, to promote personal security by improving external conditions?

Before we go into this question, it is necessary to list some concrete manifestations of personal insecurity. It cannot be taken for granted that their roots are necessarily the same in all cases, to say the least. We may also very well allow for the probability that a limited degree of inner insecurity, as distinguished from neurotic anxiety, stimulates the development and manifestation of a healthy, active personality, and that certain frustrations are socially helpful in developing additional energies for cultural development. Finally, the listing that follows can only refer to certain known or likely manifestations of personal insecurity to the extent that they occur on a mass scale. Since processes within the personality remain in the dark unless they reveal themselves in some way to the outside world, we have to hold on to tangible (and, to some extent, measurable) expressions of personal insecurity as indicators of its social incidence.

The problem far exceeds mere measurement of the frequency of neurotic behavior, which would be a very difficult enterprise anyhow as even clinical disturbances do not always reach the doctor's office, let alone minor cases. It should eventually be possible, however, to compare the changing incidence of the various manifestations to shifts in the general social atmosphere. Such a comparison would be based on the hypothesis that an atmosphere which encourages general worry or widespread anxiety (not necessarily in a clinical sense at first) is likely to offer a potential breeding ground for personal insecurity, especially if the prevalence of such a state of mind can be traced back for a generation or longer.

With this hypothesis in mind, the following manifestations of personal insecurity on a mass scale deserve special attention.

1. Neuroses. In this case personal insecurity has reached the clinical stage, though lesser degrees of neurotic behavior are quite frequent in persons who are generally regarded as healthy. In this discussion we leave out the psychotic disorders which, according to prevailing medical opinion, are of organic or toxic origin and thus cannot be expected to be traceable to socioeconomic occurrences. The latter, it is true, may well hasten, intensify, or perpetuate the external manifestation of psychotic disorders.

Even if we confine ourselves to neuroses, the problem remains very complex. To begin with, there are numerous types of neuroses, and it is possible that the degree and manner in which they are connected with socioeconomic happenings vary greatly. In a general way, Freud points out that the neurotic ego "is no longer able to fulfill the task set to it by the external world (including human society)." He also speaks of the "influence of civilization among the determinants of neuroses," in which "the demands of civilization are represented by family education." [8] However, the terminology applicable to the types of neuroses remains unsettled and fluctuates considerably. It is quite

likely that new types of neuroses continually appear on the scene
while others fade away, and that some of them, such as hysteria, are
more capable than others of spreading by a kind of social infection.
There is also the highly important question of the comparative incidence of neurotic disorders (or any given type of them) in the
various strata of economic society and in the various socioeconomic
systems.[9]

Unfortunately the statistics of neurotic disorders are in an unsettled
state, but there are good reasons to believe the statement of a psychiatrist that "there is the generally accepted observation that unfavorable environmental conditions may offset the effects of the
treatment. Such environmental conditions include unemployment, an
hostile attitude of the environment towards the patient's illness or
towards psychotherapy, unsatisfactory sex conditions, domestic and
financial hardships, etc." [10] Part of the statistical difficulty comes
from the impossibility of comparing available figures from various
periods, as both the diagnoses and the disturbance types appear to
change. Neurotic disorders are, however, known to be responsible for
a sizable fraction of the enormous population on the books of
hospitals for mental disease (548,563 resident patients in June, 1957,
in public mental hospitals alone, in the United States[11]) and for a
high percentage of rejections and discharges by the armed forces, in
the United States and elsewhere, during and after the second World
War.

While the exact figure for neuroses is difficult to determine, and
partly depends on the definition, it is safe to estimate it at several millions for this country at all times. An investigation of mental health
in New York State from 1920 to 1937 came to this conclusion concerning neuroses: "If trends in hospital admissions with psychoneuroses may be considered representative of similar trends among all
psychoneurotics, whether hospitalized or not, then it is clear that there
has been a relative increase in such mental disorders since the beginning of the economic depression." [12] The same investigation also found,
with respect to mental disorders in general, that "it is not so much low
economic status as change in such status which seems to affect health."
The National Association for Mental Health reported for 1957 that
personality disorders accounted for about 15 per cent of new admis-

sions and psychoneuroses explained almost 6 per cent of new patients in our public hospitals.

Extensive data are available from the armed services on the incidence among inductees—that is, after the elimination process at induction time—of "critical scores" on various indexes of psychoneurotic traits. These data indicate critical scores, from the military viewpoint, in between one-fourth and one-third of the cross section of white enlisted men without overseas service who were investigated in early 1944. But here again generalizations concerning the general population would not be possible without great reservations.[13]

2. Psychosomatic disturbances. Certain nervous conditions manifest themselves in physical disturbances which should be somewhat easier to identify and measure statistically than neuroses in general. This applies especially to peptic ulcers, asthma, allergies, and colitis; but the trouble, from the statistician's point of view, is that at times some of these diseases are attributed to nonemotional causes. Moreover, any health disturbance is now considered by many physicians in terms of an interaction between mind and body.

It is interesting, however, to note Dr. James L. Halliday's definite claim that "in peptic ulcer the preoccupation is with security, especially economic, occupational, and financial security," . . . "Loss of employment may really 'make a man ill,' especially a man with virtuous obsessional characteristics, by provoking bodily disturbances which in turn may induce organic changes." [14] He bases these statements in part on detailed figures of morbidity compiled by the Scottish Department of Health for the depression years 1930–1938. Along with various changes in the social, age, and sex distribution of psychosomatic affections, a rise in anxiety states in the working population of Scotland during the years of mass unemployment was found to be statistically demonstrable.

Even if we allow for the unsettled questions of causation and classification in this field, there are certain indications of a connection, still to be explored in detail, between socioeconomic instability and the mass occurrence of certain psychosomatic affections. It is not within my province to discuss the question of the extent to which such effects come about indirectly through neurotic disorders or else more directly through malnutrition or bad housing, for instance, in their impact on the general condition of adults and children. It is safe to predict, however, that reliable data on the incidence and causation of the various psychosomatic disturbances, when available, will contribute much to clarification of the socioeconomic problem before us.

3. Suicides. That school of psychoanalysts which places great emphasis on the self-preservation drive tends to consider suicide in general a manifestation of neurotic personality or other types of mental disorder. If we should choose to consider the suicide rate as a piece of evidence concerning the incidence of extreme personal insecurity, great caution would be required. Certainly some people who had been assumed to be well adjusted have committed suicide because in a given life situation their past roots and aspirations seemed to them ruined beyond repair. It is also known that the evaluation of suicide in various cultures varies greatly. A Freudian psychiatrist concludes that suicide "is to be viewed . . . as a reaction of a developmental nature which is universal and common to the mentally sick of all types and probably also to many so-called normal persons." [15]

The ultimate answer will largely depend on one's philosophical orientation. It appears, however, that some suicide cases concern persons who up to that point were generally associated with a high degree of personal security feelings. Such cases have included suicides of professional psychotherapists. Other suicides are committed on what many people would consider rational grounds, for example, an incurable case of cancer. There are indications of a certain short-run correlation between objective economic disturbances, such as depressions, and the suicide rate. This does not necessarily indicate a direct causal relationship. The evidence is considerable, however, that a drastic change for the worse in the external situation tends to promote self-destructive forces.

Experts of the Metropolitan Life Insurance Company have arrived at the following conclusions: "The suicide rate shows a much wider variation from good times to bad among men past 45 than it does among younger men; women are much less affected than men by economic swings." "In the long waves there seems to be a general tendency for below-normal suicide rates to occur in times of above-normal business conditions." In 1956, 2 per cent of all deaths at ages under 65, but 5 per cent in the group between 25 and 44 years, were caused by suicide.[16]

4. Alcoholism, drug addiction, crime, accidents. Here we enter into

an area which is undoubtedly connected with the incidence of personal insecurity but which is extremely hard to define. Only differential diagnosis in each case could show whether it represents handicaps of biological endowment, general personality factors, or socioeconomic roots of personal disturbance, either lasting or temporary. If we assume that the distribution of such causes remains the same over time (an arbitrary assumption), reliable statistics of these disturbances could be of some comparative value.

Alcoholism, in particular, is now widely assumed to stem from some combination—still ill defined—of physiological, emotional, and social factors leading to compulsive drinking. Estimates prepared by the National Council on Alcoholism and related organizations indicate a total of about 1,000,000 chronic alcoholic addicts (not counting those who have never undergone hospital treatment) and another 4,000,000 heavy or problem drinkers. The United States, with 4,360 alcoholics for each 100,000 adults, is second only to France, with its rate of 5,200. Whatever the initial causes may be in each case, many researchers in this field emphasize the impact upon alcoholism of unsolved personality difficulties, of the group setting, and of social tension.[17]

5. Family disruption. This source of evidence includes data concerning broken homes, divorces, and so forth. These occurrences often reflect personal insecurity (if not some degree of neurotic condition) on the part of one or more of those involved. To that extent such data may be helpful in measuring the incidence of personal insecurity in any given period. However, family disruption sometimes has causes that are rooted in other, more objective, factors; for example, disease, random accidents, or involuntary separation due to military service.[18] Divorce has been increasing rapidly in many—especially British and continental—countries throughout the world since the early years of the century. But this trend in part reflects changes in law and custom, and thus is not an accurate measure of changes in the insecurity level.

6. Excessive job mobility. To move around from one location to another, or to change jobs and even occupations, is not in itself a symptom of personal insecurity by any means, certainly not in American culture, which is less tradition-bound, less conservative in its approach to mobility, than many other cultures. In part, high mobility in the United States simply mirrors the expanse of the country and its vast economic

opportunities; in these respects it is a sign of healthy adjustment to the needs and opportunities that are implicit in our society and culture.

Surveys by the United States Bureau of the Census indicate that about one-fifth of the population changes residence every year. Many of these merely change homes in the same neighborhood, but several million a year move from one state to another. Mobility has been greatest among young people and the unemployed; laborers and professional people exceed other occupational groups in mobility, while farmers move least.[19]

A different picture emerges, however, when we look at individuals whose geographic and occupational mobility is in excess even of a high national standard. The person who is driven by a hidden force to keep moving around, who is unable to get settled anywhere, who has inhibitions against working consistently (especially, working for money), or who suffers from work compulsions that prevent him from being satisfied with any job, definitely reflects high personal insecurity. To the extent that it is possible to obtain comparative measurements of such excessive mobility, they can be of considerable help in evaluating the incidence of personal insecurity.[20]

7. The appeal of quacks. The regular appearance of individual agitators, rabble rousers, or soul-saving would-be founders of sects is not in itself a startling social fact. It becomes, however, an important piece of evidence on the incidence of personal insecurity as soon as any or all of these quacks begin to have a definite mass appeal. Important yardsticks of such appeal are offered by changes in the extent and effect of organized prejudice, including the frequency of lynching, which some authors have actually tried to correlate directly to cotton prices; the degree of public support that witch hunts of various types receive; and, above all, the comparative success or failure of totalitarian movements or programs of all kinds. Any such tendencies reflect the incidence and intensity of self-hating with its projections upon social groups or creeds, a public need for easily available outlets for the aggressions of frustrated individuals, and the desperate desire of many persons for a party, creed, or leader that has (and always *will* have!) all the answers— somebody to hold on to not only now but in the future.

In such a situation, prominent misfits and malcontents express the mental condition of many and thus become popular leaders. Interesting observations concerning the typical frustrations and extreme insecurities of the Nazi S.S. guards have been supplied by Benedikt Kautsky, who spent seven years under their terror.[21]

The rise of a totalitarian disposition is accompanied by a mass flight into what George Orwell calls "protective stupidity." "But stupidity is not enough. On the contrary, orthodoxy in the full sense demands a control over one's own mental processes as complete as that of a contortionist over his body." [22] This goes along with setting up a scapegoat and group persecution as a mechanism of collective tension release. In this respect there is a close relation between the totalitarian mentality in our period and older forms of witch hunts, though we have greatly "improved" our techniques. A contemporary study of the Salem witch trials of 1692 describes the underlying condition as follows, "A people whose natural impulses had long been repressed by the severity of their belief, whose security had been undermined by anxiety and terror continued longer than could be borne, demanded their catharsis." [23]

The wide appeal of the prophets of hatred and intolerance—expressed in our period in the totalitarian mentality—is an important indication of widespread personal insecurity which, in some cases at least, can be traced to a critical situation in economic life of the present or past.

Under the impact of crisis, men become unusually susceptible to the acceptance of new formulations, whether or not these formulations afford objective and lasting solutions. . . . In such times of frustration and disorder, the behavior of ordinarily civilized individuals regresses collectively to the uninhibited instinctual level. . . . In cases in which positive action leading to the primary goals is barred by circumstances, a person usually indulges in individual or collective "substitutive activities," which, at times, acquire pathological features.[24]

Fears and aggressions which might have little outside effect were they confined to an individual may snowball into a devastating avalanche when they arise, on a suitable cultural basis, from socioeconomic conditions that favor their spread. (This problem will be discussed in greater detail in Chapter IV, pp. 191–203.) Reliable measurements of the totalitarian effects of a widespread sense of personal insecurity are difficult to make, but to the extent that they are available, they are important evidence.

In summary, personality disorders in the clinical sense represent but one type—an extreme one—of personal insecurity. Some clinical disorders are not reliable evidence for this discussion as they are probably rooted in nonsocial factors. Their specific manifestation, it is true, may be subject to certain influences from the social world. At any rate, combined data on the various types of personal insecurity that were discussed earlier, preferably with quantitative indications of comparative incidence, might eventually permit a correlation with the factors of socioeconomic instability listed. It is entirely possible, we repeat, that it is the *combination* of various types of insecurity that really matters—a *general* social atmosphere of insecurity that affects everybody including the upper strata.

Socioeconomic Instability and Individual Childhood Experiences

Aside from the immediate influence of socioeconomic instability upon the current security level of the individual, there is the probable long-range impact of such instability upon personality. Most psychologists today are agreed on the enormous impact of early childhood experiences upon the personality formation of each individual. There may have been occasional underrating either of organic factors and biological heritage or of personality-forming experiences after childhood. However, analytical and clinical psychology with their anthropological applications leave little doubt that the experience of an individual from the moment of birth until the age of five—especially in the rise of frustrations and defense mechanisms—is the greatest single influence in making him the kind of person he eventually becomes.

While we cannot take up the question here of how specific social patterns of child rearing and education originate and develop, there is a fair amount of agreement concerning the influence of the cultural and socioeconomic setting in which individual experiences (and possible disturbances) occur during the personality formation of a child.

The overall pattern of personality can be understood only in terms of total childhood experience plus the situational pressures of adult life [Kluckhohn].

Neuroses contain . . . unconscious and futile attempts to adjust to the heterogeneous present with the magic concepts of a more homogeneous past, fragments of which are still transmitted through child training [Erikson].

Neuroses are generated not only by incidental individual experiences, but also by the specific cultural conditions under which they live [Horney].

As a result of his life history any given person will carry into adult life a high or low ability to "tolerate" frustrations and will stand at some point on a dimension of "readiness" to be aggressive in frustration situations [Dollard].

Similarly, Joseph Wilder has pointed out that neuroses basically represent fears of one's own drives or, more specifically, of the consequences that may arise from actions rooted in such drives; the actual danger of most actions, in turn, depends on the social structure and situation.[25]

Historical changes in the general social environment are therefore bound to affect profoundly the setting in which personality formation takes place. In Western society of the twentieth century, for instance, the older patriarchal structure of the family is giving way; conscious frightening of the child has become rarer; hygiene and impersonal rules of child rearing find wider application; and family size is smaller, thus strengthening, as it were, each child's "marginal rate of substitution" or his irreplaceable worth to the parents. The trouble is that technical improvements in child-rearing methods have not been paralleled by equal advances in the psychological setting. Father is no longer God but he may become a pitiful figure; whipping is disappearing but so also is individualized attention to the child. Above all, the growth and persistence of socioeconomic instability affect the child both directly and through the adults, especially in their role as parents.

The question which then suggests itself is the specific influence of socioeconomic instability upon the incidence, in a given period, of certain typical experiences during childhood, especially during its socialization phase. There is an enormous body of clinical and other data on specific types of childhood anxieties that may mark a person for his lifetime. Some of these anxiety types (especially the changing frequency of their occurrence) actually reflect socioeconomic conditions as they affect the child and its family. In other words, the domineering father, for instance, does not come out of nowhere, especially as a mass phenomenon. While his personality was partly shaped by his own childhood experience, this is not necessarily a self-perpetuating pattern nor a vicious circle. Aside from the possibility that he might have undergone successful psychotherapy for instance, the domineering features of his personality might have remained buried under the surface or they might not have exploded in acute external manifestations if no severe frustration in his adult life had occurred. Similarly parents who long for "security" tend to become overanxious for their children, who, in turn, reflect these parental anxieties in their own personality after being prodded into early money earning or marriage.

Social workers are thoroughly familiar both with the impact of such family experiences upon individual development and with the great frequency of such influences in social life. To mention one investigation of the range of family maladjustment, a survey of people under the care of community agencies in St. Paul, Minnesota, in November 1948, showed the following results: Of 41,000 families under care, 11,000 had problems of "maladjustment," described as a composite of behavior disorders and socially unacceptable conduct. These maladjusted families represented about 6 per cent of the community; in another 4 per cent the family situation was so disorganized that the member could not adjust to it without help. The authors of the study considered this ratio about average as compared with other cities, and they pointed to "the interplay between intrapsychic and situational factors" in the practical experience of their agencies.[26]

Whenever family maladjustments and, especially, frustrations of parents are socially induced on a mass scale—say, in the course of widespread unemployment—the children frequently suffer from them during their most impressionable years. There will, of course, always be some cases of exceptionally well-adjusted parents who can take such economic frustrations in stride and continue to rear their children in a cheerful, understanding way. Even so unemployment will mostly tend to increase childhood frustrations and anxieties in specific ways; and it is the *social incidence* of personality patterns with which we are concerned here. The continuing impact of initial difficulties in the formation of the family, the father who hangs around the house with nothing much to do while the mother becomes the provider, inadequate food or housing due to lack of an assured income, kindergarten comparisons with either less or more fortunate children, arguments among older brothers and sisters about what is happening to the family—all these and similar experiences affect the child during its critical years.

Unemployment may leave permanent emotional scars on the child by dislocating family relationships, by producing quarrels, by reversing the domestic role of father and mother, by underlining the economic inadequacy and failure of the father, and by disturbing the identification processes of young children.[27]

Muzafer Sherif's investigations indicate that "the psychological effect of prolonged unemployment has been found to include a breakdown of ego-attitudes, a narrowing of the ego-boundaries, and even collapse of the ego-form." When this is accompanied by physical deprivation (on either the individual or the social level), apathy, a feeling of age, decreased sociability, and an excessive in-group feeling may develop.[28] It would be a near-miracle if such personality disturbances in parents or siblings should fail to affect the personality formation of the child very profoundly and, as a rule, adversely. When unemployment strikes, the father, the mother, or both may easily lose their ordinary roles as bulwarks of security and as guideposts for the constantly changing life situations of a growing child. Instead they may become pitiable, helpless creatures, and most children will be quick to grasp that fact intuitively.

In a way, socioeconomic instability thus appears to encourage a high incidence within families of "emergency reactions," remotely comparable to the artificial neuroses that Pavlov experimentally produced in animals—only in this case humans are involved on both sides; nobody planned the experiment that way; and there is usually no controlled observation!

The personality formed through such family or group experiences will later be exposed to certain socioeconomic incentives and deterrents to work, administer, spend, save, invest. It will react to these incentives and deterrents in ways that will depend in part on its permanent traits: it may be rigid and may, in this case, keep up an established behavioral preference despite other, "objectively" stronger incentives, or it may be adaptable and spend at one time, save at another in accordance with the conditions of the moment. It may basically represent a miser or a spendthrift, an aggressive go-getter or a submissive follower, a domineering leader or a frightened sufferer. The basic decision on dominant traits, of which the person may be unconscious, was made in his childhood, but the specific economic situations to which he is exposed as an adult supply opportunity for certain of these traits to manifest themselves.

Moreover, the socioeconomic setting of a person's childhood may have delayed-action effects on his personality which are difficult to trace except possibly through successful psychoanalysis. Not much is known about the incubation period of many neuroses, but it might be very illuminating to compare the mental health and general level of personal security in the depression generation—that is, among persons now twenty-five to thirty years old—with that of the general population or some suitable control group. A time lag may also occur in the effects of other types of socioeconomic instability, such as inflation, housing shortages, or technological changes. An additional complication, however, comes from the probability that the lag between social cause and individual effect occurs on at least two levels: it combines the impact of long-range factors (such as culture and the socioeconomic system) with that of short-range factors (such as a recent war or business fluctuation).

The resulting distribution of personalities in a given period may help explain to some extent the resistance to socioeconomic change and the frequent persistence of certain economic attitudes in an objective situation that has changed drastically. For example, the attitudes of British coal miners after a period of war, full employment, and nationalization continued to reflect the patterns acquired during the depression in the privately owned coal industry of the thirties. Another example is the rigid persistence of established seniority preferences— which sacrifice opportunity to job security—even after a prolonged period of full employment.[29] (Related problems are discussed more extensively in the next chapter.)

The emotional development of children in our society is inevitably affected by the emphasis placed by the prevailing scale of values upon financial success, which is associated with personal assertion. The economic failure of parents, siblings, or other prominent childhood figures has important emotional effects on the child. It either leads to rejection and hostility toward them, which may not come out into the open until late in life, or to hidden guilt feelings, which likewise may warp the emotional development of the person at some phase of his life.

In particular, the family experiences mentioned may affect profoundly the level of aspiration, either periodically or chronically, by reducing it to a subdued, "abnormally" low state or by driving it to an excessive, likewise "abnormal" ambition with work compulsions. If this occurs with great frequency in any given period, the entire pattern of attitudes, motivation, and incentives in economic life, as well as the level of personal security and mental health, will have been greatly influenced by socioeconomic events of the past—events which are often difficult to trace back yet explain the comparative incidence of specific behavior in economic and other situations.

One important aspect of this problem concerns the comparative frequency of strong personal insecurity among the various strata of economic society. It would be very illuminating if reliable and comparable data could be secured on the incidence of neuroses, family disruption, excessive job mobility, and so forth among skilled and unskilled workers, the white-collar group, farmers, small-business men, and corporation executives—preferably data that would include some information about the educational, financial, and status background of each family. A significant attempt in this direction was made on the local level in the New Haven study. Its authors found the percentage of neurotics among psychiatric patients to be strikingly higher in the upper classes than in the lower, but added that "certain distinguishing characteristics of the social classes are reflected in the neurosis itself." [30]

Class Structure and Frustration Incidence

It has often been assumed that, while individuals from the underprivileged strata of society (either economic or racial) are exposed to countless frustrating experiences, both during childhood and later, this does not apply in any comparable degree to persons from the more fortunate strata. There are good reasons to believe that a much smaller percentage of potential patients from the lower classes reaches the psychotherapeutic office or clinic than from the upper, as a result of both financial and educational handicaps, and that they are diagnosed and treated differently. At first glance one might suspect that the actual incidence of personal insecurity with its neurotic climax is much higher among the poor than the daily experience of psychotherapists indicates; the records of social-work agencies would seem to confirm such an assumption.

Actually things are far more complex. It is true that people near the lower end of the socioeconomic scale are more often than others deprived of external opportunities for the fulfillment of their personal potentialities; those of an upper class, on the other hand, tend to look for more in life and thus are no less likely to meet frustration in terms of their own higher standards. Even so it cannot be assumed that these factors simply cancel each other out. Above all, it is not necessarily the immediate effect of specific pressures upon the individual that matters. General lack of stability and integration in society may affect the upper-class individual no less than the one from below, only differently. In other words, in a general atmosphere of socioeconomic instability the upper classes may be as susceptible to personal insecurity from this source as the lower, only in a different fashion.

Such general handicaps to feelings of personal security, including those of groups that are supposedly happy and carefree, may sooner or later constitute a serious threat to a society so affected. The fact that there are frustrations of the upper classes, as well as of the lower, may come as a shock to the naïve type of radical. In his novel *The Red Lily,* Anatole France spoke sarcastically of "the majestic equality of the laws which forbid the rich and the poor alike to sleep under the bridges, to beg in the streets, and to steal their bread." With regard to the factors that govern the rise of personal insecurity, however, there may be a far more serious approximation to that majestic equality. A general atmosphere of socioeconomic instability, especially the constant threat of business fluctuations and wars even in "happy" years, affects the peace of mind of the upper groups too. In fact, property ownership or wealth tends to become a source of fears, which often exceed any objective threat. The wealth may, for that matter, have resulted from the compulsive money-making of a parent in the first place, in which case the underlying fears of the parent are easily passed on to the children or otherwise affect the family atmosphere.

The general condition of society may have a far greater impact upon an individual than his own economic background, at least if he is fairly sensitive. Periodic adverse conditions in society, which are at odds with his expectations (or those of his group, or of everybody), may lead to frustrations even when his own welfare is not affected specifically. The disintegration of a belief system on which he depended, or a conflict between belief systems, may have even greater effects, regardless of whether or not his own material condition is directly affected.

Such considerations apparently apply especially to collective guilt feelings of a more or less hidden nature that specifically affect upper socioeconomic groups.

Despite impressive advances in technology and living standards, our society remains full of material instabilities, intrinsic conflicts and contradictions, and manifold inequalities. The groups that run the social system feel basically responsible for its shortcomings, even if they blame them, in public, either on the lower classes or on some other convenient scapegoat and claim for themselves all the credit for the positive achievements of their society. The upper classes thus tend to be bothered unconsciously (and sometimes consciously) by a collective guilt complex, at first with reference to the inherited moral codes both of religion and of early prophets of their own social order and later with reference to the new moral code of the lower classes. In addition, there is the underlying fear of fortunate individuals or groups that their privileged positions may be lost and that someone else may come to the top tomorrow (always a possibility in a competitive society) or that retribution of some sort may threaten either in this life or thereafter.

Moreover, periodic depressions may be unconsciously accepted, by some of those whose status they impair, as a deserved punishment of both society and themselves for their "guilt." The much-praised weeding out of the inefficient then parallels atonement—or else those who perish economically are rationalized into "guilt" by the more fortunate survivors. At this point there may actually be more than a semantic parallel between economic and psychic depression. To the impersonal "laws of the market" is attributed essentially the same role that supernatural forces, which punish and reward, assume in earlier cultures. At the same time, what John Kenneth Galbraith calls "the insecurity of illusion"—the refusal to interpret the economic system realistically, plus an underlying uneasiness even in the face of actual success under that system—contributes to the frequency of malaise among upper groups.

Some of the resulting conflicts are mirrored in contemporary fiction. Norman Mailer puts it this way:

Understand your class and work within its limits. Marxist lesson with a reverse twist. It disturbed Hearn deeply. He had been born in the aristocracy of the wealthy midwestern family, and although he had broken with them, had assumed ideas and concepts repugnant to them, he had never really discarded the emotional luggage of his first eighteen years. The guilts he made himself feel, the injustices that angered him were never genuine. He kept the sore alive by continually rubbing it, and he knew it.[31]

The lower classes are plagued in a different way by guilt feelings and other factors of personal insecurity, for the prevailing scale of values in any hierarchic society tends to blame the misfortunes of the underdog on him by asserting that he, as an individual or as a group, is intrinsically inferior—lazy or dumb, for instance—and that lack of economic success or status is the well-deserved punishment for his faults. Children are often very susceptible to such an atmosphere of class guilt or to induced race awareness, for that matter; they may be greatly influenced by such factors in personality formation. This occurs especially through mechanisms of punishment designed to prevent the child from learning certain new habits and thus increasing unduly his privileges or aspirations. The establishment of status anxieties, sometimes with fearful concealment of a person's status toward other people, also occurs early. All this appears to be more frequent in some of the middle groups—with their special requirements of self-restraint—than in the lowest groups.[32] Both the frustrations and the security feelings of children and of adults are related to the group level of aspirations.

At the same time, in families with narrow resources all the members, including the children, have to face jointly many financial problems, and family experiences are shared without the interference of servants or nurses. This reassuring community may be especially effective when income is low but relatively secure. Certain disturbing factors in personality formation may, therefore, be rarer in lower groups than in higher, though the opposite is true in some other respects.

In an industrialized society with freedom of speech and organization the underdog tends to develop solidarity feelings that find their most articulate expression in the labor movement. In various parts of the world people have actually come to be proud of being a "proletarian" and they feel ashamed if they belong to an upper class. The frequent flight of sons and daughters of the wealthy into the ranks of labor or radical organizations bears evidence of such psychic unrest. So does that type of philanthropy which primarily serves the purpose of relieving one's conscience. To quote from a recent foundation report, "While we admire men with the capacity to amass large fortunes, we have come to believe that the true measure of their greatness is their capacity to dispose of their fortunes wisely in the service of the society which nurtured them. Andrew Carnegie put the matter with characteristic vigor when he asserted that it is a disgrace to die a rich man." [33] Somewhat similarly, Richard Centers found (from a rather limited sample, it is true) that the wealthy tend to classify themselves as middle class, while the poor—despite distinctly greater frustration—classify themselves more truthfully as the working class.[34] The unhappy, inferior, or guilty feelings of many a rich school boy among poorer classmates are well known to teachers.

In countries where psychic unrest in the upper strata is habitually covered up by the boastful cheerfulness of the successful businessman, adverse effects upon his personal security feelings may result in the long run. Conceivably those countries in which the existence of basic social conflicts has been more widely and openly recognized and in which attempts to deny or repress it have worn thin in recent years may offer a somewhat healthier atmosphere. Certainly there is no discernible correlation between the wealth of a nation and its level of personal security; recent years have shown examples of nations that combined either austerity and assurance, or wealth and fear—a fact which should not be construed as an argument for austerity.

It is true that in most countries and classes a number of deeply religious individuals (religious is used in the broadest sense) manage to feel secure personally even in the face of economic adversities or in a tense social atmosphere, but even they tend to worry increasingly about other people and about the world in general. Actually some religions preach insecurity in this life and eternal security thereafter, while others believe that security can be achieved in this life through righteous behavior. On the other hand, neurosis has been interpreted as a particular form of religion, and vice versa.[35]

An interesting case of a tightly knit religious community with effective safeguards of socioeconomic stability is presented by the Hutterites in northwestern America, who have long fascinated mental-health students by their unusually low incidence of personal insecurity. The Hutterites regard private property as sinful and the use of force as wicked under any circumstances; they refuse to take oaths; and they insist on simplicity in living conditions. Their children tend to become socialized by other children, rather than by older people. The Hutterites are efficient farmers who are in business contact with American or Canadian life; but they keep going without the incentives of wealth and personal power, and without the penalties of imprisonment, fines, or threatened loss of livelihood. Among the members of this sect, severe mental illness is rare and community understanding largely prevents antisocial behavior in such patients as there are. Only five disrupted marriages and two suicides have been recorded since the 1870's. No cases of parental abandonment of children, of sex crimes, or of arson or personal violence are known. It may be difficult to prove any clean-cut interaction among their collectivistic and democratic way of life, their rural atmosphere and economic security for everybody, their child-rearing arrangements, and their state of mental health, but if this is a mere coincidence, it is certainly a remarkable one.[36]

Conformity and Security

In evaluating further aspects of the cultural and socioeconomic setting in its effect upon personality development, that peculiar, powerful, and hazardous requirement of most societies, conformity, comes into the picture—sometimes overtly but very often indirectly and unconsciously. Conformity, as distinguished from the indispensable socialization of the child, refers to identification with and support of a specific system of social norms and hierarchies. It offers an assured group status and a degree of group-belonging to the individual who goes along with its requirements. It applies, in different ways, both to the lower and to the upper classes—to the former by outcasting any thought of alternatives to the existing order of things, to the latter by imposing taboos on unorthodox thought or behavior, on things that "just are not done," sometimes with the help of intricate rationalizations. By and large the upper groups believe in the socially beneficial character of their own taboos.

Most psychologists and psychoanalysts, in analyzing the factors that breed repression, especially in a child, appear to have emphasized the immediate social environment, especially the family, and to have neglected the sociocultural proscription, direct and indirect, of nonconformist attitudes and ideas, the "socially derived sin."[37] Such proscription is bound to affect the personality development of each individual in any hierarchic society, especially if its instability fosters a defensive attitude in the upper strata. This is true regardless of whether the hierarchy is of racial, caste, religious, class, or financial type. The pressure begins in early childhood; although children, like court jesters or drunkards, have somewhat more leeway in this respect than adults, the *enfant terrible* is not long permitted to ask awkward questions that imply doubt concerning prevailing institutions or beliefs.

Sooner or later the nonconformist faces censure as "immature" or "unreasonable," maturity and reason being identified with unquestioning acceptance of the existing social order, norms, and institutions. The charge of immaturity throws him back into his childhood status and thus under the authority of the "mature" conformists. Of course, the social code and the yardsticks of deviant behavior differ according to the environment, perception pattern, and scale of values. The son of a burglar may be considered by his people a traitor (or abnormal) if he becomes a preacher rather than a burglar; similarly, the socialist son of a millionaire is usually regarded by his people as abnormal or as a traitor (psychologically, the difference between these two concepts is not great). In various groups, especially those on the border of the lower and middle classes, acute fear of success occurs, because success is interpreted as a break in solidarity if not as actual aggression toward the less fortunate fellow members of the group.

A clear distinction between "normal" and "mature" and genuinely "abnormal" and "immature" patterns of nonconformist behavior is of great importance. We cannot leave it to the psychotherapist to judge the respective merits of controversial ideas; but he can find out whether the concrete attitudes of a nonconformist individual—both during and after childhood—are translated into meaningful and effective action on the social level (economic initiative or technological invention, for instance) or merely into personal frustrations and anxieties. He can also separate those attitudes which would be considered nonconformist or immature in any organized society from those which are so considered only within the social framework of a limited group or phase of history. He can similarly distinguish those individuals who actually wish to change things on the basis of realistic knowledge of the existing world from those who operate with a distorted, illusory picture of society—for example, a world populated by villains, witches, scapegoats, or perhaps devils and angels, rather than by ordinary human beings.

At any rate, the pressure for conformity in most societies, upon the child and later upon the adult, is formidable. This occurs, in particular, when the patterns and limitations of perception that characterize one culture and social group are taken for granted, when autistic factors are extended to a social scale, or when realization is lacking that other cultures, societies, or groups might "see" (or emphasize) different sectors of life and values. In Kurt Lewin's experience, "experiments dealing with memory and group pressure on the individual show that what exists as 'reality' for the individual is, to a high degree, determined by what is socially accepted as reality." [38] Conformity pressure occurs through education (in the broadest sense), respect for symbols, and other influences that help shape the concrete pattern of "superego."

This applies especially to "other-directed" societies such as contemporary America, the "lonely crowd," to use David Riesman's terms.

The conformity of earlier generations of Americans of the type I term "inner-directed" was mainly assured by their internalization of adult authority. The middle-class urban American of today, the "other-directed," is, by contrast, in a characterological sense more the product of his peers—that is, in sociological terms, his "peer-groups," the other kids at school or in the block. In adult life he continues to respond to these peers, not only with overt conformity, as do people in all times and places, but also in a deeper sense, in the very quality of his feeling. Yet, paradoxically, he remains a lonely member of the crowd because he never comes really close to the others or to himself; his inner-directed predecessor was lonely too, but in a different way; his chief company being the ancestors within—the parents whom he had internalized. [39]

The American child, to be sure, is given far more individual leeway than are children in many other societies; but he is expected, at the same time, to become a "regular guy"—to wish to (or come to) conform voluntarily without even knowing that he conforms, to internalize completely the social norms concerned. He is trained in pro-

nounced individualism, which, in the last analysis is expected however to yield almost identical results in each individual's ideas through
voluntary action—to lead to the same basic way of life, scale of values,
and pattern of perception, even at the risk of leading just as typically
to the same personal insecurities.

In our society self-respect often comes to depend on outward "success," which, in turn, tends to depend on standardized conformity or,
at least, on unquestioning acceptance of the existing social framework.
It is the imaginative utilization of existing rules that is ordinarily rewarded, not the advocacy or mere realization of any alternatives to
them. Failure to conform often means failure to "succeed," economically and otherwise; and such failure, in turn, tends to shake
the self-respect and thus to breed personal insecurity. Constant fear
of unintended nonconformity tends to have a comparable effect.

"Abnormal" Economic Behavior

The gist of the preceding discussion is that the socioeconomic
setting during childhood and later tends to influence greatly the
incidence of certain kinds of personality. Conversely, the distribution
of personalities in society affects the frequency of specific patterns
of economic behavior. More particularly, persons who are excessively
insecure or otherwise emotionally disturbed may show "abnormal"
behavior in economic affairs, such as money matters.

However, the term "abnormal economic behavior," occasionally
used in psychotherapeutic literature, may have at least two different
meanings. It may refer to deviation from certain standards that have
been set up by the group, the community, economic theory, or convention as yardsticks of rationality and regularity, if not conformity.
Or it may refer to abnormality in the clinical sense, that is, a pattern
of economic behavior based on an emotional disturbance and often
connected with unconscious influences or leading to imaginary
assumptions.

The first meaning would be exemplified by a businessman who
consistently refused to borrow investment capital in a period of prolonged prosperity because he alone considered the interest rates too
high or because he did not trust future business prospects although
everybody else did; or a housewife who insisted on laundering her
linen by hand in order to make it wear longer, even though a laundro-

mat might be easier and cheaper to use in the short run. The second
meaning would be represented by a businessman whose personal
aggressiveness was translated, not into opening up new products and
markets but into insulting his customers and alienating his associates,
by a labor leader who did not realize that he acted like a caricature
of Napoleon, by a writer who went into a deep depression when his
novel became a best-seller, by a recluse who stored his lifetime savings
under the mattress because he mistrusted everybody, or by a person
who quit every job because he was emotionally incapable of working
for money. In this last instance, earning money means competition,
ordinarily with males; it may symbolize abandonment of the security
setting of childhood.

The border line between the two concepts of abnormal economic
behavior is somewhat less distinct than one might assume at first, for
even a clinical abnormality can often be defined only in terms of the
accepted standards and values in a given culture and society. For
example, Mary Jane Ward, in *The Snake Pit*, makes the staff of a
mental ward consider selfishness in patients normal, generosity abnormal. The question is how "normal" the implied scale of values can
claim to be. By and large, however, the discussion in this section refers
to the second, that is, the clinical type, of abnormal economic behavior
to the extent that it represents a pattern of high social incidence,
rather than a purely individual disturbance.

Especially does this discussion apply to attitudes toward money.
Our cultural and social setup is by no means the only one in which
both the economic and the symbolic significance of money are very
pronounced. Goethe, in the second part of *Faust*, has Mephistopheles
ironically present paper money as the devil's own invention for greater
"security," with the words: "Ein solch Papier, an Gold und Perlen
statt, ist so bequem: man weiss doch, was man hat!"

However, both in the expansion of the credit mechanism and in
the symbolic adoption of money-making as a decisive yardstick of
personal success our socioculture has probably gone much farther
than any past society. In the conventional scale of social values, money
and financial gain symbolize personal assertion; ownership of money
is interpreted as the best if not the only way to mobility, independence,
and indirectly security.

While money thus is widely associated with success, our cultural pattern includes several layers, derived from various phases of society, of guilt feelings toward the acquisition and accumulation of money. Usually such feelings remain on the unconscious level. One such layer represents the continued influence of feudal, precapitalist standards of value in a capitalist world; both aristocratic chivalry and ascetic negation of personal gain continue to bother many an individual under the surface of his seemingly money-mad personality. So does past disdain for the lending and borrowing of money. Another layer consists of ethicoreligious standards from the formative period of Christianity (or other religions) with their emphasis on spiritual values, renunciation of personal gain, and sharing one's wealth with one's brethren. Much of this influence, of course, is quite conscious, but often it is displaced by queer rationalizations only to bother the individual concerned that much more on the unconscious level.

A third layer consists of the Calvinist or Puritan standards of thrift from the early phase of capitalism, standards which easily get into hidden conflict with the requirements of conspicuous consumption and pecuniary emulation that an arrived, industrialized capitalism often imposes upon the wealthy. A fourth layer is supplied by the pseudofeudal, *ersatz*-chivalry standards of the Victorian era—and not only in England. A fifth layer comes from the effect of short-range socioeconomic instability in fostering personal insecurity, which has been discussed earlier. Such instability is likely to be interpreted by many, again either consciously or not, as well-deserved punishment for money-making greed or cut-throat competition. A sixth layer derives from the social criticism offered by reform movements, especially those which attempt to offer a clean-cut alternative, not merely to existing socioeconomic institutions but to their underlying scale of values, including the money standard of personal success.

The older layers mentioned are illustrated by the fact that in German, *Schuld* may mean either debt or guilt. The guilt charge of money is also exemplified, in some degree, by certain approaches to philanthropy, as has been mentioned earlier. In prosperous times, at least, successful self-assertion through money-making is often followed by generous gifts to the charities and foundations, not only to save taxes but to save one's soul. First, one must prove to the outside world and, more importantly, to oneself how smart one is; the amount of money made is assumed in our culture to be the evidence. When the fluctuations and vicissitudes of a competitive economy deprive an individual of the opportunity to make money—or even to keep the wealth acquired earlier—the bottom may drop out under his self-respect as well, unless he is remarkably independent of the conventional value scale of his society.

Abnormal behavior in money matters and in other economic situations is often due to a conscious or unconscious clash of conflicting value systems in the mind of an individual. The incidence of such clashes in our society is great enough to point with great probability to an effect of the socioeconomic setup itself and, especially, the perennial socioeconomic instability. (For an example, see Appendix II.)

It would be quite useless for the social scientist to acquiesce in a purely psychoanalytic explanation of abnormal economic behavior on the individual level and to stop there.[40] Granted that such character types as the success hunter, the gambler, the gold digger, the miser, the impostor, the dependent loafer, the sucker for easy money, the recluse develop out of specific individual experiences, especially those of early childhood, two additional factors must be taken into account in order to get a reasonably foolproof analysis. The first of these factors concerns the cultural value scale and the socioeconomic setting which classify a given behavior pattern as abnormal even though another culture or society might put a premium on it. In other words, it is essential to recognize the sociocultural determination of the yardstick itself, with relatively few exceptions.

The second factor to be considered concerns the comparative incidence, in various phases and strata of society, of various kinds of personality and behavior. If the same infantile frustration, say, "psychic masochism"—to use a term employed by some Freudians—occurs everywhere all the time, how can we explain the fact that there unquestionably are and have been many more misers in some societies than in others and that, on the whole, they were considered normal and socially useful in, say, seventeenth-century Geneva while they are usually regarded as crackpots if not worse in contemporary America, though a prolonged deflationary situation might change this once more some time?

It is equally hopeless to try to explain the horror of deficit spending, governmental as well as private, on the part of many Americans

simply from personal, if not psychopathological traits due to inadequate feeding schedules during early childhood. The idea is that the
resulting unconscious frustrations make people later hang onto money
as a symbol of food.[41] Such personality effects may occur individually,
or even on a mass scale, but no one would think of regarding them
as abnormal unless and until the prevailing scale of socioeconomic
values comes to consider deficit spending permissable or desirable.
The feeding habits of American mothers did not change abruptly
during the Great Depression, but the climate of economic opinion
did!

Similar considerations regarding the changing socioeconomic causation and evaluation of "abnormal" patterns in economic life also apply
to some other kinds of personality or behavior. The gambler, for instance, is a frequent figure in the most diverse cultures and societies
(see Chapter I) but his social role varies enormously. Some of us may
be content with the broad assertion that the gambler always unconsciously wants to lose. It is probably more accurate to say that
gambling usually results from conscious or unconscious desire either
to dodge the existing socioeconomic arrangement as it affects the
individual, or to channel existing tensions into an organized outlet.
There may also be a desire to build up artificial tension where life
itself produces too little of it to be attractive.

In a competitive economy speculative "gambling" is organized and
institutionalized along specific lines. The social position of the gambler
type is thus characterized by a dichotomy. On the one hand, his
gambling drive is appreciated and possibly rewarded insofar as it
goes into speculative business initiative. On the other hand, it is
usually outlawed and punished if it is channeled into gambling per
se, without serving any real market function. Stock-exchange speculation is considered both smart and socially useful, at least as long as
it is successful. Gambling at the horsetracks is usually outlawed or
drastically restricted, although significantly it is often tolerated
unofficially both by prevailing opinion and by public agencies.

"Abnormal" economic behavior may thus be considered abnormal
only within a very specific framework of cultural, institutional, and
socioeconomic character. This does not imply that all types of abnormal economic behavior should be viewed in relativistic terms.
It does mean that some of them, possibly the majority, fall into this

category. The Zuñi culture, for instance, considers personal initiative and drive abnormal in the sense of deviant and puts severe sanctions on it, whereas our own culture rewards it.[42]

Attitudes toward gold are another interesting example of normality standards that are subject to sociocultural change. Until the early eighteenth century gold and, in a lesser degree, silver were the recognized standard of wealth in both a good and a bad sense. Gold was the standard and symbol of financial success as well as of sinful greed. With the development of an economy based on credit and paper money and with the disruption of the international balance-of-payments mechanism by two World Wars and a major depression, gold lost much of its former economic importance, especially in the domestic affairs of nations. But in an atmosphere of socioeconomic instability it still stands as a symbol of security and real value for many. This is one important reason why governments of the most diverse ideological denominations are anxious to maintain it as backing for their currencies—even when no real economic reason warrants it—and why it is still hoarded whenever public regulations permit it, if not in defiance of them.

A further example of relative standards of normality is offered by the incidence of work compulsions in our period. This incidence mirrors in part the economic dynamics of a competitive society where moderation or standstill threaten destruction, where survival is deemed to depend on expansion, and where seeming personal adjustment is often achieved at the expense of other people's real maladjustments. In other instances, however, work compulsions overcompensate a strong unconscious need of an individual to relax and be cared for, or reflect outright emotional disturbances. The exact border line between a healthy activity impulse and a pathological work compulsion can be defined only in terms of concrete sociocultural values.

These considerations illustrate the interaction between socioeconomic instability—especially when it comes into conflict with a long-range scale of values—and excessive personal insecurity. The social incidence of the latter, in its specific and changing forms, is influenced by the occurrence and kind of the former. If and when personal insecurity of specific types develops in society on a large scale, it is then likely to backfire and to affect the prevailing patterns of economic behavior, even to the point of making a new social rule out of patterns that were formerly considered abnormal or, at least, an individual exception.

Avenues of Research

The hypothesis formulated in this chapter assumes that socioeconomic instability experienced during childhood and later influences personality formation and behavior patterns. It thus has a decisive impact upon the rise and incidence of various personal insecurities in our society. Widespread insecurity in turn influences individual and group behavior in economic and social situations. Such interaction is indicated by impressive, if scattered and incomplete, evidence from both economic and psychological sources. Convincing proof that this hypothesis is correct (or incorrect) would require more extensive data than are available now. The following paragraphs are designed to suggest the main avenues of further search for convincing evidence one way or another.[43]

1. Survey data. Brief sample interviews cannot hope to uncover the whole story, but they can help greatly by revealing the comparative spread of subjectively felt insecurity during various periods in a given population and in specific social groups. This can partly be garnered through reference to socioeconomic factors that directly affect the level of personal security; for example, through questions about feelings of financial security. In addition, indirect questions can be asked to bring out the general atmosphere in society as reflected in individual attitudes, as well as the incidence and distribution of certain personal phobias, worries, or expectations that may have a bearing on this problem.

Many such questions would have to be of a projective type, and serious problems of interviewing method, coding, and quantification would undoubtedly be present. Even so, the application of survey techniques to patterns of personality and behavior in their interaction with economic life looks worth while. The kinds of questions to be asked might include some on the perception of the world outlook in general; planning for the future of the family; a comparison of children today with those of the respondent's childhood; nervous feeling; the effects of minority status; the relationship between the income and a sense of personal achievement; membership in social or group organizations with its advantages and drawbacks; evaluation of conformity and independent thought; receptiveness toward authoritarian or totalitarian solutions; geographic, occupational, and social mobility and its psychic effects; various aspects of feeling settled; personal-security aspects of specific types of business and consumption such as real-estate ownership, insurance, liquor, movies, fashions, advertising; attitudes toward money, such as hoarding, gold, saving, investment preferences; and various related questions.

The limitations of survey methods are: (1) that they are usually not well suited to bring out unconscious factors even when the interview succeeds in breaking through the outside screen of camouflage and rationalization; (2) that they are largely confined to contemporary data in a few Western countries with freedom of speech and do not lend themselves easily to historical or anthropological comparisons; (3) that they require a complex and expensive machinery even where they are applicable. All this is said, not in order to argue against surveys but in order to delineate their legitimate applications in the field with which we are concerned here.

2. Psychiatrists, lay analysts, clinical psychologists, psychobiologists. Few members of these groups are likely to keep detailed case records and fewer will be willing or able to make them available, even with all identification removed. A wealth of important material might, however, be opened up here by extensive questioning, especially of all kinds of psychotherapists, on the known, possible, or probable connection between specific socioeconomic influences and personality disorders in their clinical experience. For the thoughtful psychotherapist "is concerned when the rules and the underlying and supporting culture-complex are so incongruent and so peculiarly contradictory that they give rise in some people at least to states of mental disorder—and probably in everyone to some measure of insecurity." [44]

At the very least, valuable information concerning the socioeconomic aspects of recently treated disturbances (and perhaps concerning long-range trends in the types of neuroses) might be utilized and compared in this way, although it is doubtful whether these materials would be suitable for tabulation. Some such materials are available in the various journals of psychiatry, psychology, and sociology; but an attempt at more systematic utilization of psychotherapeutic experiences through the interviewing of practitioners should be well worth while. Ample allowance should be made, however, for differences in the classification, interpretation, and treatment of the personality disorders concerned and in the socioeconomic knowledge and philosophy of the psychotherapists to be questioned.

Actually psychotherapists have much to gain for their own clinical and scientific purposes from greater knowledge and understanding of socioeconomic factors. Psychotherapists so often have had to unravel economic rationalizations in the behavior of disturbed persons that they seldom have got around to studying the range of genuine economic reasoning. Many have had even less acquaintance with the intricate links between culture, socioeconomic system, and individual personality dynamics. Last but not least, they have not always realized that their own interpretation of man, and their standards of personal success, normality, and mental health, may unwittingly be colored by the economic society and group in which they have been brought up.

In evaluating the basic influence of the family in the personality formation of individuals, disregard of the economic position of the parents and their role as providers can lead a psychotherapist astray. Similarly, he needs to be interested in certain community, work, and old-age situations that easily encourage pathological behavior in predisposed individuals. The socioeconomic background of a patient may have an important bearing on his response to treatment in general or a particular method of it.

Knowledge of the prevailing socioeconomic values would also make the psychotherapist understand (if not excuse) the financial and administrative shortcomings of the facilities for treatment and research in this field. Psychotherapists, it is true, have often repressed in their own minds the problems of cost of treatment, and of class discrimination in it, with possible prejudice to the realism of their therapeutic methods. The mere fact that the psychotherapist is usually paid for his services—at greatly varying rates—can easily warp the therapeutic situation if unconscious guilt feelings, conflicts, or rationalizations are allowed to develop from this situation in either the therapist or the patient.

The psychotherapist, it is true, can often recognize the pathological motivation of "abnormal" economic behavior without having had any elaborate economic training. But he will often need a great deal of socioeconomic knowledge in order to avoid therapeutic errors and to understand the patient's family, work, and community setting, and his general life experience. Such knowledge would help in preventing the therapist from learning economics chiefly from his patients, or misinterpreting his own economic function as mere help to the patient in making money more effectively. He would also be more wary when he is called upon to direct a patient toward specific economic goals such as entering father's business, keeping away from risk, or supporting a given ideology. In summary, the contact with the approaches and research needs of economists may turn out to be very fruitful for psychotherapists from their own point of view.

3. Social-work agencies. The experiences of psychiatric social workers and the activities of social-work agencies in general offer a potential mine of information on the problem before us. In particular, it would be very illuminating to compare the types and incidence of those cases which are referred to psychotherapists with other cases that reach the social-work agencies. In the latter case, the cause of the trouble is presumably socioeconomic only, while the former type represents an interaction between socioeconomic and personality factors of disturbance. It would be very interesting to plot the frequency of the various types of trouble against the specific socioeconomic background and family conditions concerned. It would likewise be most illuminating to compare a representative sample of children from unemployed (or formerly unemployed) families with other disturbed children. Here again, many scattered data exist and quite a few have been published, but a full utilization for the purpose of this kind of investigation apparently remains to be made.

4. Clergymen. Personal insecurities of almost any kind, including the main types discussed earlier, are brought to clergymen, whose need for both socioeconomic and psychological training has received much emphasis in recent years. Extensive interviewing of clergymen on their experiences with the socioeconomic background of personal insecurities might be of considerable value.

5. Mental-hygiene agencies. Data from such agencies as the National Association for Mental Hygiene, the Association for the Advancement of Psychotherapy, the Veterans Administration, and the armed services (especially from selective-service experiences), when assembled, integrated, and compared with survey data available,

might be invaluable. The Association for the Advancement of Psychotherapy, for instance, issues a questionnaire to patients which includes questions regarding the socioeconomic background of the family.

6. Mental institutions. Public mental hospitals usually have some information about the financial standing of their patients, though this in itself is not an adequate definition of their socioeconomic background. This also applies to some private institutions, with the additional qualification that they usually cater only to patients from the upper-income class and thus do not represent a cross section. The questionnaires submitted, for screening purposes, to job applicants at mental institutions may also contain some lessons for wider application.

7. Employment agencies. From the experiences of employment agencies with vocational guidance, with data on the incidence of work inhibitions and excessive job mobility and with various personality tests, valuable information on the relationship between socioeconomic and personality factors might be gained.

8. Insurance companies. Records of the life-insurance business (and of other sources of vital statistics) on the trend of divorces, mental disorders, and suicides can be of some help, at least if it is possible to separate statistically the neurotic disorders, and possibly the "insecurity suicides," from others. Insurance data also permit conclusions concerning other aspects of personal insecurity feelings as, for example, by comparison of the emergency-protection aspect with the savings features of life insurance.

The Survey Research Center found, from a regional survey, that the protective aspects far exceeded the savings features in the minds of people—both those who were insured and, in an even larger degree, those who were not. Especially did this apply to the protection of dependents. The lower income and educational groups emphasized protection even more than the others. In this survey, 43 per cent of all privately insured families felt that they carried too little insurance; even in the group carrying the most insurance ($20,000 or over) the percentage was still 28. Only 3 per cent of the total thought they carried too much insurance; this proportion was no less true of those covered by social insurance than of others.[45]

9. Age-group data. Information about the condition of specific age groups may be very illuminating in this kind of an investigation.

Above all the experiences of school clinics for mental hygiene or child guidance may be helpful, particularly when they list parents' income or other socioeconomic data. At the other end of the life scale, explorations in gerontology, especially in the attitudes of various age groups toward the growth in life expectancy and in the social proportion of old people, may also contribute to our evaluation of personal insecurity in its socioeconomic incidence. In between these two groups, special data (for example, from the armed services and the Veterans Administration) regarding the mental health of the middle-age groups including the depression generation can be helpful.

Conclusion

In answer to the second question posed in the Introduction, we may state that impressive indications point to socioeconomic instability as a leading factor in explaining the changing incidence and distribution of strong personal insecurities, which may then backfire upon socioeconomic attitudes and behavior. This hypothesis rests on serious grounds, but it is not easy to prove in an irrefutable way. To begin with, the frame of reference for such concepts as stability, security, flexibility, or adjustment lacks reliable and widely accepted definition at this point, both in socioeconomic and in psychological studies. Moreover, the relationship between the two sets of factors is complex; there are evidently some types of insecurity that are not rooted in socioeconomic conditions and that originate in strictly individual factors of personality (organic ones, for example). There are, on the other hand, a good many cases in which socioeconomic instability fails to be accompanied by personal insecurity on the individual or group level. Allowing for these two types of cases, however, we find indications of a wide area of overlapping which strongly suggests a far-reaching interaction.

Extensive research would be required in order to test this hypothesis convincingly—for example, by measuring the changes and variations in expectations, aspiration levels, and motive patterns which accompany major developments of socioeconomic instability either immediately or later. Much light could be thrown on the problem by utilizing and integrating all the potential sources of information mentioned, even though only part of the latter would lend itself to fool-proof verification and, especially, to quantitative presentation.

For proper perspective, such evidence from our own period will require checking against any comparable information that can be ascertained from historical or anthropological sources. While we obviously cannot hope to measure *ex post facto* the extent of personal insecurity in a feudal society of the past, for example, there is much indirect evidence that would permit fruitful comparisons with our own period.

What matters from the viewpoint of social policy is to break any vicious circle that may have resulted thus far from a constant interaction between socioeconomic instability and widespread personal insecurity. If it should be possible to establish the exact pattern of such interaction, the next and decisive possibility might be to work out a psychoeconomic therapy on a wide social scale. Such a procedure, not to be confused with mere group therapy, could then attempt to bring about both healthier minds and healthier institutions at once. At this point we appear to be quite far from any general agreement on the nature of the evil or on the task we face, let alone the solution or even the identity of the prospective sociotherapists; but exploration of the possibility of a combined reform of institutions and attitudes appears promising.

Chapter IV

Economic Reform
and the Human Mind

IN ONE WAY or another, the fateful interaction between socio-economic instability and personal insecurity has absorbed the attention of many of those who have not given up hope that the condition of mankind can be improved. A good many psychologists believe that such improvement can best be achieved by educating or curing a sufficient number of individuals in the right way. The Marxian school and some other approaches to social thought, on the other hand, assume that with a suitable change in socioeconomic institutions the individual will automatically achieve or regain his peace of mind.

Although both assumptions contain a certain nucleus of truth, neither one seems entirely satisfactory in the light of recent advances in both economic and psychological knowledge. A good many economic reforms have miscarried despite intrinsic merits because the value systems, attitudes, and motives of the populations concerned were not taken into sufficient account. At the same time, the soundest approaches to education—let alone any attempt to cure individuals one by one through clinical treatment—have run into insurmountable difficulties on the practical level in the absence of a suitable economic, social, and political setting.

144

There is need, therefore, for an integrated approach to economic and other institutional reforms; an approach which would take the psychological and cultural characteristics of the population concerned into constant account, along with its economic features. This need was expressed in the question raised in the Introduction under (3). The first condition for such an approach is clarity concerning the motivational factors that make persons and groups support, tolerate, or oppose economic reform in general or a particular type of it. Such insights should then be integrated with the social factors, such as the degree of economic stability, that influence the incidence of the various reaction patterns in a given society, group, or period.

Some of these social factors have been discussed in the preceding chapter. It is the purpose of the present chapter to show more specifically the connection between a given socioeconomic setting and the incidence of particular kinds of personality and ideology, such as conservatism, reform, or revolt; to point out that attitudes toward economic reform, far from being determined by rational-logical processes alone, reflect a belief system rooted partly in general character traits of the person concerned; to apply these considerations to the basic difference between revolt and reform attitudes in economic life, with special attention to patterns of the labor movement and to various types of economic planning; to discuss both the lure and the danger of the totalitarian mentality in economic life; and to emphasize the necessity of keeping needed economic reforms in line with the psychocultural setup of the population concerned.

Personality and Ideology

Ideas on economic conditions and needs, like other ideas, do not occur to a person by accident, nor do they necessarily impress people merely because somebody has presented them. The receptiveness of an individual to specific ideas, especially those which imply social change, is conditioned by the general pattern and development of his perception, which in turn reflects the basic structure of his personality. In this discussion we are concerned only with those personality-shaping influences that foster specific attitudes and ideologies in the sphere of economic life. We also remain interested in the impact of economic conditions upon personality formation, some aspects of which have been discussed in the preceding chapter.

Personality could be defined as "the individual's organization of predispositions to behavior."[1] Emphasis is usually placed on its unique and persistent traits, which may show similarities among many persons in the same society, on its dynamic orientation toward the environment, and on the continuous though varying interaction between each individual and the society he lives in. Apparently many essential traits of personality are acquired in early childhood. The total personality formation, however, is determined by a combination of biological, group, role, and situational factors during lifetime.

The concrete functioning of a personality is largely characterized by the urge for self-expression and for a reduction of tensions. It makes all the difference in the world in what specific ways such reduction is achieved—whether important conflicts are repressed leaving the entire personality dominated by a basic anxiety on or below the conscious level; whether conflicts find a pseudo-solution by purely external adaptation; or whether they are resolved in a productive and socially fruitful manner.

Because of such differences the *incidence* of specific kinds of personality in various societies is greatly influenced by prevailing socioeconomic conditions, of the past or present, that is, by the probability that a child (and, in some cases, an adult) will experience certain frustrations, conflicts, satisfactions, or norms. At the same time, the meaning which the individual will typically attach to such experiences will vary with his perception and values.

This is not meant to be a subscription to the child-rearing theory of basic personality, not even in its more refined forms.[2] To begin with, while childhood experiences are extremely important in personality formation, certain happenings during later periods of life may also have a substantial share in this continuous process. Further, typical experiences both during childhood and later may differ significantly within the same society according to the class or subculture (racial group, for instance). The child-rearing methods, of course, do not come out of nowhere; they are determined and changed in a large degree by economic factors. Such factors include the method of soil cultivation as it affects family life, population trends, and property relations. Moreover, some decisive influences upon childhood experiences—both typical and unique influences—stem from medium-range or short-range events such as wars, famines, slumps, inflations, oppression, revolution, technological innovation as well as from long-range cultural factors. Recognition of the latter need not blind us to historical and institutional influences of a more immediate nature. Last, but not least, modern industrial cultures are generally far more complex and dynamic than the culture of, say, the Tanala or Comanche. As a result, the interaction between culture and the individual personality is now less direct and less definite than the interaction between socioeconomic processes and the individual personality.

In other words, in order to understand the personality formation in any specific case, especially as it affects attitudes toward economic change, we must consider the interaction of cultural setting, socioeconomic factors, and strictly individual endowment or experiences. These three kinds of influences may reinforce, balance, or weaken one another in a given person depending on their direction and intensity. Certainly a purely cultural theory of basic personality could not hope to explain fully the attitude of an individual toward economic reform in his period. Such a theory might admittedly be of some help in explaining the incidence of certain ideas, their general reception, and their effectiveness, but it would need supplementation by an analogous account of socioeconomic (that is, shorter-range) influences upon personality.

Such socioeconomic influences include, especially, the class situation and the group membership in which the individual finds himself embedded by virtue of his birth or family position. The family, and later the playmates, the school, or the church, transmit to him an "objective" role expectation which he internalizes currently, thus making it subjective as well. If and when he does not do so sufficiently —and this is not an infrequent case in our dynamic and mobile society —extra tensions and conflicts result. Similar conflicts may arise between the level of aspiration of the individual or family and the objective opportunities which are available on the basis of socioeconomic position.[3]

Education, in a broad sense, serves largely the function of training children in the prevailing ways in which society sees, overlooks, or associates things. The "size of the world" in which a person lives, or his life space, his value system, his application of causality, and his pattern of identification and ego involvement are all significantly influenced by the socioeconomic order and by his family's specific role in it. This need not mean, of course, that he will always conform to the prevailing social standards; individual sources of discontent may modify his attitudes, especially in combination with other persons from the same group or subgroup. Particularly is this true in or after critical situations in society with a quasi-traumatic effect.

Even if full allowance is made for the great importance of the socioeconomic and cultural background, including status and role expectations, experiences of a strictly individual nature still retain a certain share in shaping the personality. Each person lives in a unique family setting and undergoes life experiences that are not exactly paralleled by those of any other person. Even though the incidence of authoritarian fathers in a given society may be enormous, some will always be more authoritarian than others; the relations between children and mother or among siblings always vary somewhat; and the specific combination of traumatic or other experiences—say, a fire, an accident, an impressive acquaintance—is never exactly repeated by another child. The combination of individual endowment and experiences with cultural and socioeconomic influences determines, first, the general setup of a given personality including its level of maturity and, second, its propensity to develop specific socioeconomic attitudes, its receptiveness toward emotional and intellectual forces which lead to ideological involvement of one kind or another.

Kurt Lewin, Solomon E. Asch, and others have shown that social attitudes and actions interact with perception. The possession of correct knowledge—even if based on firsthand experience—does not automatically rectify distorted perception, especially if the latter is rooted in a definite group pattern. Similarly, individuals tend to accept new values and beliefs through identification with a new group, not the other way around. The degree of flexibility and independence with which a person reacts to his own experiences, his ability to learn from them in contrast to mere submission to the intellectual authority of others, the very capacity to believe intensively in definite values and ideas—all these express basic traits of personality.[4]

An individual will thus accept or reject a specific "ideology"—meaning a system of ideas based on the prevailing norms of a group and its body of common beliefs—according to his own personality constellation as of a given date. The cultural and socioeconomic setting concerned make it *likely* that many individuals within any particular group will accept a specific ideology based on the social values of this group. Because of individual variations, however, there is no predictive certainty about this process in any one case. At the very least, there will be individual differences in the intensity of opinions, loyalties, or prejudices, and in the readiness to question or reinterpret the social values.

In other words, the cultural and socioeconomic heritage enters decisively into the value system of each individual in determining the *probability* that he will accept or reject a given ideology; but the question whether a specific individual will actually accept it, and with what degree of involvement, will be decided by his unique traits of personality. We can only mention here the broader question of whether or not ideologies should be interpreted as a "superstructure" upon socioeconomic systems or classes, perhaps in some parallel to the role of the superego in the conceptual system of Freud. Another interesting question is whether the decisive binding force of an ideology is in an original myth of a group or institution, in the substitution of a desired world for the real one, or in any other factors.

Regardless of the exact answers to such fundamental questions, the general processes of ideological change have a direct bearing on attitudes toward economic reform. If the personality traits that were acquired in childhood determined fully the ideological attitudes of each person for the rest of his life, no real question would arise. It is clear, however, that for most persons this does not hold true.

At the same time, psychological and political evidence alike indicate that attempts at change of socioeconomic attitudes through factual arguments affect incomparably fewer people than do emotional appeals that are addressed directly to frames of reference. The attempted shock effects of totalitarian propaganda, regardless of its specific brand, aim precisely at this target. Objective economic events, however, may sometimes produce a shock effect too. Bankruptcy in a family business, long unemployment shared with many other members of the group, or loss of family savings during an inflation may result in a change of the frame of reference either directly or in the wake of propaganda that hits precisely this sensitive spot. Unless such a hit is scored, propaganda will be ineffective no matter how vocal or technically accomplished it may be.

It is important to realize, however, that the propensity of individuals to change their ideological attitudes is partly a function of the social setup. Individuals in a society with a high degree of mobility and fluidity tend to be less insulated against such shifts than are individuals in rigid and firmly entrenched societies. The threshold of attitudinal change varies according to the cultural and socioeconomic background.

If we apply these principles to ideological variations in our own period, what attitudinal differences among personalities exist today in relation to economic reform? The experiences of the last few decades indicate that the decisive difference in contemporary Western societies is that between the totalitarian and the democratic types of personality. These concepts are used here merely to characterize polar extremes. In reality every person, of course, represents some combination of both these traits and many others. The relative preponderance, however, of either totalitarian or democratic traits in each individual and group today is of crucial importance.

Self-absorbed persons and, especially, self-haters, with the possible exception of some negativistic, passive types, tend to become intolerant, black-or-white, fanatic proponents of a "cause," which is no less likely today to be an economic one than a political or a religious one. Their self-hate is projected to groups, institutions, or beliefs; the "cause"— perceived as *the* panacea to the exclusion of any legitimate alternative —serves as a desperate device to which they cling in the absence of genuine safeguards of personal security. Late conversion, based on an attitudinal shock which disturbs earlier roots of personality, is especially conducive to such zealotry.[5]

Persons with mainly democratic traits, on the other hand (the concept of democracy is used here not in its political sense but in that of character structure), show, above all, open-mindedness, that is, readiness to change or adjust their attitudinal system in line with important new experiences. This includes prominently experiences of an intellectual type, without, however, succumbing to a constant drive for conformist adaptation to the fashion of the moment. Society itself can either encourage or discourage, either reward or punish such personality traits, especially through its educational philosophy and system.[6] Here again, the *incidence* of persons with mainly democratic traits depends on the cultural and socioeconomic setting, though there are modifying factors in each individual.

In summary, it would make little sense to ask whether personality determines ideology—perhaps through strictly individual traits of biological heritage and childhood experience—regardless of a person's socioeconomic position, or whether this position determines the ideological preferences of a person without regard to purely individual experiences and traits. Neither assumption would be realistic. The personality pattern *is* decisive in shaping the ideological attitudes, but it is not the ultimate determinant, socially speaking. The given social arrangements—class structure, economic institutions, living standards, the degree of economic stability—act upon the family and the education process. These arrangements thus determine the *probability* that individuals in a given society and group will be exposed to specific types of frustrations and compensations and that certain patterns of aggression will be tolerated or even encouraged while others are not.

In other words, while the ideological preference of a person is largely shaped by his individual experiences during childhood and later, the probability that he will undergo specific types of experiences is determined by the socioeconomic structure including his own group situation. The ideology of a person is individually determined; the incidence of individual ideologies of any specific type is socially determined.

This brings us to the question for which this section has really tried to prepare the ground. Which specific traits of personality are conducive to affirmative, critical, indifferent, or oscillating attitudes toward economic reform in general, disregarding at first the differences among its various possible types?

Reformers, Conservatives, Apostates, Indifferents

Two extreme opinions are often presented in answer to the question just mentioned. One of these opinions denies any definite relationship between specific personality traits and ideological attitudes and considers the latter either accidental or based entirely on intellectual values that were acquired from experience, study, and insight. At best it is admitted that personality traits may be relevant for the *role* of a person in any movement he happens to join—his rise to leadership, for instance. The other extreme opinion considers the ideological attitude of an individual to be fully defined in each case either by his biological heritage or by his childhood experiences, class situation, or transcendental predetermination.

The alternative to both extremes is based on personality factors in each case but gives due credit to the part of social influences in determining the *incidence* of the various reaction patterns in a given period. This approach could be applied to the most diverse kinds of public figures in various societies—to demagogues, politicians, profiteers, preachers, moralizers, totalitarians, pacifists, altruists, indifferents—if we wanted to apply our own concepts to other cultures as well. This discussion, however, will be confined to attitudes toward economic reform in contemporary Western societies. The principal types concerned are the reformer, the conservative, the apostate, and the indifferent. Important subdivisions could admittedly be made in each case. Moreover, significant differences exist not only in the content of ideologies and reaction patterns—that is, change, preservation, or vacillation—but in the degree of involvement.

Before proceeding to a detailed discussion of these differences, a renewed warning may be in order at this point against any attempt to explain ideologies purely from individual traits. It would be hopeless to disregard the social setting that first underlies the formation of such traits in the minds of people and then confronts these traits as they manifest themselves in practice. Father haters in the Sioux society, for instance, may acquire their characteristics for reasons quite different from those of father haters in mediaeval England or contemporary Italy; the overt manifestation and social reception of such attitudes may likewise be quite different. Allowing constantly for such sociocultural distinctions, we may venture the following generalizations concerning the main ideological types in the field of economic reform in the West today.

a. The reformer. The term reformer is used here in a broad sense, meaning a person who is actively and genuinely interested in extensive change of specific economic conditions regardless of whether or not this is felt to affect the social order in general. The term thus comprises potentially the whole range of methods from the gentle missionary to the merciless revolutionary. Nonconformity toward existing conditions or institutions, in contrast to antisocial egocentrism in rebellious form, is the yardstick to be used here. This concept of reform includes backward change or reaction no less than forward change, but it is the latter kind upon which the present discussion will be focused.

It appears that reform attitudes typically go through two phases, not necessarily in a strict time sequence. The first phase is characterized by introversion and idealized images, the second phase by extrovert group action during which such images are applied from the self to the outside world. The first phase may originate in specific frustrations during the period of personality formation. This phase need not necessarily reflect a neurotic situation, but occasionally this may be the case. Such frustrations may be of a strictly individual type (say, witnessing an accident without being able to help); or they may be due to a socioeconomic situation (say, lack of adequate food in the family due to father's unemployment). They may, finally, arise from more hidden and indirect malaise and guilt feelings of a class or group, which may be an upper one no less easily than a lower one.

In other words, attitudes toward reform, and the corresponding behavior, may reflect a varying combination of individual factors and group situations: John is a reformer because he has adopted the attitudinal framework of his parents, who are reformers; Mary is a reformer because she is at odds with her parents who are conservatives; Joe is a reformer because he has a conformist character and everybody in his group (perhaps a lower one) is a reformer; Ruth is a reformer because she has a nonconformist character and wants to get away from her group (perhaps an upper one). Moreover, a nonconformist person is allowed a varying range of deviation depending on the culture, society, and group before being forced out of his original role or membership.

If we allow for such variations, the two main sources of proreform attitudes are, first, group conformity among persons who have shared frustrating individual experiences, especially those due to economic handicaps of the group; and, second, nonconformity on the part of persons from more privileged groups, who project individual frustrations to the social scene. In the latter group, the desire for a kind of group solidarity which they miss in their own stratum and which they rightly or wrongly associate with lower classes, or with reform movements, is especially important.[7]

This disposes of two mechanistic approaches to the problem under discussion: first, the belief that proreform attitudes usually indicate a more or less neurotic disturbance of personality, while social conformity reflects personal adjustment; and, second, the assumption that attitudes toward reform are a mere function of the objective economic situation of the group concerned, so that reform aims would disappear automatically with economic improvement. Both assumptions contain a nucleus of truth; both, however, have often been subjected to unwarranted generalizations which have obscured the actual complexity of the problem.

This complexity is mirrored in the wide range of reform attitudes that was mentioned earlier. Why do so many people in our period become *economic* reformers, rather that prohibitionists or adventists, for example? The main reason is probably in the central value position of economic issues in our society as distinguished from, say, the Middle Ages or other spiritually oriented societies. The unsettling and bewildering effect of business fluctuations, in particular, has tended to focus the attention of reformers upon economic issues. In many individual cases, moreover, the nature of the initial frustration or of the subsequent projection may emphasize, in a person's mind, the field of economic action more readily than religious or artistic problems; or it may lead to a combination of several such fields of interest in one reform program.

Similarly, the question of why John Doe becomes a mild gradualist while Joe Doakes goes in for fierce revolution can only be explained in terms of individual personality traits against the background of the culture, society, and group concerned. "Revolution" itself may turn into destructive, vengeful revolt in one case, long-range nonviolent reconstruction of society in another. Moreover, a movement which starts out in a revolutionary vein may become bureaucratic, conservative, or reactionary, while some of its supporters continue to believe that it remains what it was initially. Conversely, mild gradual reforms may unwittingly add up to great changes, or they may increase in momentum sufficiently to generate a new social order.

Revolution, in its underlying mentality, may thus lead either to reform or to revolt. Any far-reaching change in society due to more or less deliberate group action can be classified as revolution, especially when it is speedy; but the eventual content of revolution may be either constructive or destructive (or both, in either order). In practice, many revolutions contain both elements. That is why revolutions tend to split sooner or later into two camps, on psychological lines; one of the factions then devours the other. In nearly every revolution there is a showdown between those who are after genuine socioeconomic change and those whose main personal need is really vengeance and a destructive form of tension release. The same applies to counterrevolutions.

This fundamental divergence of psychic needs is especially clear in the history of Marxian movements. A first look at personality factors in the early development of Marxism shows that, of its two founders, Karl Marx was the son of a forward-looking, respectable intellectual, a converted Jew; Friedrich Engels' father, on the other hand, was a Calvinist with grim, harsh, and somewhat bigoted traits. The differences in family and group environment were considerable, yet the actual combination of effective personality factors in each of the two men came to associate the two very different personalities in a lifelong joint effort.

It would be quite foolish, however, to expect either type of personality traits necessarily to exist in present-day Communists: the latter range all the way from landless peasants in Pakistan to conformist bureaucrats in the Soviet Union, and from these to neurotic types in Western countries, who unconsciously wish to be persecuted and punished.

The case of Gerhard Eisler exemplifies the fact that family background, while important, is only one of several variables in shaping a person's ideological history. Eisler and his sister Ruth Fischer are of mixed parentage; they were brought up in Germany and Austria under financial stress in the family; both became active Communists and carried on an exciting life on party assignments; but the sister was expelled from the party as early as in the mid-twenties and became a bitter apostate, while the brother remained a faithful party activist throughout the decades that followed. Another brother, also with Communist sympathies, became a successful composer. Individual modification of the joint family background turned out to be of decisive influence at some juncture in life.[8] The nature of assignments—and, consequently, the personality requirements—for international Communist activists have changed greatly since 1917: appeals by Communists for economic reform now mostly serve as mere instruments for the expansionist aims of Russian foreign policy.

At the other end of the ideological scale there are Mahatma Gandhi and his successor, Acharya Vinova Bhave, preaching home industry and land reform without violence, trying to convince others through their own example of frugal life and individual sacrifices. Whatever the personal background that shaped their ascetic and pacifist ideas of social reform, they appear to fit somehow into the cultural setting of India. They would be considered eccentric, if not worse, should they appear at Hyde Park in London or at Union Square in New York. Here again, the personality traits that shape the reform attitude and role of an individual must be seen against the background of his society and culture in order to be interpreted in a meaningful way.

This principle applies to reform attitudes in Western society too. In the late forties an inquiry was made among a number of labor leaders in the United States concerning the factors that had led them into the labor movement.[9] While the labor movement in this country cannot generally be associated with economic reform, there are many points of contact between them, as will be shown later. Significantly, some of those questioned answered by looking back to their own past, while others offered a "rational" explanation in programmatic terms, thus marking important differences in perception. The answers included such statements as "I am a trade unionist because, so to speak, I was born one. My father was a member of the Knights of Labor. . . ." "My early training and upbringing had emphasized the desirability of servicing the common man in his effort to realize his rightful place in a just society. . . ." "I am in the labor movement because work is an activity indispensable to man's survival." "My father was perhaps as near the typical 'small business man' in the Middle West as could be found, except for some peculiarly unorthodox social and religious ideas. . . . I became convinced that there could be more men like my father if the real meaning of the Christian faith could be properly expounded." "I started to work when I was 10 years of age as a clothing worker. . . . The labor movement philosophy has become my life work and I enjoy it." "How I became a worker at an early age was no matter of early choice or decision. . . . It stemmed from the lack of security in our family. . . . Not enough has been said or written about the act of joining the union as a step to maturity." "I was born and raised in a 'labor' family. . . . I was taught—and it is my firm belief—that the labor movement is carrying out more of the teachings of the Carpenter of Nazareth than any other group in our nation." On the conscious level, proreform attitudes leading to active participation in the labor movement were derived from childhood impressions and family influences in some cases, religious or ethical beliefs in others, solidarity needs in still others. In each case individual experiences were integrated with social or group values of one kind or another.

b. The conservative. The essence of genuine conservatism is emphasis on the preservation of traditional, still existing, institutions and values whatever they may be. This emphasis distinguishes conservatism from reaction, which endeavors to undo history and thus represents a reform program of a kind. A contemporary historian draws the line somewhat differently: "The conservative conserves discriminately, the reactionary indiscriminately. . . . By 'tradition' the conservative means all the lessons of the past but only the ethically acceptable lessons. The reactionary means all the events. Thereby he misses all the lessons." The same author describes the principles of conservatism as follows: "Proportion and measure; self-expression through self-restraint; preservation through reform; humanism and classical balance; a fruitful nostalgia for the permanent beneath the flux; and an 'obsession' for unbroken historic continuity." [10]

This may be an excellent description from the historian's point of view, but the psychological border line between conservation and reaction is in a somewhat different place. The genuine conservative is characterized by resistance to change either forward or backward, except that he may be willing to undo very recent changes. Conservative attitudes are thus not identical with conformity, though they overlap with it. In a social situation that is stable and settled, conformity and conservatism are nearly identical. On the other hand, when the social situation is very fluid and change is the slogan of the day, conformist persons may join the radical majority movement of the moment while conservatives will keep resisting change. In the Soviet Union today, for that matter, it is the conformists who become Communists, and the idols of conformists have been Stalin and Khrushchev, respectively. Here again individual attitudes must be evaluated against the background of prevailing values and institutions.

In most societies, personality traits that are conducive to conservative attitudes include, above all, strong adherence to a traditional body of social or group norms, which serves as the central frame of reference. Selection among arguments for and against change is very rigorous and usually inclined toward rejection of change. Social norms are strongly internalized, and social perceptions including the power of imagination are delimited by them. The resulting frame of reference is largely habit-bound and rather rigid; most attitudes are persistent, and innovations meet vigorous opposition. The values and practices of the group enter strongly into the ego attitudes and, especially, into the personal aspirations of the individual concerned. Social conservation becomes identified with the maintenance of personal role and status, of "good standing" within the group or society far in excess of a mere desire for security of possession. A weakening of the concern with status usually marks a weakening of conservative attitudes as well.[11]

If and when economic trends or fluctuations occupy a central position in social life, resistance to economic change becomes one of the main measures of conservative attitudes. An example was provided by experiences during the postwar productivity drive in western Europe under the impact of American aid. Among the obstacles to this drive in various countries, technological conservatism was less important than the fear of employers that they would be required to work out production problems with the trade unions in a new way, thus giving up some of their old status privileges.

Economic conservatism may in fact become the focal point of ego defensiveness in our period. It is, above all, the fear of the unknown or untested that bolsters the resistance to economic change today. Preservation of the known, however imperfect, is preferred by this kind of person to innovations which may involve conflicts of values or, at least, genuine decisions. Essentially one variety of the security needs discussed earlier is at the root of such horror of economic change.

In extreme cases the healthy scrutiny of the untested that is implicit in genuine conservatism may give way to pathological mistrust. The following passage from an anthropological source is illustrative: "Tradition is as neurotic as any patient; its overgrown fear of deviation from its fortuitous standards conforms to all the usual definitions of the psychopathic. This fear does not depend upon observation of the limits within which conformity is necessary to the social good." [12]

The stickiness of old norms, however, is a function of the sociocultural setting no less than of personality factors. Certain societies encourage nonconformist or, at least, innovating attitudes, while other societies penalize them. There is no convincing evidence that society is *always* designed to restrain predetermined, native impulses of man, as one branch of the Freudian school of thought assumes.

Objective changes from stable to unstable conditions in economic and social life have been especially frequent in the contemporary world. Individual conservative attitudes thus tend to foster more frequent and intensive conflicts of values than they did in many societies of the past.

c. The apostate. Attitudes toward economic reform and belief systems in general show countless examples of conspicuous shifts occurring sometime during a person's life cycle. There is an important difference, however, between one great conversion in life and constant vacillation. The individual who keeps shifting from one belief system to another is likely to be an insecure person who looks all his life for something to hold on to without ever finding it, or without trusting it very long whenever he momentarily thinks he has found it. On the other hand, the person who undergoes one sweeping ideological change sometime during his life may be driven by a variety of influences. A genuine change in attitudes may have occurred, either abruptly under the impact of a drastic, traumatic experience or more gradually under a prolonged impressive influence. As an alternative, a basic attitude (hateful aggressiveness, for example) may merely have shifted its object and focus without undergoing any change in its basic quality.

The history of apostasy, in economic beliefs and otherwise, shows many examples of the different cases mentioned which should carefully be kept apart. A shift from a conservative to a proreform attitude or vice versa, for instance, is quite dissimilar in psychological quality from a shift, within a totalitarian mind, from communism to fascism or vice versa. The possible kinds of apostasy range in the underlying traits of personality from extreme rigidity to excessive vacillation. Somewhere between these extremes is the possibility of genuine readiness for an attitudinal change that is based on new experiences of either an emotional or an intellectual nature.

Some light is thrown on the roots of apostasy by the relative frequency of cases in which leaders of sweeping reform movements—or else totalitarian pseudo-reform groupings and postrevolutionary dictatorships—have been of foreign extraction or have come from marginal areas of a nation. The mechanism of conflict between national and group or family setting, with the overcompensation involved, is not difficult to discern. The Corsican Bonaparte came from the fringe of France; the Austrian Hitler from the fringe of Germany; the Georgian Stalin from the fringe of Russia. In the upper Nazi hierarchy, Slav names such as Hadamovsky, Skorzeny, Globocnik, and Suchanek were not rare. Here again, generalization should not be overdone, for these individuals have been outnumbered in each case by leading figures of old ethnic stock. Striving for overcompensation of an alien background, in other words, was clearly not the only driving force in the rise of individual leaders, but the frequency of such cases in history and the penetrating vigor of these persons in asserting themselves against great initial odds are worth noting.

Many instances are known of sons of ideological leaders adopting a creed different from that of their fathers and often diametrically opposed to it, but no adequate evidence is available concerning the comparative frequency of such cases. Perhaps a sufficient number of detailed family stories will be available at some future date in order to determine the incidence and attitudinal mechanisms involved.

Somewhat more material is available on the various collaborators with foreign totalitarian regimes. One of the most interesting cases is that of the Belgian Hendrik De Man, who rose from the labor movement to a leading role in the democratic government only to collaborate with the Nazi occupation forces during the second World War. His earlier theoretical work had attempted to put socialism on an ethical and idealistic basis as against the scientific claims of Marxism. Conceivably his defensiveness toward attacks from these quarters, coupled with pointed opposition to the Marxian belief in "inevitable" development toward socialism, broke his power of resistance toward the right-wing extreme.[13] General lack of a durable frame of reference, plus the shock effect of Nazi occupation, resulted in ultimate failure to live up to the ethical principles professed earlier. Possibly De Man was impressed by what looked like a confirmation of his earlier criticism, or perhaps he merely rationalized a basic opportunism into belief in a "socialist" driving force in nazism. At any rate, in this case as in many others, brilliant intellectual gifts did not prevent betting on the wrong horse.

Probably the largest single group of apostates in our period is that of the ex-Communists. The mental processes which lead a person to embrace a totalitarian creed of any kind will be discussed somewhat later. Likewise we are not concerned at this point with those persons in Western countries who sometime in the past stumbled into the Communist Party from sheer ignorance and who later became ordinary voters and democratic citizens like millions of other people. We are discussing here the professional, full-time ex-Communist of today whose involvement pattern remains entirely centered around that movement even after he has left it, somewhat along the lines of what Freudians call *Hassliebe,* hate-love.

Arthur Koestler describes impressively the collapse of the middle-class idyl of his family when he was a child and the following guilt feelings and resentments against the rich, which led him to communism. "But when I was liberated I did not know that I had ceased to be a Communist." On the other hand, Ignazio Silone, who left the Communist movement relatively early and became a moderate socialist, relates his initial childhood experience as follows, "I grew up in a mountainous district of southern Italy. The phenomenon which most impressed me, when I arrived at the age of reason, was the violent contrast, the incomprehensible, absurd, monstrous contrast between family and private life—in the main decent, honest, and well-conducted —and social relations, which were very often crude and full of hatred and deceit."

Obviously this is only a fraction of the personality story in either case. However, in the former case the uneasy background of the Jewish middle class in central Europe; in the latter case the hateful social relations of a poverty-stricken rural population were essential both in the initial decision and then—with increasing life space and social experience—in the change of creed. In Silone's case the conversion led to middle-of-the-road politics; in Koestler's case general preoccupation with communism remained decisive even though his ideas on the subject had changed.[14]

In a period in which support of communism is no longer an abstract creed or ideology but often involves concrete action in the service of a foreign government, the specific motives that underlie such ideological fluctuations are especially interesting. Whittaker Chambers in his autobiography analyzes the background factors that led him first into communism and then out of it. As a child he was often told by his mother of the agonies she suffered at his birth, and this made him acutely unhappy. He hated his original names and never had any real friends. Father, a pseudo-artist, was unable to accept any affection; his parents had not wanted any children and resented him. The grandparents were morbid; grandmother suffered fron paranoid delusions. Father's unemployment further impaired family life. Chambers himself got into communism in the course of his search for a faith: "I wished to serve—I did not particularly care how." In his testimony during the Hiss trial, Chambers added, "My brother's suicide set the seal on my being a Communist. I was a Communist before, but I became a fanatical Communist after that." Later, when his faith in communism had been bitterly disappointed, "my need was to be a practicing Christian in the same sense that I had been a practicing Communist"; it was a need for "daily mysticism."

Without attempting here to evaluate other aspects of Chambers' story, this is a fairly clear case of personal guilt feelings being projected into the ideological scene. Atonement is aimed at through boundless involvement in communism—first as its supporter and then as its enemy, without any great change in the underlying psychodynamics.

The "confessions" of indicted ex-Communists in Soviet trials reflect quite impressively their fascination with a totalitarian creed even after it has turned against them. It is their perception of loyalty, in this case toward the party, that makes them do otherwise inconceivable things —not merely drugs and torture, though these apparently have also been used.[15] The same personality factors that led such persons to embrace this particular brand of totalitarianism in the first place usually remain with them even after they have run afoul of its rules or hierarchy. This discussion, we repeat, applies to full-time ex-Communists, not to persons who got into the party by accident or misinformation and have long since turned to other pursuits and interests.

Klaus Fuchs, the atomic spy in Britain, represents an extreme case of apostasy rooted in an unresolved conflict of value systems. The son of a Lutheran pastor who tended to associate Christianity with communism, Fuchs made a substitute religion out of that supposed program for economic reform that had become a cloak for Russian expansionism. On his mother's side there was a strain of mental disturbance in the family; his own childhood had been spent in a German society which had been disrupted by inflation with subsequent mass unemployment. Work on atomic energy had added to these stresses the moral conflicts to which many scientists are subject these days. In the confession he read in court, Fuchs stated, "I used my Marxian philosophy to conceal my thoughts in two separate compartments. One side was the man I wanted to be. . . . It appeared to me at the time I had become a free man because I succeeded in the other compartment in establishing myself completely independent of the surrounding forces of society. Looking back on it now, the best way is to call it a controlled schizophrenia." It was neurosis more likely than schizophrenia, but in any case the Fuchs affair represents a drastic case of personal conflict and disturbance leading to an extreme version of apostasy in the form of treason.

d. The indifferent. Perhaps this is the largest group of all. It consists of at least two types of persons. The first type includes those with low general capacity for ego involvement of any kind, as a result of either native endowment or early training. The second type comprises those who are potentially capable of strong feelings or enthusiasm, but who, in discouragement, have given up the quest for economic improvements that they or their forefathers had long been striving for unsuccessfully. In the latter group defeatism about social problems reflects a feeling that they are inscrutable or unmanageable.

In either case an escapist attitude tends to develop; it seems better to get away from all the trouble than to stick one's neck out. Moreover, those who *spell out* social or economic evils are easily made responsible for them by others—just as the meteorologist who predicts rain is often perceived as its originator; in parts of Germany and Austria meteorologists are popularly called *Wettermacher.* Essentially indifference is an extreme form of attempted escape from responsibilities for social initiative or action. Of course, the whole problem comes up only where culture and society permit real choices on the part of the individual. The *incidence* of indifferent personalities or behavior is socially determined in any case.

Far from representing a purely intellectual weighing of the merits of a given program, attitudes toward economic reform are anchored in the total personality of the individual concerned within the social setting. It is true that the personality of some individuals emphasizes intellectual weighing, but the essential attitudes of many more people are derived mainly from emotional, rather than intellectual, experience. In a degree which varies from person to person, attitudes toward economic reform reflect not primarily intellectual convictions but a belief system.

Economic Reform as a Belief System

The traditional assumption has been that economic ideas are ordinarily worked out and confronted according to their intellectual merits. This assumption is exposed to strong qualifications as soon as one realizes the importance of personality factors in shaping individual reactions toward such ideas. The very capacity to perceive or stress the intellectual side of economic issues is inherent only in a limited number of persons, and in a varying degree. In everybody's mind there is some emotional element, often a decisive one, in influencing his attitude toward social issues in general and economic reform in particular. Even among those who are quite convinced that they proceed in a purely scientific-objective way there are, at the very least, important differences in perception and involvement.

Personal needs (or "interests") are often rationalized into objective needs of society and reform programs. The incidence of specific personal needs, it is true, is in part socially determined. The fact that a reform attitude originates in some people's personal needs does not mean that it cannot be objectively justified. Actually personal needs and socioeconomic requirements quite often coincide, and fortunately so; but this is not necessarily the case in each instance. The fact that John Doe advocates a certain type of reform with great personal involvement proves neither that he is a neurotic nor that his program is objectively wrong. Either condition, on the other hand, *may* be true in individual cases.

Neither personal adjustment to an unhealthy society nor sustained blind hatred as a general attitude can ever offer the right solution even if such hatred should happen to underlie a sound reform program. The kind of reformer who is most likely to bring genuine progress is the one who manages to channel his personal needs into a reform program that is realistic and objectively justified in the light of widely accepted standards of knowledge. This judgment will admittedly depend somewhat on the standpoint of the observer.

In our period personal needs are focused more often on economic reform ideas than they used to be, and less often on new religious cults, for instance, though there are quite a few of the latter too. This trend can be explained in part from the puzzling and overwhelming nature of economic problems in our period, and in part from the fact that many traditional religions have lost the capacity to arouse strong ego involvement in great masses of people. Even so, the difference between economic and religious reform is less absolute than it might appear at first. Some programs of economic reform represent an implicit protest against materialism or individualism much as certain religious ideas do; other economic programs aim at better social conditions for individual development much as some church statements do. It is true that the growth of reality systems that are empirically derived has stripped religion of some of its traditional areas of action, perhaps more so in economic life than elsewhere.[16]

Yet the use of bone-dry, "objective" statistics, models, or theorems barely conceals the unwitting missionary needs of many economists who really are frustrated or wayward reformers. This consideration applies equally to the emotional needs of antireformers; for either wishful images of *laissez faire* or the escapist types of abstraction easily lend themselves to rationalizing away any social need for economic reform.

Many examples, including autobiographies of some outstanding economists, could be quoted to show the close if mostly unwitting relation between economic thinking, no matter how abstract, and general belief systems. Not surprisingly, the outstanding contribution to economic thought in recent decades, Keynes's *General Theory*, ends with a chapter entitled "Concluding Notes on the Social Philosophy toward Which the General Theory Might Lead." At its very end Keynes offers this credo, "Practical men, who believe themselves to be quite exempt from any intellectual influences, are usually the slaves of some defunct economist. I am sure that the power of vested interests is vastly exaggerated compared with the gradual encroachment of ideas. . . . Soon or late, it is ideas, not vested interests, which are dangerous for good or evil."[17]

Conversely, religious spokesmen sometimes come to discover the significance of economics for their beliefs. This is exemplified by the following passage from a letter which the author received some time ago from a southwestern rural community: "I am theorizing that our civilization and our own country should get away from hit-or-miss living and build on the certainties of the sciences, and that economics is one of the essentials. Philosophers and politicians cannot do the job. I have been a Baptist preacher for 61 years, and am deeply concerned in the welfare of the *genus homo.*"

The significance and incidence of any specific type of economic ideas, we repeat, can only be understood if we interpret them in the context of related belief systems. The term belief is used here in the sense of "an enduring organization of perceptions and cognitions about some aspect of the individual's world." [18] This includes knowledge, opinions, and faith. Attitudes toward economic change are almost inevitably implied even in the most abstract body of economic theory; they mirror the underlying belief system that served as starting point for such theoretical considerations, often below the conscious level. This applies no less to ideas which implicitly emphasize resistance to change than to those which tend to favor change; it applies to reactionary ideas about economic policy no less than to radical, and vice versa.

If this were not the case it would be difficult to understand why even the most impressive body of factual data nearly always fails to convince a sizable number of people with specialized knowledge, as well as people without it. Actually the significance of available "facts" is perceived very differently, depending on the attitudinal and belief system. This explains the frequency—so exasperating for the non-economist on the fence—with which economic experts tend to disagree emphatically regarding the meaning of "objective" evidence including figures.

To restate the point just made, the basic inclination of certain people or groups toward economic reform in general, or some specific kind of reform, as opposed to basic resistance on the part of others to any economic change, reflects extensive conflicts of ideologies and reform ideas. Karl Mannheim has contributed much to our understanding of the differences in perception implicit in various attitudes toward reform and change. In his own terminology, ideologies are complexes of ideas which direct human activity toward the maintenance of an existing order; utopias, on the other hand, are complexes of ideas which tend to generate an orientation toward change of the existing order.

The concept "ideology" reflects the one discovery which emerged from political conflict, namely, that ruling groups can in their thinking become so intensively interest-bound to a situation that they are simply no longer able to see certain facts which would undermine their sense of domination. There is implicit in the word "ideology" the insight that in certain situations the collective unconscious of certain groups obscures the real condition of society both to itself and to others and thereby stabilizes it.

The concept of *utopian* thinking reflects the opposite discovery of the political struggle, namely that certain oppressed groups are intellectually so strongly interested in the destruction and transformation of a given condition of society that they unwittingly see only those elements in the situation which tend to negate it. . . . In the utopian mentality, the collective unconscious, guided by wishful representation and the will to action, hides certain aspects of reality. It turns its back on everything which would shake its belief or paralyse its desire to change things.[19]

Regardless of whether or not we wish to adopt Mannheim's terminology, it is important to realize that whole social or intellectual groups may have mental blocks arising from limitations of perception —limitations which largely reflect their own life experience and which may foster wishful thinking or rationalizations on a group scale. That is why support of any type of economic reform, or opposition to it, represents a definite belief system. It is not a haphazard or strictly individual one. Common or typical experiences within a social group make for a high or low incidence of specific belief systems in this group and in a given society.

To the extent that it evaluates the factors that make for a high or low incidence of certain ideological dispositions, a discussion of economic belief systems can hope to be scientific.[20] Neither blind confidence in the persuasive power of superior reform ideas nor diffident reliance by intellectuals upon the healthy instincts of others—the proletarian, the businessman, or the farmer, for instance—could be expected to replace the functions of attitudinal analysis.

The main lesson of such analysis is that new social values and economic programs crystallize on a group scale when socioeconomic conditions breed many individual experiences that break down earlier frames of reference and create others. The fact that economic beliefs of this or that kind are not confined to scattered individuals and that community or parallelism of experience often leads to similar patterns of personality and beliefs worries those who mistrust mass movements as such.[21] They assume that mass movements are always based on the same frustrations, insecurities, suspicions, and hatreds and that they are always essentially unhealthy in a psychological sense. Yet it is one thing to recognize the emotional and attitudinal basis of reform programs in general and the belief-system character of economic reform in particular; it is quite a different thing to jump to the unwarranted conclusion that such programs—or, at least, the social movements designed to carry them through—are essentially all alike, namely, delusive and destructive.

It would be quite impossible to discuss here all the various belief systems in history which have emphasized economic reform. They have included abstract utopias such as those of More, Bacon, Campanella, and Rousseau as well as practical utopias, which have tried to achieve the same programmatic goal through actual example (Lanark; New Harmony; and, in our period, the Communauté Boimondau in France, a producers' co-operative for watch casings). It is interesting to note the concentration of many contemporary guides to utopia, such as Father Divine, Dr. Townsend, and the Oxford Group, on a quest for some kind of security, rather than on equality or freedom as comparable movements in earlier periods did. A combination of divine protection with individual security of economic arrangements is especially popular.[22]

Some other programs promise freedom from the economic frustrations which in the past have often resulted from initial handicaps of status coupled with a low degree of social mobility. In the Kibbutzim, the agrarian collectives in Israel, for instance, the element of a productive purpose in life—economic improvement, against exceptional odds, mainly through the power of a rejuvenated national faith—has been of great importance during their formative period.

Sometimes economic programs represent belief systems in an unwitting way. This applies, especially, to many antireform ideas. General disinclination toward any innovation in economic institutions or policies reflects a specific kind of belief system, especially if a mirage of the past is involved. Another example of an unwitting belief system that affects economic ideas is offered by those Freudian psychologists who cannot perceive any real sense in economic reforms, or in other institutional reforms in society, for that matter. To their mind, all that really matters is a cure of the individual from the evil burden of the unconscious.

Quite a different case, within the area of economic belief systems, is offered by Marxism. Here a sweeping socioeconomic reform that is based on scientific necessity as far as its own assumptions are concerned actually contains strong elements of faith. The political practice of Marxian movements over the last century has given these belief factors ever greater importance.

This is not the place to attempt any general evaluation of Marxism either as an abstract system of thought or as the starting point for great political changes in the world. We are concerned here only with its psychological assumptions, effects, and limitations. An essential trait of historical materialism was to assume that the ideologies of men were shaped by the prevailing economic arrangements in general and by the given class situation in particular. Ideology was conceived of as a superstructure upon socioeconomic institutions, especially those connected with the production process. Concentration of capital and disintegration of the middle classes were expected to convert the overwhelming majority of every population into proletarians sooner or later, and the development of a revolutionary-collectivist ideology was considered to be an inevitable effect of such proletarization. Scientific analysis, therefore (science being largely associated with the discovery of objective laws), seemed to indicate an indomitable trend toward a collectivist reconstruction of society.

At this point the attitudinal effect of Marxian theory upon its supporters came to the fore. The "knowledge" that they were right, that historical necessity was on their side—in other words, that they could not be conquered despite occasional setbacks—had an attitudinal effect comparable to that of a talisman or else of a fatalistic religion such as Islam. On the one hand, a somewhat personified deity called history looked down on them with the expectation of glorious performance and with the promise of eternal praise; on the other hand, the supposedly inevitable character of their ultimate victory tended to have a paralyzing effect at times. While they moved they had a horror of being left behind by history, but the assumed knowledge of historical necessity sometimes prevented them from moving at all.

Fundamentally many of the subsequent showdowns in the proletarian movement mirrored the cleavage between the revolutionary and the passive effects of an unwitting fatalism, or else the psychological contrast between an intellectual reform program and an emotion-bound belief system. After the first World War, however, the application of the Marxian system of thought to the cultural characteristics of the Russian people changed the basic nature of various Marxian movements in other countries as well. Largely under the impact of the Soviet experience and mentality, some of these movements increasingly became the focal point for one type of totalitarian personality (the other one being fascism). Still later—especially from the thirties onward—this strange mixture of "scientific" theory and totalitarian mentality was put into the concrete service of Russian expansionism. Concealed by seven veils of semantics, some abstract concepts of Marxism had been put to a use that their originators had hardly anticipated. A system of social theory and an economic program had been adapted to help rationalize a substitute religion of a superstitious, cruel, and essentially primitive character. The nineteenth-century rationalism, which had been the intellectual starting point of Marxism on the conscious level, had been transformed into its opposite.[23]

This amazing and devastating change does not undo certain contributions to economic psychology which the original, theoretical Marxism rather unwittingly made. Marxism had hardly any notion of the actual impact of unconscious and nonrational factors upon attitudes, motivation, and behavior, nor of the enormous variety of cultural value systems and perception patterns. Actually victories of Marxian movements were to occur mainly in backward, semifeudal countries, instead of the industrialized ones which Marx and Engels had had in mind. Yet Marx and Engels had pointed out that ideas did not come to societies or groups out of nowhere, nor out of a purely accidental heritage of individuals; and that many human traits were subject to the impact of socioeconomic conditions, especially frustrating ones.

Hardly any allowance, however, was made for modifying influences on the individual level and for the malleability of the human mind in general. Marxism implied that classes—the upper classes, at least—

always followed instinctively their own "interest" even when they subjectively believed they were acting in the common interest. The mentality of a ruling group was thought to be rather rigidly determined once for all by its established function in the production process. Actually we have witnessed some developments in which parts of feudal classes survived economically by joining capitalist top groups or converting themselves into such groups—in Japan and Germany, for instance. It is an interesting question whether a comparable process of adaptation might not apply to substantial parts of capitalist management in the course of further changes in the socioeconomic system.

If Marxism had remained a theoretical system of armchair predictions, it might have bypassed some of the psychological pitfalls mentioned. Theory in this case, however, served as a basis for social movements, and some of the latter eventually converted the intended scientific predictions into a substitute religion. The assumption of historical necessity and of a resulting invincibility became the basis for a continuous revivalist pep talk within the movement. The psychological backbone of this creed was broken in central and western Europe when the formative period of the socialist movement came to an end and governmental responsibility began in democratic coalitions, as opposed to the totalitarian dictatorship in Russia. Belief in long-run invincibility then became the source of political illusions and an unrealistic perception of the world. A millennium which remains imminent right here on earth from day to day and from year to year is a psychological impossibility.

Later on, voluntarist criticism within the socialist movement in western Europe aimed at overcoming the paralysis of action by making the character of socialism as a belief system more conscious than it had been. Hendrik De Man, who was mentioned earlier, criticized the rationalistic nature of Marxism and attempted to put the labor movement on a sounder psychological basis by interpreting the predicament of the worker in terms of inferiority feelings, oppressive atmosphere, lack of proper working motivation, solidarity needs, and even religious symbolism. In De Man's own case, however, abandonment of the belief in an "inevitable" victory, of the "scientific" basis of the socialist movement, led to demoralization and, eventually, to collaboration with nazism. Some people need a belief in historical necessity, or in fate, in order to act themselves; they must feel supported by science if they are to acquire enough personal security to act, while others may be paralyzed by waiting for "history" to act for them.

In summary, attitudes toward economic reform always reflect a specific belief system, even when reform programs are presented in purely intellectual or scientific terms or when they are summarily rejected. The incidence and intensity of people's adherence to any specific set of economic ideas is in large part explained by the prevalence of certain kinds of personality. This prevalence, in turn, depends on the cultural and socioeconomic setting of the period concerned and its recent past. Beliefs concerning economic reform are shaped neither by accident nor by direct influence of the class situation alone. The specific way in which cultural, socioeconomic, and group conditions typically act upon personality formation in each period influences indirectly the frequency of various attitudes toward economic reform. At the same time, general belief systems and reform ideas are likely to turn toward economic issues whenever the latter assume a central position for the society, group, or individual concerned.

Thus far the term economic reform has been used in its broadest sense, referring to either gentle or vehement pursuit of real desires for economic change. A clearer distinction now needs to be made between the main attitudinal influences upon the actions which each actor perceives as aiming at economic reform but which may have very different roots and effects. Such a distinction is of crucial importance for the understanding of the present-day world.

Reform versus Revolt

In evaluating the various types of contemporary attitudes toward economic reform, the decisive difference is that between productive and destructive orientation—a difference which, in turn, reflects the level of personal maturity. Some of the underlying frustration experiences which helped shape the personalities concerned may have been similar in both cases, but the manner in which such influences are channeled differs basically in the two types mentioned.

Cases in which one of two brothers or sisters became a conservative, the other a radical are not infrequent; likewise, one of two siblings may become a rebel, the other one a mild reformer even though the family setting is the same. The particular position of each child within the family, the different timing of their upbringing, shifts that the entire family may have undergone meanwhile in its economic position or social status, changes in the general atmosphere in society, and, of course, variations in strictly individual heritage or experiences may result in destructive orientation in one case compared with productive orientation in the other. Some allowance might be made here for creative destructiveness—tearing a house down in order to make room for a better one—but the border line is often difficult to draw.

Clinical experiences indicate that destructive attitudes toward society usually reflect displaced destructiveness toward one's self or, still more deeply hidden, toward a parent who is felt to have weakened the self. Some Freudians actually attribute any revolutionary attitude to loss of a father image and, with it, of respect for authority in general.[24] This looks like an overstatement and oversimplification, but sometimes there actually is a "tendency to experience internal processes as if they occurred outside oneself and, as a rule, to hold these external factors responsible for one's difficulties." [25]

In the final analysis, it is realism in one's social reactions that is decisive in determining a productive orientation toward reform. The last word on what is realistic admittedly represents a philosophical issue, not purely a clinical one. On the social scale, an especially important case of lacking realism in critical or revolutionary situations of either a national or a class character has often arisen from the failure of ruling groups to realize that "the children have grown up." History is full of such cases: Britain's experience with its American colonies, the blindness of the feudal class before the French Revolution, the disintegration of the Hapsburg Empire, Holland's desperate last-minute attempt to hold on to Indonesia. On the other hand, Britain avoided its earlier paternalistic mistakes in the final arrangements for India and Burma.

On the individual level the pattern of either productive or destructive attitudes toward social and economic reform is not necessarily set once for all. Such attitudes may change in certain individuals under the impact of important experiences. Attitudinal patterns are even more subject to shifts on a group scale. This is one reason why degeneration of revolutions is a frequent phenomenon in history: the revolution often devours its own children, or some of them. Once a revolution has won, some of the same aggressions which prompted it tend to turn from the defeated enemy to one's own comrades; potentially creative aggressions turn into destructive ones. Partly under the influence of leadership by intellectuals, economic platforms and arguments are often used to rationalize the underlying attitudinal conflicts within a movement. The actual roots of such crises in its group dynamics are likely to be emotional rather than economic.

Revolt, or rebellion, as a general attitude is essentially "against"; reform is essentially "for." Revolt attitudes shift their object easily, perhaps from a father to a king and from the latter to one's own comrades of yesterday. Genuine reform attitudes in the sense of social realism are generally characterized by relative insignificance of unresolved aggressions and, especially, of destructive propensity. Reform attitudes center around concrete objects—in our period around extensive change of specific economic conditions, in particular. Such attitudes are grounded on a basic belief that people can be persuaded and, thus, on confidence in people generally, prominently including one's self. In this sense it might be said that reform-mindedness represents a more "rational" approach to socioeconomic problems than does revolt-mindedness. Similarly, reform attitudes reflect a personality in which intellectual reactions tend to be more influential and emotional reactions to be better controlled than they are in persons with a revolt attitude. This difference explains both the strength and the weakness of reform attitudes: in critical times, when emotional impatience prevails, they tend to have little popular appeal or influence compared with revolt attitudes.

Yet any change in economic arrangements that is to be of lasting character must be based on reform-mindedness, never on aimless revolt against everything and everybody. Genuine economic reform is incompatible with destructiveness. Its general approach is that of "progress," in the sense of gradual and durable improvement of specific economic institutions. Progress admittedly is an elusive and much-misused concept that requires a constant warning against semantic pitfalls.[26] Even so, an attitudinal orientation toward specific socioeconomic goals, as distinguished from mere rationalizations of a basic destructiveness, is generally descriptive of reform aims in the sense of progress.

In our period, such goals include genuine interest in high living standards for everybody, even at the risk of making the social levels of aspiration rise faster at times than the material means of satisfaction. But a genuine striving for reform is also characterized by the quest for a meaningful life beyond purely material improvements, by keen perception of social welfare needs despite possible differences concerning their concrete traits, by appreciation of individual freedom including that of group organization, and by a desire to avoid gross inequalities and to extend democracy from mere in-group or in-class arrangements to a general attitude.

At which point, however, do such aims of improving society through reform actually turn into general rejection of the social order? At which point does the latter attitude shift from the rejection of specific institutions, with the intention of replacing them by better ones, to a destructive attitude toward society as such? Quite frequently what appears to some people to be a radical change in the economic order is interpreted by others as a necessary corrective designed to save a system which would otherwise be endangered. People who consider themselves conservatives may be perceived by others as reformers; the opposite may also occur. The Keynesian school of thought, especially its economic policy, is a case in point; antitrust legislation is another one; the New Deal was a third one. For decades, partly under the influence of Marxian ideas, the type of property arrangements preferred was considered the decisive border line, but with the growing diversity of public intervention methods, including taxes, this yardstick has become less and less foolproof.[27]

The real criterion of reform, therefore, is not institutional but attitudinal. Genuine reform programs differ from conservatism in that there is no basic fear of change. There is, instead, intellectual openmindedness toward economic and social innovations. At the same time reform programs differ from revolt attitudes in that there is no destructive attitude of general opposition to everything that exists. Similarly, at the point where conservatism shifts into reaction a destructive attitude sets in toward actual or suggested reforms. Individuals or groups that basically lack confidence in themselves tend to perceive social-security laws, soil conservation, public housing, health insurance, or widespread education not as healthy correctives in society but as a fundamental threat to their own status or security, if not to fundamental values.

Such attitudinal differences also apply to those reform programs that are designed to reduce the monotony or fatigue of industrial work, to improve the methods of employment, compensation, and discipline, and thus to raise indirectly the social status, life outlook, and personal-security level of the worker—without necessarily changing the property relations in society in any fundamental way. The work of the International Labor Organization aims at somewhat similar results; international information, model legislation, and agreements are designed to make things easier for reformers in domestic politics everywhere. Whenever the sociopsychological situation in a country is latently ripe for improvements in working conditions and social protection, the activities of the I.L.O. are intended to help in administering the final attitudinal shock to such groups as may stick to the last to their privileges or prejudices. Yet the basic orientation in this case remains directed toward gradual reform, not toward radical change in economic systems or uncritical international equalization.[28]

Socialism, on the other hand, involves a basic attitude that favors change in the economic system as such, even though, when it comes to concrete measures, the institutional reforms proposed often differ little from corrective actions. The semantics involved in the shifting concept of socialism reflect the emotional meaning attached to it by its friends and foes alike: basic attitudes either favoring or opposing change clash with one another.

There have, however, been additional clashes of attitudes and emotions within the socialist camp itself. This fact helps to explain the various splits that have occurred in it historically. In early socialist movements *both* attitudinal types were represented indiscriminately—reform and revolt, productive and destructive orientations alike. Early in this century Vilfredo Pareto formulated a distinction between real, religious, theoretical, metaphysical, and scientific systems of socialism; to his mind, these systems represented very different types of mentality regardless of the way in which the leaders and followers of each movement perceived it.[29]

It is true that the ideological splits between revisionism and orthodox Marxism in Germany around the turn of the century and between Mensheviks and Bolsheviks in Russia far exceeded in significance a mere clash of personality patterns; actually a good many of the persons involved changed their ideas sooner or later. However, the element of conflicting kinds of personality and basic attitudes was strongly involved in these clashes. Lenin's theory of cleavage between labor aristocracy and true proletarians was too simple a rationale for the subsequent split between Socialists and Communists, especially in Western countries. The difference was not primarily in the economic situation of the individuals concerned; or it was only insofar as the economic family background had an indirect relationship to the incidence of various patterns of personality in each group. Essentially the split reflected the difference between reform and revolt attitudes and the preponderance of either democratic or totalitarian traits in the personalities of activists, especially in the social movements to the West of Russia. Those whose basic attitudes did not fit into the movement they had either chosen or stumbled into were sooner or later expelled, purged, or neutralized. The movements themselves, of course, did not stand still and their personality requirements kept changing too.

Those conflicting attitudinal elements in early socialist movements are perhaps best exemplified by the two leaders of French socialism during its formative period before the first World War, Jules Guesde and Jean Jaurès. Guesde, a convinced Marxian, was a rigid revolutionary who neither offered nor expected mercy. Jaurès, sensitive and humanitarian, perceived socialism in terms of action and goal, not of scientific necessity. He was basically optimistic concerning human beings, and socialism was for him a requirement, not for an abstract society, but for the development of the individual. ("Ainsi il est bien vrai que, pour les socialistes, la valeur de toute institution est relative à l'individu humain. . . . C'est l'individu humain qui est la mesure de toute chose, de la patrie, de la famille, de la propriété, de l'humanité, de Dieu. Voilà la logique de l'idée révolutionnaire. Voilà le socialisme.") In a somewhat similar vein a recent British publication defines the socialist goal as "a society so organized as to provide each one of its members with an equal opportunity for the development and expression of his personality." [30]

The attitudinal content of socialism has been gaining ground during recent years in Britain, on the Continent, and to some extent in the new socialist parties of Asia, as the old institutional emphasis has worn thin. Traditionally, socialism had been identified with a broad democratic movement, based chiefly on the labor class, for public ownership and planning of all the means of production. Changes in property relations, in the direction of collectivism, were seen as the backbone of any real improvement in social conditions and in individual opportunities for the underdog.

This yardstick of socialism no longer holds true. For one thing, Western and, to some extent, Asian socialists have discovered that there are many other, often better, means of social control over economic life than public ownership with central planning. They have often come to prefer monetary and fiscal policies, supervisory boards, social welfare measures, or co-operative forms of organization to outright nationalization with its bureaucratic dangers and power concentrations. They also stress ever more social equality, public education, and nonmaterial values such as the quest for a richer, more aesthetic, and generally more meaningful life amidst a mechanized civilization. In underdeveloped countries socialists emphasize, like nearly everyone else, the need for speedy economic development, and they wish to channel it in such a way that it will benefit the peasant and worker. But they generally go along with their Western comrades in stressing democratic methods and attitudes as distinguished from the totalitarian planning and mentality of the Soviet countries. Both in Europe and Asia, socialists think of themselves increasingly as representing a certain frame of mind, rather than a specific mode of property relations.

After several decades of international experience with Communist policy and mentality, most students of reform movements have abandoned any idea that communism is just socialism in a hurry; the two movements are now increasingly viewed as qualitatively different in their basic attitudes. The reconstituted Socialist International has declared that it does not assume an inevitable world trend toward its goal, that it does not require strict conformity of opinions within its ranks, that it believes in mixed and flexible policies and incentives in economic life, and that essentially its reform aims are moral.

The coexistence of two basically incompatible attitudes—reform and revolt—in one movement turned out to be impossible. Actually the showdown accounts for a considerable proportion of the international troubles in our period. To judge from every indication available, cultural and institutional factors must have fostered a great incidence of rigid or destructive minds in Russia; social rewards in the form of power awaited them there. A number of such minds, however, exist in the contemporary Western world too, even though their party complexion may be different. They are recklessly trying everywhere to suppress constructive and understanding personalities, whose existence is psychologically intolerable to them.

Up to this point, the discussion in this chapter has mainly been concerned with the psychological forces that make people adopt specific attitudes toward economic reform. To sum up this part of the argument, movements for economic reform reflect differences in belief systems and in the prevailing kinds of individual attitudes. It would be misleading, however, to consider attitudinal differences as such a full explanation of such movements; disputes on the intellectual level and very real conflicts of group interests also matter a great deal.

In modern times most revolutions—revolutions in the exclusive sense of far-reaching, long-range change of basic institutions—have comprised a varying representation of both polar types of attitude: the destructive attitude of revolt as self-purpose and the constructive attitude of deliberate change to the better. This distinction overlaps with the difference in emphasis between intellectual and emotional reactions but is not identical with it. Reform attitudes almost inevitably contain a strong emotional element, and revolt attitudes may at times use intellectual tools, for instance, in their propaganda techniques. Yet reform ordinarily shows a relative preponderance of intellectual influence (not necessarily influence by intellectuals) as compared to revolt.

Perhaps the essential trait of reform attitudes is a genuine belief that socioeconomic institutions can be and should be improved. This is in contrast not only to conservative attitudes but also to a basic belief in spontaneous progress, along the lines of nineteenth-century liberalism. Optimism concerning man in general, which was at the root of the latter attitude, still persists, but it is now based on the possibility of considered change through social action, rather than on an assumption of automatic progress.

Some pessimistic restraint now comes from the psychologists—both from those who point out that change from within matters no less than change in institutions (and perhaps much more) and from those who emphasize the difficulty of any change from within. The old belief in the power of reason has weakened. Contemporary experience has shown that in times of revolutionary change constructive reform may get snowed under by destructive revolt, that impatience may be either creative or damaging to society, and that majorities are as easily induced by success as vice versa.

Such experiences have made the contemporary reformer a less sanguine man than was his intellectual ancestor in the nineteenth century. However, certain experiences of the opposite type have also taken place; some organizations with a basically conservative approach to the economic system, such as labor unions in North America, have turned out to foster socioeconomic change unwittingly.

The following sections will be concerned with recent institutional outlets for constructive and destructive patterns of attitudes toward economic reform. The two kinds of outlets to be discussed—namely, labor movements and totalitarian movements—are emphatically different in nature even though they sometimes overlap. However, not only do both of them channel existing attitudes into specific institutions such as fraternal solidarity groups or political parties, both also tend to become important factors in the social setting that will determine the prevailing kinds of personality and ideology in the generation to follow. This does not represent any comprehensive attempt to explain the general role of institutional factors in determining the social distribution of personalities. It seemed worth while, however, to analyze the role of two institutional factors of special importance. The first one to be discussed is the varying pattern of labor movements.

Psychological Patterns of Labor Movements

The conventional interpretation of labor organizations, by their friends and foes alike, perceives trade unions and, in some countries, the consumer co-operatives that are associated with them, strictly as an instrument designed to assure economic betterment of the worker. Earnings and working hours are ordinarily considered the main yardstick not only of the worker's level of living but of the achievement of labor organizations. Labor parties, wherever they exist, often function as the political arm of the trade unions even where such parties officially have a program or philosophy of their own.

It is not, of course, intended to dispute the importance of the fight for better wages and shorter hours as an essential goal of union activity, especially in countries or periods in which the living standard of the workers is low. Yet the dynamics of the labor movement cannot be understood without recognizing the impact of additional, psychological factors, some of which may not be conscious. Many veterans of the labor movement agree that the element of group solidarity, either of a whole class or of occupational units, has been decisive in holding organizations together and giving them a life goal. Gains in social status and self-assertion for the individual member often result from successful group action of the unions regardless of whether or not such action is strictly economic in character.

Organization may thus serve as a self-purpose in a sense, not only by offering thousands of members new functions or advancement opportunities within the movement itself, but by raising the workers' feelings of acceptance, achievement, and self-assertion in general. This may be the case regardless of whether or not the objective working conditions show any striking improvement, though there is some degree of interaction between these two kinds of occurrences. Insofar as the labor movement helps by changing the kind and degree of security feelings and social belonging of the workers, this movement always represents a kind of economic reform and, at the same time, a belief system. Objective economic successes are important in bolstering such feelings, but the latter are not necessarily rooted in tangible successes and may survive a long series of defeats.

Psychological differences of considerable importance, however, exist among labor organizations according to, first, the range and explicit character of their ideas about economic reform and, second, their general interpretation of group roles in society, especially class distinctions. Without attempting here to discuss the class concept in any detail, we may define class in terms of a combination of objective socioeconomic facts and of belief systems. More accurately, a class reflects a community of attitudes and beliefs based largely on common or parallel experiences in economic and social life.

The correlation between objective socioeconomic situation and the prevailing attitudes and beliefs of a class or group is by no means perfect, but it appears to be extensive. Some authors feel that the pattern of association among individuals, or the experience of sharing certain social norms, is the decisive factor. Others point out that in most class societies the position and role expectation of the family matter more than that of the individual. Still others emphasize that the historical rise and fall of classes have usually been due to changes in the importance of their social functions; such changes have affected the morale as well as the objective position of families and individuals.[31]

The class role of labor in a capitalistic society is on the whole characterized by an absence of rigid barriers to individual mobility and, at the same time, by unstable employment and status. Marx had assumed that increasing proletarization of industrial societies, along with ever-greater instability and poverty, was bound to produce in the workers' minds an ideology of solidarity and collectivist aims. Class consciousness, it is true, was not necessarily associated by Marx with objective class status in its early stages. Such consciousness, however, was expected to result from that status (or to be aroused easily) sooner or later, at least in the working class.

The Marxian expectation of increasing proletarization of society has not been borne out by developments in the Western world; but even if it had been, it is another question whether proletarian class consciousness in the Marxian sense would have resulted automatically. Nevertheless there is a nucleus of truth in that theory. In the preceding chapter we attempted to show how typical life situations in families of a given group tend to produce a high incidence of the corresponding patterns of perception and reaction, though modifying factors of personality formation apply to each individual. Wage labor, slum conditions, low status rating, unemployment, and general helplessness of families will affect profoundly the worker's child in an early industrial society, and in this sense his objective economic situation will produce a high probability and incidence of certain decisive experiences.

To this extent the Marxian assumption of objective conditions shaping subjective attitudes is realistic. It tends to overlook, however, the range of modifying factors in individual cases and also the impact of cultural differences among populations—differences which affect the propensity toward co-operative solidarity, for instance. A low standard of living, while potentially an important factor in personality formation, by no means tells the whole story. Noneconomic experiences with humiliation or oppression, on the individual or family level, may be no less influential, and they may occur even under a relatively high standard of living.

In fact the sensitiveness of workers toward perceived attempts at group humiliation may increase with better living standards, rising levels of aspiration, and successful union organization. Paternal attitudes of management—discussed in the first chapter, pages 36–38—may arouse increasing resentment in a workers' population that has reached a relatively high level of income, status, and organization. The same applies to defensive or rigid behavior of managerial personnel; needless to say, union officers are not always free from such behavior either. The enormous literature on industrial relations teems with instances of the emotional immaturity involved in seemingly economic conflicts, especially on the part of individuals or groups who feel their leadership position challenged.[32]

In other words, the economic progress of labor has been at odds with the Marxian theory of impoverishment, but this progress has not led to a calming down of the emotional relations between management and labor to the same degree. In fact, the hopelessly underprivileged worker of the past, who was "accustomed" to oppression and instability, was often less restless than is his economically advanced counterpart today. The level of aspiration has risen faster than the level of economic progress. There is, however, an important difference between the social attitudes of workers and labor organizations in America and in Europe. In America the resentments, aspirations, and conflicts have remained largely within the perceived framework of the existing economic system; in Europe—and some other parts of the world—they have historically resulted in conscious and emphatic support of a fundamental change in the system as such, which, of course, has not been exactly identical with the American in any case.

This difference explains in part why the American labor movement is almost entirely a trade-union organization. Labor parties and consumer co-operatives, which are so important in Britain and Scandinavia, for instance, are practically absent in the United States. Not only does the labor movement here concentrate on unionism, but it has confined itself traditionally to the most direct goals of unionism—better wages, working hours, and safety provisions. As far as the conscious level is concerned, the ideological element has been conspicuously missing, or else it has consisted in clean-cut support of the existing economic system. The framework of union activity has been capitalism, American style, and the goal of such activity has been a larger slice in the pie, not a different pie.

The underlying issue, however, exceeds wages and hours, and it concerns attitudes no less than money. A considerable degree of labor identification with private enterprise tends to develop in American society whenever management persuades itself to treat its workers and their representatives like grown-ups and equals, but paternal attitudes of management in our period may bring intensive emotional reactions on the part of labor almost regardless of the economic issues at stake.

At the same time, extensive improvement in the living conditions of the worker has often been perceived as a qualitative change in the economic system, implicitly amounting to far-reaching reform. This feeling has applied even more to gains in self-assurance and status as a result of organization, as such, and of successful union fights. Since the Great Depression, general economic issues—employment goals, social security, housing, public utilities, foreign trade and aid, price and credit policy—have found increasing attention among unionists. Economic programs for immediate action have sometimes been quite extensive without usually being associated by labor with an attempt to reform the system. Undoubtedly the job, rather than institutional innovation, still presents the central frame of reference even though the relative emphasis on it has somewhat diminished.

Shall we assume, therefore, that job consciousness will always be the natural focus of the socioeconomic interests of American labor, and perhaps of industrial labor everywhere? This was the gist of the famous Perlman theory.[33] According to this theory, labor would continue to pursue job-control aims and would not concern itself with the social order or with control of management; scarcity of job opportunities would remain the basic fact facing the unions; political action, if any, would always remain far less important for the unions than immediate economic goals. Essentially this was a static theory. It was expected to prevail in the long run on the assumption that the basic mentality of workers would always remain the same and that any modifying attempt by intellectuals would therefore fail sooner or later.

We are mainly interested here in the psychological assumptions of Perlman's theory. It represents one of the many cases in social science in which an interesting special theory was offered with the dubious claim of being a general theory. There is little doubt that the cultural and institutional setting of American labor, especially during the first half-century of its federal union organization, was quite different from European conditions. Should one have jumped to the conclusion, however, that the attitudes, motives, and behavior either of average workers or of union leadership were always to remain the same in the United States, and that the same mentality was likely to prevail eventually in Italy, Norway, India, and Argentina regardless of sociocultural differences? How reliable could a general theory hope to be that made little allowance for attitudinal differences toward economic reform among laboring people in various periods and cultures?

Moreover, traditional job consciousness among American labor has often concealed indirect support of economic reforms, especially on the nonconscious level. It has been claimed, approvingly, that the labor movement in America is the real conservative movement of our time.[34] It is probably more accurate to say, however, that in their actual effect the job-conscious American unions have promoted far-reaching economic reforms over the last few decades. This has been true, especially, in forcing management into greater productivity, in securing more leisure time for the average American, and—last but not least— in encouraging a money flow sufficient to assure high employment over prolonged periods, though armament needs subsequently turned this monetary corrective into an inflationary menace. Unwittingly the unions may thus have encouraged almost revolutionary innovations in technology and business methods, even while being interested on the conscious level only in immediate gains for their members within the traditional framework of economic institutions.

The question, however, is whether the emotional strain under which such results have been achieved has not been excessive. Amazingly enough, industrial conflict in the United States, where the labor movement does not ordinarily attack the economic order, is often more bitter than in some of those countries where the labor movement is distinctly anticapitalist. Some of the emotional factors involved in periodic industrial conflicts have already been mentioned. Wage increases, or other union successes, imply a raise in the relative social position of the workers or the unions, regardless of whether or not the marginal efficiency of capital warrants such gains for labor. Wage demands often come from highly paid groups of labor, not merely from the low-paid ones. Appetite comes while eating; increased self-confidence and status consciousness keep raising the level of aspirations.

The old belief in individual opportunity to get ahead in life has worn off sufficiently to produce a need for a substitute—for the opportunity to get ahead collectively, through group action. Whenever the latter opportunity is denied or challenged by management in the interest of its own status, either actual or desired, strong emotions are aroused; for many people refuse to be reduced to apathy, passivity, or reliance upon rewards after death. Most persons in our culture hang on to the socioeconomic life goals they perceive as valid for themselves. If they cannot pursue them individually with real hope, then they are likely to try collectively.

The recognition of these underlying status needs and aspirations has given rise to a new discipline that is concerned with the motivation of workers, especially in its effect upon productivity; wage incentives are increasingly considered but one stimulus among many. New approaches to working motivation are sometimes thought of as a kind of economic reform without change in property relations. Raising the worker's morale (that is, making him happy on the job) is thus interpreted as economic reform through psychological methods.[35]

Do industrial conflicts, then, represent mere misunderstandings that can be cured by proper psychological treatment? This would be a very distorted way of looking at such conflicts. To be sure, there is no lack of "misunderstandings" in industrial relations, as in other spheres of life—shortcomings in perception, especially in seeing the other fellow's point of view, and misinformation in an objective sense, mistaken assumptions about the factors that govern individual or group behavior. This kind of misunderstandings can often be relieved by morale studies and practical application of the findings. Yet conflicts about relative group status, about personal security feelings, or about self-assertion projected to a group or class scale are just as "real" as a scramble over money. Moreover, such conflicts often stem from institutional maladjustments. In other words, there is some real hope in improved knowledge of the dynamics of the individual—in his specific role as worker, union officer, or manager—and in detailed study of the interpersonal relations involved. Such adjustments in human relations, however, should not be interpreted as a device to avoid needed institutional reforms, to dull the interest of workers in such reforms, or merely to increase the rate of profit. Any such interpretation contributes to the mistrust by labor organizations of industrial psychology.

On the other hand, some supporters of economic reform in America, and many more abroad, have overlooked the perceptive, emotional, and involvement factors that are implicit in industrial conflict; or they have assumed that a change in property relations would automatically take care of these factors. Various experiences, including those in nationalized enterprises in Britain and on the Continent, have shown that the psychological factor in economic reform cannot be neglected with impunity any more than can the institutional problems involved.

In Europe labor movements seldom assumed in the past, on the conscious level, that any reform short of a basic change in the economic order could be really successful. This was especially true of those continental countries in which Marxian thought was influential, even if we disregard here all the Communist-dominated organizations. Actually social-democratic trade unions and parties carried through or supported many specific reforms while challenging the economic system itself. In these instances fundamental criticism of the system was often accompanied by a constructive program of reform on the level of daily action.

Even so the national differences in the *conscious* attitudes of labor toward economic reform, especially that kind which aims at changing the existing system itself, are of psychological interest. In the United States the labor movement indirectly promoted greater economic reforms than it either intended or realized. In Britain and the Commonwealth countries, at the same time, the labor movement followed mainly a Fabian program of specific reforms in the fields of social legislation, health services, education, housing, rural rehabilitation, public utilities, and co-operatives. Later a moderate amount of nationalization was added to the program, but the emphasis of British-type labor movements, with gradual broadening of the concept of labor, remained on slow change and the power of persuasion, not on an unbridgeable cleavage between economic systems or a sudden break in power relations.

Such cleavage or break was the traditional assumption of most of the labor movements on the Continent including the non-Communist ones. The official programs of socialist parties and trade unions were for many years based on the basic belief perhaps best expressed in the title of one of Karl Kautsky's pamphlets published around the turn of the century: *On the Day after the Social Revolution*. Right after the social revolution—ever less thought of in violent terms—a new era was to set in, not only in economic institutions but in the attitudes and motives of human beings. Reforms under capitalism were considered useful only in the sense of making the working class more fit for the transition to socialism. Compared with the labor movement in America and, in a lesser degree, in the British countries, continental labor conspicuously lacked identification with existing institutions, on the conscious level. Probably the main historical explanation of this difference lay in the strong precapitalist legacy of Europe—feudal oppression, class rigidity, backward middle classes, and lack of appreciation of manual labor.

In their actual policies, however, many of the European labor movements acquired a far-reaching identification with existing arrangements in society as an increasing number of institutions—especially social legislation and civil rights—fell in line with the "immediate" aims of the movement, as distinguished officially from the "ultimate" ones. Some of these groups began to wonder whether they should think of themselves as the gravedigger of capitalism or as its physician. The social dangers implicit in preventing the existing economic machinery from functioning without promptly replacing it by a new one came to worry them increasingly. Interestingly, some labor movements that had started out with an attitude of rejection of existing institutions gradually built up greater feelings of responsibility toward them, at the expense of pressure-group mentality, than certain movements that had identified themselves with the existing economic system from the outset. A vague expectation of a final break with the present lingered on in the minds of those connected with the former type of movement; but this break came virtually to assume the meaning of a beyond, which, for that matter, had always been emphasized in the religious branch of the European labor movement.

What then is the psychological significance of the labor movement as a whole, especially in its attitudes toward economic reform, allowing for the important differences in the cultural, historical, and economic backgrounds of the various countries? Struggle for the organization of labor has accompanied industrial development everywhere; the timing, extent, intensity, and forms of such organization, however, have varied considerably. The economic goal of raising the living standard of the workers has clearly been vital, especially in the early phases of industrial societies. In addition, however, it has everywhere been an essential purpose or effect of labor organization to give the worker a sense of belonging, an opportunity to identify himself with a group of his own kind, and a general frame of reference.

In this sense, as well as in the impact of extensive labor organization on managerial efficiency and on social legislation, the mere fact of such organization represents a kind of reform. What Marx called alienated labor [36]—the worker alienated from recognized and appreciated functions in society and even from his own fellow workers—is thus transformed into a formal group that seeks collectively and aggressively for self-expression, independence, reduction of social inequality, and greater personal security. This remains true in general despite certain union practices, such as slowdowns and featherbedding, which tend to impair the new feeling of social utility and personal assertion resulting from fruitful group action.[37]

The basic need for collective self-assertion and status explains the fact that the most bitter fights between labor and management in many countries have not been waged about money but about the principle of union recognition in contrast to the old paternal attitude of management. Eventually the tables are sometimes turned; management virtually comes to strive for recognition by the unions. Strikes and lockouts often reflect a struggle for mutual or public acknowledgment of group status, power, and social utility. Sometimes such conflicts are an important device to let off steam and, at the same time, to strengthen the internal coherence of the groups concerned. Labor organizations which are strictly of the traditional union type tend to suffer from an organic handicap: they are essentially negative, or "anti," and are dependent on the management for their existence. When a company or shop is discontinued, the end of the union or local has come unless it has some outside functions, no matter how strong it may be internally.

The union tends to represent a conflict structure; the sanctions that it must always have ready against management may also hurt its own members and the consumers. This fact results in a kind of insecurity which seldom disappears completely as long as purely unionist goals in the traditional sense prevail, that is, short-run concentration on wages and hours. For this reason general welfare aims, political interests, and various union enterprises sooner or later come to supplement if not supplant the original goals. In those countries where the labor movement establishes political, educational, or co-operative organizations of its own, its psychological structure is broadened. This is true even when the movement is not conscious of thus implicitly transferring economic reform from the beyond to the society of the present.

The specific psychological setting of the various labor movements is reflected in the types of leaders produced. The extensive literature that has been built around the problem of labor leadership can only be mentioned here.[38] It is full of material on the personality factors that make for active interest and successful leadership in the labor movement under given sociocultural and historical conditions. It also discusses the attitudinal framework that is conducive to a conception of unionism as an approach to economic reform, rather than an opportunity for personal or material assertion of a few leaders.

In summary, a labor movement that mobilizes in its members real ego involvement, at least periodically, represents a kind of economic reform in itself; for it helps many workers in overcoming frustrations that are rooted either in industrial occupations as such or in their "low" position in society. Participation in the labor movement, and the solidarity feelings that go with it, tend to give individuals new involvement objects and values. This occurs at a time when many people cannot derive adequate satisfaction either from purely financial incentives or from the traditional joys of creative and durable work, either from the promise of rewards after death or from temporal work for love, à la Father Divine, either from competitive or from cooperative stimuli as such. Moreover, the labor movement reflects the security strivings of large population groups in industrial societies which have witnessed the psychological as well as the economic disaster that goes with mass unemployment.

In his emotional needs for organization the worker is sometimes joined by recruits from the upper or middle classes, who wish to participate in what they perceive as a great community of solidarity. Labor organization thus tends to expand in various countries into a national movement for economic reform even if its conscious starting point was a nonideological or almost conservative desire for a moderate redistribution of the national product. This trend in organized labor toward a national reform program has been much slower in the United States than in Europe. Cultural and historical factors have resulted in far greater identification of American labor with the existing socioeconomic system if not always with the specific enterprise concerned. On the conscious level, belief in the individual opportunity and social mobility which this system offers has remained great even while the actual impact of the labor movement encouraged far-reaching reforms.

All this, however, is outside the crucial problem of *pseudo-labor movements*, which use supposed labor interests and reform aims as a cloak for attitudes of a very different kind, especially as a mask for totalitarian mentality. The main types of such mentality are communism and fascism.

Totalitarian Appeal and Economic Reform

Both the Communist and the Fascist brands of totalitarianism contain certain elements of a program for economic reform. In fact, an economic program, in the alleged interest of labor or the "toilers," has officially been the principal rationale of communism, and similar elements have been quite significant in the rise of nazism. Measures against unemployment, programs of industrialization, the expropriation of certain groups or types of property, the redistribution of land, tax reforms, and regulation of foreign trade have been regular features of totalitarian programs, though none of these measures have been an invention or exclusive province of the totalitarians.

It would be quite misleading, however, to regard such initial ideas of economic reform as the real explanation either of the dynamics or of the wide appeal of totalitarian movements. Some people, it is true, are attracted to them mainly by these proposed remedies for economic evils, but this type of supporter is unlikely to stay with totalitarian movements very long. For the bulk of the followers, the economic reforms proposed represent a rationalization of deeper emotional needs, not the real basis for political support.

This fact emerges readily from a comparison between contemporary totalitarianism and older forms of autocracy. Through the ages monopolies of power and of ideas, based on convictional certainty, have been frequent. In many societies of the past conformist exclusiveness was internalized to the point of making any deviant pattern of thought appear to the average person as sinful or insane. The mediaeval knight, serf, or priest could not even perceive any such thing as free thought—a freedom for "wrong" ideas to compete with the "right" ones!

In modern Western societies, however, the cultural and institutional setting of such attitudes is quite different. Individuals who have been brought up in the values of freedom and yet desire to escape from it reflect extreme personal insecurity. The roots and manifestations of such insecurity, and its interaction with socioeconomic instability, were discussed in the third chapter. For the present discussion, the totalitarian outlet for personal insecurities is of particular interest.

The essence of the totalitarian mentality in our period is emotional inability to bear criticism or even a real discussion, along with an uncontrollable urge for an unshakable frame of reference to which one can always hold on in the midst of an otherwise confusing and unstable world. Such a mentality reflects an excessive and rigid urge for definiteness and stability in the environment, with intolerance of any perceptive ambiguity, and a constant if sometimes unconscious striving for absolute *certainty* even at the risk of self-deception. Such an urgent need for definiteness on the level of perception is often accompanied by impatience for action regardless of consequences. The title of a Nazi pamphlet was *Besser falsch handeln als gar nicht handeln* ("Better to Act Wrongly than Not at All"). At the same time, authoritarian-guided relief from responsibility, from the necessity to make individual decisions, seems to promise a peace of mind that acutely insecure people often despair of finding in any other way.

Basically persons with a totalitarian propensity are characterized by deep unresolved frustrations, often rooted in family experiences during childhood. Such frustrations may lead to self-hating along with hidden needs for parental affection, which are then projected to the social scene. Picking of scapegoats and *Führer* veneration result. A political party, social movement, or economic panacea may offer an organized outlet for such needs and may even put a premium on neurotic or psychopathic traits. Blind authoritarian discipline and sacrifice come to be happily accepted by many in fulfillment of an unconscious craving for parental protection even if it includes punishment (or *because* of it). A hidden fear of children by parents also appears to occur with some frequency in contemporary societies, thus adding a new source of personal insecurity in adults; but this is another story.

Identification with the authoritarian leader or hero momentarily gives the insecure person some of the emotional hold he had been missing. At the same time he tends to develop a perceptual block and strong resentment toward the mentality and aims of those who resist a similar breakdown of their selves and a totalitarian resocialization of their adult personalities. They are perceived as a danger to society in refusing to join the ranks of the insecure with their collective fear of freedom and in demonstrating implicitly that all human beings need not be that way.

The excessively fear-ridden, as a group, are emotionally incapable of bearing the presence of those who are not. At the same time, whenever totalitarians of any denomination succeed in spreading a mentality of fear and a receptiveness to ideological panics, they have scored a victory for *all* such denominations no matter which one of the latter may win the next election or immediate public support. Uncontrollable mass fears are the indispensable basis of any type of totalitarianism. Mussolini knew what he meant when he said, paraphrasing what other authoritarians had expressed before him: "I do not care about their love as long as they fear me." [39]

Perhaps a totalitarian propensity in a strict sense is not very frequent as yet in Western societies, but its nearest relative, the authoritarian mind, has been found to be fairly widespread. The features of the latter have been described by Max Horkheimer as follows: "Mechanical surrender to conventional values; blind submission to authority together with blind hatred of all opponents and outsiders; anti-introspectiveness; rigid stereotyped thinking; a penchant for superstition; vilification, half-moralistic and half-cynical, of human nature; projectivity." Similarly, Else Frenkel-Brunswik summarizes as follows the traits of authoritarian personality in the light of the research carried out by the California group: "self-alienation, mechanization, standardization and stereotypy, piecemeal functioning, intolerance of ambiguity, lack of individuation and spontaneity, and a combination of irrationality with manipulative opportunism"; "it is this externally over-adjusted type of person who is internally much less adjusted than the democratic-minded individual." [40]

In our period the totalitarian—an extreme version of the authoritarian—is quite likely to use economic programs far more frequently than did his forerunners in earlier phases of society. Essentially, however, economic arguments or institutional programs of any kind provide mere rationalizations, for totalitarianism is basically a primitive religion with some totemistic traits, a perverted messianic element, and a relapse into barbaric mob behavior. This substitute religion shares with some older creeds an antiscientific, anti-intellectual attitude which is fundamentally at odds with the requirements of genuine economic reform. Totalitarianism, however, has not learned tolerance or even understanding of other people's mentality, as many other creeds have in varying degrees.

On the economic scene initial improvements sometimes occur under a new totalitarian regime when it takes over a society ridden by economic backwardness or disruption. Recent history shows conspicuous instances of totalitarian regimes that started out with the promise of economic progress in the sense of increasing equality but wound up with extreme inequality to the point of establishing a class of slave laborers. Totalitarian methods of rapid economic development, it is true, have been conspicuously successful, largely in a technical sense, whenever they have been applied to backward pre-industrial populations.

In modern Western societies a high incidence of strong personal insecurities has accompanied certain processes of social disorganization and the various forms of economic instability discussed in Chapter III, such as the ever-present threat from market competition, business fluctuations, unemployment, changes in money value, housing shortages, the old-age problem, technological innovations, and industrialized warfare. In these societies strong personal insecurities are often expressed in a propensity to embrace some variety of totalitarianism. Contemporary society, however, with its background of pronounced encouragement of intellectual individuality, cannot take totalitarian attitudes for granted as some earlier societies did, nor can it afford to accept the rise of such attitudes as unavoidable in any sociopsychological situation. For any sweeping disintegration, in the wake of totalitarianism, of the social norms that are usually associated with civilization, any revolution of nihilism, any wide appeal of psychopathic heroes who take care of people's personal fears by making them the prevailing and, indeed, the only recognized pattern—any such trend can be fatal in a period of mechanized large-scale production with its striking instruments of mass communication.

Once a totalitarian atmosphere has developed, any discussion of

economic reform is immediately displaced from the level of intellectual evaluation to that of a primitive version of theology. The
suspicion of unorthodox economic ideas or reform preferences becomes a favorite starting point for heresy hunts. Not that such hunts
depend on the actual occurrence of unorthodox thought or behavior.
Their essential element is the uncontrollable emotional need for
witches that characterizes the totalitarian mind. If it cannot find anything resembling real sinners, it will create them in its own imagination. Witches and confessions are indispensable as an outlet for the
fears and security needs of totalitarians; whoever declines to confess
refuses the accusers relief from their insecurities. Lack of "co-
operation" on the part of whoever happens to be accused thus comes
to mean sabotage and betrayal—of the security needs of the totalitarians. The real purpose of forcible confessions, regardless of whether
the coercion is physical or mental, is to enhance the beliefs and
security feelings of the accusers. Sometimes this comes to apply to
strongly insecure or totalitarian-minded defendants, too, regardless of
possible innocence; confession relieves them of any hidden guilt feelings, especially those stemming from lack of successful resistance
toward the inquisitors.

Essentially the purpose of obtaining such confessions is to "explain"
the root of evils and to make sure, by the confession as such, that
these evils are now removed. Confession thus serves as a kind of
incantation—to plead innocent means to invite the wrath of the
demons. The factual guilt question involved—in our period quite
often economic beliefs and their meaning—is irrelevant and serves
as a mere irritant if brought up by old-fashioned defendants who
have not caught on to the game. That is why any denial of charges
or any criticism of totalitarian investigators is automatically considered a proof of subversion: it means refusal of personal security
to the investigators.

The witches are most effective in their security-promoting function
if they were originally of the accusers' own breed, if they were considered "loyal" in the past; Satan was originally an angel. The mutual
tension-relief operates best if a community of emotional starting
points underlies it. In addition, this type of collective tension-relief
also serves the purpose of creating a particular kind of "mass"—the

one that only a community of fear can cement. Refusal to confess, that is, to share these mass fears is thus interpreted by the totalitarian as an antisocial act.[41]

Basically, we repeat, the totalitarian mentality reflects the emotional inability of excessively insecure persons to bear criticism. Mere discussion of controversial ideas or institutions, in the economic field in particular, is perceived as a tool of antisocial propaganda if not subversion. Totalitarianism "solves" economic and other problems by removing any possibility of a legitimate alternative to its own preconceptions, not only legally but psychologically—by denying the very existence of such problems under its own rule outside the perverted imagination of deviants who supposedly are always few but never are allowed to die out.[42]

It is part of the tragedy of our time that such a mentality has spread in the name of communism and anticommunism alike, and that it has often met only weak or brief resistance among the rank and file toward the compliance requirements concerned. Such requirements were rationalized both into individual beliefs and assumed objective needs of society. It is the ultimate aim of totalitarianism to make an accomplice out of every individual, at least in the psychological sense of coming to share the guilt with the totalitarian movement and, especially, with an established regime of this type. That is why totalitarian inquisitions always insist that everyone exposed to them become an informer.

In practice, the psychological differences among the various denominations of totalitarianism have been slight even when their economic programs or political semantics seemed to be irreconcilable. In Western countries, at least, the choice of denomination appears to be a secondary matter, or else to show oscillations, in persons who have a strong totalitarian propensity.

The most elaborate brand of totalitarianism in our period, however, is undoubtedly communism. The key to the understanding of its role in the present-day world is not in the intellectual, political, or economic origins of the movement but in its psychodynamics, including attitudes and beliefs. Undoubtedly there are strong, if mostly hidden, elements of an attitudinal and belief system in the original structure of Marxism despite its claim to purely scientific analysis. It would be quite hopeless, however, to look in the writings of Marx and

Engels for an explanation of the twists of Soviet ideology and policy in our period. Only censored editions of Marx are available in the Soviet Union today, and there is reason to believe that Stalin or Khrushchev would have liquidated Marx had the latter lived long enough to see what uses had been made of his doctrine.

Moreover, the socioeconomic starting point of Communist movements should not be confounded with their subsequent features. The justified grievances of the working class in industrialized areas (especially in newly developed ones) and, above all, the exploitative legacy of feudal and absolutist regimes in backward countries, are frequently at the root of an initial mass appeal of communism in large parts of the world. Nevertheless, its frequent origins in actual needs and goals of economic reform should not blind anyone to the basic role of communism as an international tool of Russian power policy and, at the same time, as an all-embracing substitute religion in its psychological meaning to the individuals afflicted.

Actually the common cover of Marxian or pseudo-Marxian semantics conceals the existence, within the world of communism, of three phenomena of quite different orders. First, there is a genuine movement for economic reform with radical methods, mainly in countries with a feudal-aristocratic legacy, landless rural masses, and a need for sweeping redistribution of land, industrialization, and protection of workers from ruthless exploitation. Such reform goals are not essentially Communist in character, but the Communists easily manage to appropriate them, largely by default of other political and ideological groups. In recent years, the combination of such economic ideas with nationalist slogans has been especially effective in China and elsewhere.

Second, there are the Soviet Russian Communists, after decades of unchallenged power and ideological monopoly. In the Soviet Union today and, in a lesser degree, in some of its satellite countries to the west, the Communists represent largely the conformist or indifferent types, not the revolutionaries or malcontents. In a monolithic structure like the Soviet regime, with a large majority of people who have never known any other order of things, it must take quite an unusual amount of independence, nonconformity, or rebellious personality to oppose the Communist regime. Essentially it is the individual with a conformist or, at least, a conservative personality who now supports the Communists in the Soviet Union, although continuing industrial and scientific development must leave some approved outlets for imaginative initiative for the time being.

Third, there is the person with a totalitarian propensity in Western countries that have long known freedom of thought and democratic discussion. To go totalitarian in a free country takes an extreme amount of personal insecurity resulting in a pressing need to hold on to someone who supposedly will always have all the answers. The frequent occurrence of such needs in a country with traditions of intellectual freedom indicates strong disruptive influences in social life, such as a high degree of recurrent economic instability. This was pointed out in Chapter III, especially in the section on "The appeal of quacks," pages 116–118. Wide support for either communism or other shades of totalitarian mentality under Western conditions is a symptom of a sick society.

The three kinds of Communist attitudes overlap in some places and are subject to shifts in their relative importance in the various countries affected. At any rate, Moscow and Peiping hold them together and utilize them as best they can.

The following description of the rise and fall of a Russian Communist is illustrative of mental processes in totalitarian persons:

The Party gave him a psychological backbone which he did not otherwise possess. He was a man without initiative and he felt safe in the Party; it offered him a certain position he could never have won on his own. . . . During the revolution and the years of civil war they had been attracted by its revolutionary ideas and, once inside, a cleverly devised system saw to it that they never drifted away again. Their choice was between membership of the dominant group, which included a comfortable and secure position, and the terrible threat of complete moral and physical destruction if they ventured to depart by as much as a hair's breadth from the Party line.[43]

The totalitarian identification, once acquired, often continues even after an individual has been purged; he is afraid of losing his frame of reference without being able to replace it by a new one. Hence the paralyzing effect of totalitarian purges upon many people who are objectively innocent of the charges raised against them; they can fight against perceived enemies but not against perceived brethren even if the latter made a "mistake." Conversely, the accusers perceive suspected dissidents as "suffering from a psychological dichotomy which will split and destroy them 'spiritually.' . . . The internal strains to which they are subject will be too much for them both as individuals and as a party." [44]

Among the individual patterns of totalitarian propensity in Western countries, the people most likely to be attracted to communism, rather than to other shades of totalitarianism, are the strongly guilt-ridden persons. Communism, as distinguished from fascism, has its social starting point in lower-class aspirations, and it keeps rationalizing the emotional needs of its followers in this old way. This practice tends to attract certain individuals from upper and middle groups of society who unconsciously wish to repent for individual or group sins. Driving the Communists underground probably increases this masochistic attraction and strengthens the allegiance of the initiated, the "knowing," to each other and to the cause. At the same time, Communists appear to have a basic contempt for fellow travelers, who do not commit themselves to the movement formally and, above all, psychologically, and who may even be really interested in economic reform, rather than in an all-embracing substitute religion.

The fascination that communism holds for its active members often, as we have said, continues after they have been expelled or have left the party on their own. Ideologically the positive charge in their minds shifts into a negative one, but psychologically little changes in such cases: the black-and-white mentality continues, and in their whole perception of the world there is still nothing more important than communism. The explanation, of course, is in the fact that the same personality traits that led them into communism in the first place are still there even though their good standing with the ruling party clique of the moment has been impaired.

The social and historical starting point of communism, as we pointed out, is in lower-class aspirations. Fascism, on the other hand, originates typically in aspirations of the upper and middle classes, especially where the middle classes are of precapitalist origin. It then comes to attract a number of persons from various strata who identify themselves with a social élite but are frustrated in their conscious or unconscious desire for high social status. Here again a program for economic reform serves to rationalize basic totalitarian propensities, even though society may objectively be in need of actual reform. While the socioeconomic roots of fascism are different from those of communism, however, the psychological disposition of the individuals afflicted in Western countries is (or comes to be) very similar. Actually, interchange of ideas, methods, and allegiances between these twin movements is by no means infrequent despite the bloodthirsty language they like to use against each other.

The socioeconomic conditions which typically enhance the mass appeal of fascism include national inferiority feelings based on perceived humiliation (in the wake of military defeat, for instance); uprooted precapitalist groups surviving into an industrialized society, such as aristocratic landowners or small handicraft; disgruntled intellectuals who form a frustrated would-be élite; an aimless or cynical youth in search of leaders and goals; strong concentration of economic power along with failure of the economic system to function properly, especially a sequence of sweeping deflations and inflations; actual or imagined threat to the economic order from radical currents or an extensive labor movement; fear of loss of the paternal role and, at the same time, collective guilt feelings on the part of the upper classes; cultural and national characteristics that favor conformity, especially in the absence of deeply rooted experiences in democratic give-and-take; and, last but not least, any factors that generally foster a high incidence and intensity of personal insecurities.

Economic reforms, we repeat, often rank high in the official programs of Fascist movements and in the initial policies of Fascist regimes. This applies to employment policy, community improvements, housing, drainage and irrigation, land reforms, monetary changes, and so forth. Basically, however, such reform programs are entirely subservient to the emotional urge to find outlets for the mass fears found or aroused. Reform goals are cynically sacrificed to this urge whenever they are no longer required for purposes of plausible rationalization. Persons who are attracted to a Fascist movement mainly by its economic program, and not by its images of hatred and power, will soon run afoul of its demands and mentality.

Fascism cannot be genuinely interested in economic reforms because of its consciously anti-intellectual character, its endeavor to arouse strong and blind emotions in its followers, its "know-nothing" attitude toward any scientific approach to human problems. The persecutory mob, not the revolutionary, is characteristic of fascism at an even earlier stage of development than it is in communism. Economic factors, not excluding real goals of status defense of individuals or groups, are only of indirect importance in the rise and policy of fascism, to the extent that economic frustrations contribute greatly to the state of fear that underlies fascism.

These considerations also apply to the related area of attitudes usually summarized under the heading of group prejudice. Attributed traits and various stereotypes concerning certain groups (especially minorities) may be offered as the "explanation" of high prices, bankruptcy, exploitation, or inequality. The underlying state of mind, however, is not really rooted in any specific shortcomings of the economy or in lack of economic information, although tensions resulting from socioeconomic instability influence it greatly in a longer run. Norbert W. Ackerman and Marie Jahoda describe the emotional predispositions to group prejudice as anxiety, confusion of the concept of self, fear of the different, and conformity. The corresponding defense mechanisms transform the underlying anxiety into aggression against a collective scapegoat.[45] Fascism attempts to drive such displacement processes to the extreme, on a mass scale: it sets out to change and broaden the scale of social distances in its followers in such a way that actual economic relations and needs are distorted sadistically in their minds. This or that minority group permanently or periodically becomes the great villain, replacing the concept of objective economic conditions to be studied and changed.

In summary, any serious spread of the totalitarian mentality—either of the Communist or of the Fascist type—in contemporary Western societies indicates a wide incidence of strong personal insecurities. Such insecurities, in turn, reflect in large part a recurrent socioeconomic instability, as was shown in the third chapter. Yet totalitarian attitudes are not genuinely directed at economic reforms which might in due course remedy such instability. Essentially totalitarianism mirrors a psychic state of fear on a mass scale. Its Communist variety has its historical starting point and frame of reference in the lower classes; in the Fascist variety upper-class or middle-class values are used in a comparable way. However, in essential traits of the mentality and in psychic needs there is relatively little difference between the various brands of totalitarianism in Western societies. In each case economic reform is used as an initial or periodic device to gain attention and support among masses who actually need improvements. Sooner or later, however, economic reform becomes a mere object of rationalizations—if not conscious deception—on the part of totalitarian movements.

The question that emerges from these experiences of our generation is how to replace the totalitarian mentality, especially when it occurs on a large scale, by genuine striving for needed reforms. The reduction of socioeconomic instability eventually will help to diminish the incidence of strong insecurities that foster a totalitarian propensity, but this might take a generation or longer, and in the meantime the vicious circle of instability and totalitarianism might continue. Attempts to "disprove" the delusions of real totalitarian addicts, to show that their fears are objectively unjustified, would be psychologically hopeless. Such a procedure, however, may influence some persons who have no real totalitarian propensity and who fell into the orbit of totalitarian movements by accident or by genuine mistake.

Well-meaning liberals, who have been trained in logical argumentation and who strongly believe in its power, are quite likely to be ineffective in counteracting the real totalitarian mentality. Likewise, turning the fears and hatreds of those afflicted against each other, thus leading their mentality *ad absurdum,* may sometimes have occurred in history when a mass hysteria had nearly run its course and merely awaited a final blow; but ordinarily this is an uncertain and hazardous procedure.

The real task is to eliminate uncontrollable fear—not fear of anything in particular—as a mental condition and a snow-balling occurrence among the masses. By far the most promising method is action through key persons, reference groups to whom people look for guidance, and legal devices which demonstrate to those afflicted that prejudice, hatred, and violence are at odds with basic values of society, and that the totalitarian, far from being embraced by a new fraternity, is likely to find less acceptance and assurance than the democratic person. In this process, an attempt could be made to imbue the unhappy totalitarian souls, as a group, with a greater degree of personal security than they have had. Institutional reforms—prominently including some economic ones that will be discussed in the next chapter—can eventually contribute much to changing the attitudinal framework of persons with totalitarian propensities and, still better, to preventing the rise of such propensities on a mass scale in the future. This, however, is likely to be a long-continued process, rather than a quick cure once for all.

Planning, Planners, and Incentives

Actually it has been claimed that organized economic reforms, especially those which involve any type of planning, are likely to foster the totalitarian mentality and policy. The best type of economic reform, so the argument runs, is the one which comes about spontaneously, through the mechanism of an unfettered economy; any other attempt at reform will wind up in a vicious circle of economic intervention and totalitarian mentality. We shall not discuss here the general aspects and fallacies of such theories. This was done in an earlier book by the present author, which also attempted to draw a clean-cut distinction between various types of economic planning and control.[46]

The present discussion is concerned only with human factors and limitations in economic reform, especially to the extent that such reform may involve changes in industrial incentives, a growth of government action, or increased centralization of economic decisions. The assumptions made in this discussion are the following: First, there is need for some type and degree of economic reform everywhere—even in the most prosperous countries—in order to keep increasing the level of productivity, to build safeguards against excesses of depression and inflation, and to improve the housing situation, the use of basic resources, and the condition of substandard groups. Second, it is far better to carry out needed reforms in a well-considered and integrated way than to do it on a hand-to-mouth basis. Third, economic reforms can be implemented in such a way as to strengthen the democratic participation and responsibility of citizens. These three principles are combined in the concept of democratic planning as the approach to economic reform. The degree of public ownership, which looks to many people like the main issue involved, will actually vary from country to country and period to period. It is by no means the essential yardstick of reform, planning, or democracy.

Economic reform can—and often must—proceed in a piecemeal way; economic planning is an attempt to integrate new measures with one another and with as many existing institutions as possible. Planning means essentially anticipation, followed by integration of independent ends and means, with a view to eventual action. This applies to planning on almost any level—the household, the firm, the public budget, the local or national government, international units.

It is uncertain whether or not individuals with a high degree of integrating and "planning" capacity in their personality are more likely than others to support planning in economic and social life as well. On the latter level there are usually additional factors of an emotional nature, especially in attitudes toward government intervention, which were discussed in the second chapter. As a symbol of father, the image of a paternal state may arouse emotions which make for perception of public measures in either a less or a more favorable way than the objective situation warrants. The state may thus become an object of blind hate or naïve veneration; worst of all, it may turn out to be even more remote than a private owner, thus disappointing the faithful children. This problem of identification and communication is the crux of the planning problem and, indeed, of any public policy in a complex society.

Planning, at the same time, is a much broader concept than socialism, with which it has often been associated historically. Actually the planning orientation may be applied to the individual, local, or social level, to private or public property. The kind of mentality—that is, of perception and goal direction—matters here far more than the institutional setting. The planning orientation stresses the systematic, "rational," intellectual, and perhaps scientific approach, even though it may not always succeed in making the best use of this approach in practice.[47]

Social goals of one kind or another are always implicit in economic planning. In this sense, the latter always includes some noneconomic purposes and functions. Apparently planning aimed at specific social targets—preparedness or industrial development, for instance—is likely to arouse greater public support than planning directed at the maintenance of economic balance in a general way or at sustained high employment. The latter type of planning—a program of countercyclical measures against excesses of deflation and inflation—has, however, come to be widely accepted in Europe and has gained much ground in the United States since the Great Depression. Such an attitudinal change, it is true, has often been unconscious and has manifested itself more readily on the practical than on the verbal level.

Even so, any strict centralization would arouse great resistance in Western countries. Planning has the best hope of success there if it aims at establishing favorable conditions for specific economic action that is desired from individuals, groups, or firms, rather than at direct decisions from above. Planning thus becomes largely identified with anticipation of the attitudes and motives of management, labor, and consumers, and with the setting of an attitudinal and motivational framework that favors the kind of individual or group decisions the policy makers have in mind. This kind of planning need not assume "rationality" in any conventional sense, but it must explore systematically any prevailing patterns of "irrationality" in order to be realistic.

This applies especially to the problem of incentives. Capitalism has traditionally assumed that the pressures of a competitive market would beget top efficiency in managers and workers. Critics of capitalism, on the other hand, have long claimed that stronger identification with the economic order on the part of the population, or of the decisive classes in the production process, would increase the satisfactions of work and of achievement and would thus strengthen the incentives for efficiency. J. A. Hobson, for instance, saw the essential challenge of economic reform precisely in the necessity to develop stronger incentives than capitalism had been able to do.[48]

At any rate, any economic reform of the planning type would need to grasp the emotional influences that are involved in the various types of economic decisions. Some of these influences could then be consciously utilized in the interest of accepted social goals. Opponents of any such reform claim that by eliminating the market mechanism, with its mutual correctives for workers, managers, and consumers, the door would be opened to arbitrariness. On the other hand, supporters of certain reform programs assert that by putting economic decisions on a scientific basis, including the use of applied psychology, the new economy could be made far more "rational" than the old one has ever been; planning boards would proceed according to the requirements of marginal analysis in economic theory, while private business firms today do not. The practical experiences available thus far are not yet conclusive.

One of the main controversies along these lines concerns the work incentives for an industrial labor force. Is competition for jobs and earnings doomed if government intervention is increased? And can we hope for any work efficiency in the absence of such competition? Practical experiences and psychological considerations alike indicate that the problem is far more complex than these questions assume. It is true enough that the necessity of working for a wage is an important incentive, especially for unskilled laborers and for workers in early industrial societies. However, one price that society has to pay for cheap labor supply is its high turnover and instability. Lack of involvement in the work to be done, and personal insecurity due to low and uncertain status, tend to result in excessive mobility and low productivity.

Perhaps this problem of how best to stimulate the involvement of people in their work, their interest in getting things done, and their sense of achievement will turn out to be the crux of any conflict of economic systems. Attempts to increase the personal involvement in industrial work through profit sharing have seldom had much success. The workers and, especially, the unions have tended to suspect the motives of management in such experiments, and the financial participation offered has not sufficed to break down this basic attitude and has sometimes strengthened it further. On the other hand, noneconomic forces which aroused strong emotions of a productive type have occasionally created the kind of involvement that made economic planning or innovations a success even when financial sacrifices or handicaps were involved. The experiences of the Kibbutz movement in Palestine, at least until the rise of complications from party politics and rapid heterogeneous immigration, are a case in point.

This is not meant to minimize the impact of financial incentives in specific social constellations; it is meant to emphasize the great *variety* of incentives that may make economic processes—including innovations based on public action—either effective or ineffective. It was shown in the first two chapters that financial incentives are part of a complex motivation, within which they often reflect or symbolize deeper needs of people, especially a striving for self-assertion, personal security, or social status. Financial incentives are important, but they are apt to be disregarded or unconsciously neglected whenever they are at odds with such deeper needs. Unless, therefore, economic planning or other reforms are associated by most individuals with national, social, or group interests that concern them personally, such measures will have a small chance of succeeding.

It is worth noting here that some populations in our period have access to a huge body of statistical data, at least in a popular version, and may have a greater cultural tendency than others to being interested in quantitative information. In such populations "planning through publicity"—some people might prefer to call it simply economic education—could have considerable effectiveness. Conversely, absence or disregard of such information among the rank and file may result in attitudinal resistance toward planning measures regardless of whether or not they hold intrinsic merit.

British experiences during the postwar period have an important bearing on this whole issue. These experiences, to be sure, have been in the nature of scattered economic reforms, rather than of planning, despite the presence of a Planning Board and Planning Staff. Moreover, the legacy of the war and the far-reaching disintegration of the Empire supplied modifying influences of great significance. This is not the place to attempt an evaluation of British postwar reforms in general; the purpose of the following remarks is merely to point out a number of lessons from an economy that underwent a great increase in public intervention within a few years—an increase which was not drastically reversed with changing the party composition of the government.

British experience shows that men do not automatically work harder for the government than for a private employer, if indeed anyone ever believed this. The opposite assumption, for that matter, would be just as untrue. The really decisive factors appear to be, first, the degree of identification and ego involvement that management—either public or private—can arouse in the workers; second, the group norms, especially those expressed in the prevailing standards of trade-unionism, which the workers recognize as their own. The British experience indicates that unless nationalization (or public regulation, for that matter) is accompanied by a strengthening of the workers' identification with the plant or with the job to be done, nothing much will change. Such changes in identification may occur either directly in each worker or, more likely, through the medium of newly developing norms of trade-union behavior. Without such basic changes, major attitudinal shifts on the job cannot be expected to arise.

Purely financial incentives turned out to be effective only if and when there was psychological readiness for a positive response; otherwise they sometimes backfired. In some cases higher wages brought greater absenteeism; extra leisure was preferred to an increase in weekly earnings. Situations in which such preferences for leisure by one key group (say, the coal miners) forced other groups into similar behavior turned out to be especially difficult to handle.

Lack of effective communication between the central management of nationalized industries and the workers on the local level was found to be fatal to the latter's identification with their productive assignments. In addition, the unions had lost their traditional function of preventing exploitation by the company and braving the management in the interest of their own members; and they had not acquired a new clean-cut function. Unions were still perceived by their members and officers as instrument for the gain of immediate advantages, and they were wary of appearing as a new kind of company union. Labor supply for the coal mines was at first difficult. The existence of a Labour government, while it lasted, had not automatically brought a higher status for the holders of such jobs or any intensive identification with the state.[49]

All this should not be interpreted as an indictment of the British reform experiment. Actually the economic recovery of Britain after the war was a marked success, and most of the Labour reforms enacted were accepted as permanent by the Conservatives, with only slight alterations. The British experience does teach, however, that any institutional reform program, whatever its merits may be in other respects, is bound to run into serious headaches if it disregards the changes in attitudes, motives, and group norms which it either involves or requires.

In other words, any institutional reform is only as good as the motivation of the people who carry it out including those in executive positions. This is true in the planning type of reform even more than in other types, for the planning approach requires specific personal qualities, which have been pointed out earlier. In a sense, any type of extensive economic reform now means adjustments in the selection principle for managerial executives. Compared with such adjustments, property titles are of far less importance in the economic process today.

If an institutional arrangement encourages the selection and promotion of the "right" kind of people to executive positions, it will be effective. "Right" here means not only technical competence but adaptability, co-operation, the ability to make essential decisions and to delegate others, and an absence of authoritarian or rigid traits. One of the main arguments used against private enterprise, especially outside North America, has been precisely the selection of economic executives on different grounds, for example, ruthless egotism or family connections. Conversely, it has been claimed that under any type of economic planning or noncompetitive arrangements "the worst come on top"[50] because of the attraction such assignments exert upon bureaucratic, sterile, and authoritarian minds.

Now a strong case could be made for the belief that bureaucratic management is unavoidable in a huge, complex society; Joseph A. Schumpeter even claims that "bureaucracy is not an obstacle to democracy but an inevitable complement to it."[51] The problem in this case is reduced to the decision whether bureaucracy should mainly be a public one (civil service) or a private one (corporate hierarchies). But this is not the crux of the issue. We are concerned here, not with bureaucracy as an institutional arrangement but with bureaucracy as a state of mind. Its characteristics can be described as rigid adherence to set impersonal rules, especially restrictive ones; lack of sufficient perception of or appropriate response to changing conditions; inertia and remoteness; a safety-first attitude along with overconformity; and excessive identification with the administrative hierarchy, based on assured tenure. The typical bureaucrat has the greatest inhibitions against admitting an error (which would be implicit in changing an economic plan, for instance); he is insensitive toward both intellectual qualifications and emotional factors in complex issues. For an intellectual person to be squeezed into the strait jacket of a bureaucratic machine is a process full of frustrations; it is a serious problem in a period when economic administration and, especially, economic reform cannot dispense with intellectual guidance.

It is quite true that certain institutional arrangements may tend to put individuals with bureaucratic traits of character into top positions or to reward such qualities in some way. Conversely, persons with the traits described may actively seek an outlet for their personal needs through administrative power over people, or perhaps through perfectionist planning. However, this may also happen in a competitive economy and in the absence of either public planning agencies or economic reform. Bureaucracy as an institutional development should not be confounded with the bureaucratic mentality. Both may affect either public or private organizations—planning agencies either of the government or of large corporations. There is no automatic guarantee against it, only the general possibility of encouraging a non-bureaucratic spirit in all human endeavors.

At the same time, there has been some neglect by advocates of economic reform and, especially, of economic planning of the distinct possibility that bureaucratic persons might gain from the institutional changes proposed. Likewise, there has been too little emphasis on the necessity in a democratic society of staffing executive positions with persons of productive orientation, adaptability without conformity, and organizational gifts without authoritarian traits. Economic reform of any kind will be a failure unless it improves the selection of executive personnel, from the viewpoint of human qualities, over earlier methods of selection. In turn, the ultimate decision on who is to do the selecting, and according to what standards, will be reached in the showdown of *political* forces and the social power groups behind them.

In summary, the planning type of economic reform poses some special problems of personality and motivation. Regardless of whether or not any formal changes in property relations are considered necessary, any attempt by democratic societies to integrate needed reforms into economic planning will depend for its success on the selection of suitable personalities for the executive functions involved. Even so only real involvement of the population—especially the labor force—in such reforms and a high degree of identification with them will promise achievement.

In addition, the type of reform to be chosen, and of the incentives, rewards, and penalties that go with it, must take into account the cultural characteristics of the population and its prevailing scale of social values if such measures are to be realistic. What is perceived as a reward in one society may be interpreted as a penalty or meet indifference in another; what is interpreted as regimentation by one nation may be readily accepted by another. In one country or group, beating the law is considered evidence of smartness even when the most essential measures are at stake; in another country or group, co-operation with public policy is taken for granted even when this policy is disapproved by some of those affected. Likewise, certain populations have a greater cultural propensity for semantic lags than others. Some populations may in practice readily participate in a substantial amount of public planning but may be extremely reluctant to admit that they do it. In addition, there are, of course, attitudinal differences among individuals and groups in each nation regarding public intervention and social innovation, and corresponding conflicts of codes may easily arise in the minds of some people.

In other words, no one program of economic planning—or nonplanning, for that matter—will be applicable to all sociocultural conditions or will make everybody happy. Psychological adaptability, not to be confounded with conformity, will be an important testing ground for the individuals, groups, institutions, and policies that are affected by any such program.

Economic Reform and Attitudinal Change

What types of economic reform are psychologically realistic in our own period? Unless we assume that we live in the best of all possible worlds right now—an assumption which few people would care to make—or else that any attempt to improve economic conditions through human action is preposterous, some kind of reform will be considered necessary nearly everywhere. Some people will advocate economic planning of this or that type; others will recommend a change back to *laissez faire;* still others may put their faith in the simple ways of the Puritans or in technological innovations at some future date.

The point is that no one type of institutional arrangement can hope to succeed at all times and in all societies just because it looks to some of us like the most advanced or logical. Only by taking into account the differences in cultural and historical heritage, scales of value, perception patterns, group distribution, and status needs can economic reform promise success at a given time and place. This principle by no means precludes the possibility of economic policy agreements on an international scale; but no one type of institutional arrangement, no matter how successful it may have been in one or more countries, will always fit populations with a different background.

Competition, co-operation, freedom, planning, profit, welfare, efficiency, joy of work, thrift, investment—these are all concepts or symbols which mean much to one population and little to another or which assume quite a different meaning when transplanted from one region or social group to another. In one society, concern with the common welfare may be taken for granted and may even enter, through a back door, into theoretical concepts of economics.⁵² In another more rigid society both the upper and the lower strata may assume that given economic arrangements are transcendental, superhuman devices designed to benefit the upper strata only. In one case the little fellow is, sentimentally perhaps, considered the real focus of reforms; in another case he is disregarded, if not held in contempt for his economic failure. In all of these cases the concept of economic reform refers to *intentional* extensive change in economic conditions, as distinguished from the concept of economic growth, which applies mainly to *spontaneous* processes of expansion, however defined in detail.

The crucial dilemma of such intended change in those countries which need it most—the ones ordinarily classified as backward or underdeveloped—arises from the possibility that reform may destroy old values without immediately replacing them by other, equally firm, ones, thus fostering personal conflicts on a mass scale. On the other hand, lack of reform will often perpetuate disease, exploitation, or savage superstitions.

Another dilemma of many underdeveloped nations is rooted in the lag between their aspirations for economic development and a higher level of living on the one hand and the actual degree of their attitudinal readiness for the changes involved on the other. The aspiration for better material conditions is now almost universal. The traditional assumption of both the "developed" and the "underdeveloped" populations that the latter were doomed by nature or history to remain in this condition has been widely abandoned. Populations that have long been ridden by poverty, disease, and illiteracy no longer take their condition for granted, nor do the wealthier nations assume that this condition is inevitable in the interest of an international division of labor, the law of comparative advantages, or the white man's burden. Clichés about the innate laziness or inefficiency of entire populations have also become far less fashionable in the West than they used to be.

The causes for this world-wide change in attitudes and aspirations are many. The rapid decline of colonialism has been partly a cause and partly a symptom of this change. Other influences came from the initial defeats suffered by the Western powers during the second World War, especially in East Asia, the stimulation of industrial growth in countries like India during both world wars, the demonstration of industrial technology by the occupation armies, and, above all, the example of Soviet Russia (and, later, Soviet China) in rapidly developing their economic and industrial strength no matter how one felt about the totalitarian methods used. Modern means of communications helped disrupt the old complacency and resignation toward economic and social evils. Pressure from a rapidly rising population in many areas upon food supply and land tenure was no less important.

But the actual readiness to translate these aspirations into social action and change has often lagged behind. Some of the obstacles to economic development, it is true, have been chiefly economic in character, such as lack of a sufficient supply and formation of capital, absence of substantial savings in a poverty-stricken population, shortage of efficient credit institutions, hectic fluctuations in the world market prices for raw materials, barriers to the international exchange of goods and services, and exhaustion of a soil that had been misused for generations under the pressure of a rising population and outmoded systems of tenure.

Noneconomic impediments, however, have probably been even more important. Some of these, to be sure, look economic at first sight, but their actual roots are psychological, social, and cultural. Perhaps the most widely discussed among these impediments has been the shortage of a spirit of enterprise, in the broad sense of individual initiative, readiness to experiment and innovate, and willingness to assume responsibility for economic decisions. In this sense the spirit of enterprise is not necessarily confined to private business, though historically it often has been. Many experiences show that this spirit cannot be reproduced at will in an underdeveloped area—certainly not by the preaching of foreign advisers—no matter how badly it may be needed. Often there simply is no class or group of people who have the right kind of curiosity and the ability to perceive industrial and commercial opportunities. Usually there is no lack of people who would like to get rich quick, but this attitude is far remote from a spirit of enterprise.

Another noneconomic obstacle to economic development has come from the political habits and traditions of many countries. Although their desire to develop is often motivated by nationalism, especially the wish of new nations to create an economic basis for their new independence, this does not necessarily mean that there is real national coherence. Ethnic or religious minorities may not feel any sense of solidarity with the rest of the nation, or may not be fully accepted. A new bureaucracy may be more anxious to preserve its jobs than to encourage economic development.

Readiness to step up productivity, even to perceive the connection between such change and a higher level of living, may also lag behind economic aspirations. A rise in productivity is often viewed as harder work in the interest of the wealthy; the latter often interpret it this way themselves. Sometimes a change in the traditional organization and habits of work seems to threaten the established structure of society; factory work may tear families apart and make strangers work together in spite of different cultural traditions. An advanced method of drainage or irrigation may meet insurmountable resistance in populations that objectively need it very badly, if such a method seems to conflict with their assumptions about ancestors or marriage or life after death, or if it implies deviation of some individuals from the rest of the community, or if it tends to arouse personal insecurities in any other way. But if the spiritual leaders of the community can be either persuaded or effectively replaced in their frame-of-reference function, the same reform will find co-operation and perhaps enthusiasm.

In other words, economic development inevitably involves important changes in perception and attitudes. Unless the population concerned is convinced that the new institutions proposed, including technological innovations, are beneficial, feasible, and worth the effort in terms of social prestige as well as of material comfort, the finest airport, steel mill, or model farm will do little good. And unless people's motivation for economic action shifts accordingly—for example, from safeguarding an established level of subsistence to a drive for continuous accumulation of investment funds—the jungle may soon grow over airports, steel mills, and model farms supplied by foreign aid. To quote the International Development Advisory Board, "Development is a state of mind. People have to develop themselves before they can change their physical environment and this is a slow process. . . . Habits of thought and of conduct are the most stubborn obstacles to development."

The United Nations concluded similarly,

Economic progress will not occur unless the atmosphere is favorable to it. The people of a country must *desire* progress, and their social, economic, legal and political institutions must be favorable to it. Economic progress will not be desired in a community where the people do not realize that progress is possible. Progress occurs only where people believe that man can, by conscious effort, master nature.[53]

The United Nations study then points out that men are in general unlikely to make efforts where they cannot secure the fruit of their efforts, for example, where civil disorder is chronic. The demands of the family may discourage initiative. Private enterprise and communal property may be at odds with each other. Custom or law may prevent productive innovations. A rigid social system may deny equality of opportunity to members of certain groups, or may deny to many enterprisers the resources they need. Rapid economic progress cannot take place unless the leaders of a country at all the levels—intellectual, spiritual, economic—desire it and are willing to pay its price.

This means that economic development must not be conceived of as a purely technical enterprise. Even with adequate economic preconditions, such as financial organization, capital supply, technological advice, and foreign aid, no economic development will occur with lasting success unless the attitude of the people favors progress, initiative, enterprise, social change. The opposite is also true, of course: a favorable attitude alone will not suffice if the technique of economic development is faulty or inappropriate for the country in question.

The very fact that mankind in our period consists of so many different types and levels of economic and cultural development accounts in a large degree for the difficulties encountered in making the world livable for everybody. The remedy, however, cannot lie in any attempt to make this multitude of institutions and cultures conform to the historical experiences or contemporary predilections of one nation. The real task is to develop a kind of world that would be acceptable to all those societies that are not bent on the destruction of others. If we allow for this necessity, a variety of economic and cultural forms will be with us for all foreseeable future even if the specific kind of reform called economic development should make fast progress from now on.

The question of economic order, in the Western sense, may well turn out to be far less important than the fact of economic development itself. From the viewpoint of backward economies, both American capitalism and Russian communism are infinitely advanced in a technological sense, and both offer assistance to others in building highways, power dams, or steel plants. Both the practical and the ideological choice may depend on the degree of cultural understanding these populations expect to find in their prospective helpers. Actually future historians may conclude that the real function of totalitarian economies, in a number of hapless countries, has been a ruthless and barbaric kind of concerted capital accumulation in the interest of rapid economic development, with the help of a semiconscious mentality of aggressive nationalism.

Regardless of the economic order and ideology professed, the cultural characteristics of each population concerned are of fundamental importance in determining its response to development measures. One such cultural factor consists of the degree of what W. Arthur Lewis has called "the will to economize," that is, the will to concentrate national energies on the constant improvement of material conditions. The Hindu and Buddhist cultures, with their emphasis on ascetic or transcendental values, have not been very conducive to such concentration, while the North American culture has.

A related cultural influence has been rooted in the role and evaluation of material wealth within the general framework of values. In traditional China the way to social prestige was through learning not through wealth; in the Soviet Union it has been through Communist party activities; in the United States it has been mostly through success in business.

A third influence comes from the prevailing attitude toward material effort, especially toward work. In certain cultures work is despised altogether, or it is considered an attribute of the lower classes. This is quite clear in slave societies but is by no means confined to them. An equally important factor is the presence or absence of habits of systematic and regular work, which are not necessarily associated with the good life.

A fourth cultural influence is the evaluation of experiment, innovation, and risk-taking. Where age-old convention frowns on such behavior, economic development will meet greater resistance than elsewhere. One kind of experimentation is the search for foreign contacts and experiences, a search which is appreciated in some cultures but not in others. In cultures where the majority shows little "will to economize," a religious or ethnic minority may become the leader in economic development. The Huguenots and the Jews in

Western Europe during the seventeenth and eighteenth centuries are points in case. In other cases, however, it may be the minority that falls behind economically, for example, the French-Canadians.

A fifth factor of great importance is the cultural attitude toward "knowledge." Where all the knowledge is regarded as being comprised in past documents of tradition or religion, economic or other innovations will be considered superfluous or damaging. On the other hand, where prevailing cultural values favor the unbiased examination of new opportunities, economic development will proceed more readily.

The security feelings that are often rooted in certain traditional ways of doing things can be affected adversely by innovations no matter how superior the latter may look from an "objective" point of view. When steel axes were introduced among the aborigines of the Cape York peninsula in Australia to do the job of the traditional stone axes, only better, the group relations and the magic associated with stone axes were lost and severe social tensions and anxieties developed. Elsewhere, superior seeds or foods were rejected because the resulting flavor lacked the emotional and symbolic appeal of more traditional foods, or because the innovation seemed to destroy old group differences in nutrition such as caste privileges.

Disregard for established social relations in the community that is to be changed and improved may easily frustrate projects that are excellent from a purely technical or economic point of view. This is especially true of the effects of industrialization upon society and culture. The conversion of a peasant into an industrial worker may not only encounter difficulties of a technological type, such as change to the regular pace of work which the machines require; it may also destroy the old family ties, religious observances of the old community, services to ancestors at prescribed times, and other elements of the traditional culture. It may lead to fears and unhappiness, thus impeding economic improvements and reforms that look perfectly rational and self-evident to the outside observer or technical expert.

Entire populations or specific social groups may oppose increases in production because such increases are, rightly or wrongly, interpreted as a threat to the social function or prestige of groups that traditionally have enjoyed high status. When Europe was "underdeveloped," highly qualified handicraftsmen with a tradition of guild privileges often opposed the introduction of factory methods and mass production, and some vestiges of this opposition still remain. Elsewhere the high cultural valuation of land ownership has been an obstacle to the investment of commercial or financial gains in industry; new wealth has often been used for more land purchases, especially in Latin America, instead of being invested in industrial development based on a spirit of enterprise.

When economic development is attempted on a sizable scale despite all the problems discussed, there still is a danger of destroying established cultural values and community arrangements without replacing them, in the minds of the population affected, by other values and arrangements that it finds equally acceptable and meaningful. A vacuum is thus created in their system of beliefs; they have nothing left to believe, no standard of behavior to which to hold. They become frustrated, insecure, tense, perhaps nihilistic. Their energies are released in socially harmful ways, such as crime, alcoholism, drug addiction, gambling, or mental disturbances. The degeneration of native workers in the industrial and mining towns of South Africa, with the help of fanatic racialism, is a case in point.

All this, of course, is not an argument against economic development or any other kind of socioeconomic reform. But it shows the necessity of applying economic standards and "rational" methods from North America and Western Europe only with great caution in other areas. Only a real effort to adjust development policy to the culture, value system, and social structure of the population concerned will lead to lasting economic change for the better. Economic development, in other words, represents in large part a long-range process of attitudinal adjustment even where available techniques would objectively permit a much faster pace in our period than was possible in the past. Certain cultures, it is true, are less resistant toward economic change than others. Thrift, imitation, and systematic approaches to economic change have come easier to the culture of Japan than that of India, for instance. But the fact that a population group catches on more readily than another to advanced techniques of economic development does not necessarily mean that it will permanently retain its early advantage, or that it is intrinsically superior.

The needs and aspirations of the underdeveloped nations are in the spotlight of international economics and politics at this time, but much of what has been said on the psychological, social, and cultural bases of economic change applies equally to reform needs in more advanced countries. Serious attitudinal problems were encountered in Europe, for instance, during the productivity campaign conducted under the European Recovery Program after 1947. French farmers were reluctant to replace horses by tractors, first, because many of them took it for granted that a farmer had to have a horse anyway, and, second, because effective use of tractors, especially in small-holders' or hilly areas, was often possible only on a co-operative basis, which was at odds with their deeply ingrained individualism. Elsewhere, traditional standards of living or of group stratification, the inelastic efficiency of labor, or rigid habits of spending and saving prevented any easy change in economic methods.

Generally, therefore, cultural and group attitudes toward change constitute the crucial problem of economic reform. Clarity about this fact should not be misinterpreted as advocacy of a purely psychological treatment of people or groups without any institutional change. Sometimes such a change almost automatically molds the attitudes of the people concerned, but this is rare. Only if an attitudinal change has already taken place under the surface, will a new law provide the final shock that will bring the new attitude into the open and make the new arrangement work. In the absence of such an attitudinal change laws will often remain ineffective. In some instances, an institutional innovation may anticipate a trend and may thus promote an attitudinal change.

When traditional attitudes are deeply rooted, however, institutional programs or changes may fail altogether through disregard of such attitudes. In the early days of the debate about socialism somebody discovered one day that there could be no socialism without socialists. In a somewhat similar vein, but with converse emphasis, both Werner Sombart and Joseph A. Schumpeter suggested later that capitalism would die from a withering away of the capitalist spirit. Lags between institutions and attitudes do occur, and frequently they have dire consequences for the groups affected. However, we are mainly concerned at this point with those attitudinal changes which may lead to conscious support of needed institutional reforms. In order to overcome nostalgic traditions, any kind of economic reform must give people the feeling that it is meant and able to help *them*, that it is not designed merely to build up lifeless resources, and that the action of the people is the really decisive element of such change.

This presupposes an attitudinal readiness to listen, to re-examine habits and values, to overcome an earlier commitment to social norms of a different character, and, more generally, to recognize implicitly the historical relativity of institutions and values. Both the cultural and the personality factors that guide individuals in any given society are not always conducive to such flexibility of mind; even in relatively dynamic societies like ours the incidence of rigid personalities is always considerable.

Wherever economic changes are needed and intended, above all they will require effective action upon the leadership groups in the society concerned and, in each group, upon those individuals who provide the frame of reference for the others. If and when it is possible to unfreeze in their minds the old values, to establish and stabilize a new perception, economic reform will take place as a group procedure without arousing any serious resistance. On the other hand, it would be hopeless even with the best objective program to try "to develop an economics without people and without culture," to use Kurt Lewin's formulation.[54]

Conclusion

The third question from the Introduction can now be answered to some extent. Most people are agreed in a general way that economic conditions and arrangements can stand much improvement even in the most prosperous and advanced countries of the world, let alone that majority of populations who live in abject poverty, ignorance, and oppression. Specific attitudes toward economic reform, however, are not necessarily guided by the objective needs of a person, group, or society, nor is behavior that actually leads in the direction of reform always meant to serve such a function.

On the individual level, the configuration of attitudes and beliefs concerning socioeconomic conditions, which is summed up in the concept of ideology, depends largely on personality traits. At the same time, the incidence of specific kinds of personality is greatly influenced by the cultural and social environment of the past and present. At first sight the fact that a person becomes a conservative, a reformer, an apostate, or an indifferent seems to be rooted merely in the general structure of his personality. Socially seen, however, this structure does not come out of nowhere. It results from life experiences. Therefore the incidence of a given personality pattern mirrors the *typical* life experiences, under prevailing sociocultural conditions, of people in various societies and groups: a headhunter, a serf, a knight, an industrial worker, a farmer, or a corporation executive. Strictly individual factors may, of course, modify the influence of the group setting.

The social incidence of various kinds of personality greatly influences the prevailing patterns of either support for economic reform or opposition to it. The programs concerned, of course, usually present themselves as purely intellectual systems or as group interests of objective validity. Actually we are faced here with a conflict between belief systems to which strong emotional involvement is attached by most of their supporters. In our period, reform attitudes are more likely to center on economic issues than they used to do in the past. The reason lies in the overpowering and confusing features of a developed industrial economy, including its lack of transparence and its resulting difficulty in inspiring confidence. However, cultural and personality factors affect noneconomic types of reform also.

The central position of economic issues in our period accounts for the importance of the kind of mentality that is to prevail: a productive reform attitude oriented toward genuine economic improvement or else a destructive revolt attitude in the guise of economic programs. Some degree of genuine reform is often implicit in the existence and functioning of democratic organizations, as the history of some (though not all) labor movements shows. Through its own dynamics such a movement may provide its members with a sense of belonging and achievement, which changes their entire life experience quite aside from improvements in their material situation, which the movement may also help to produce.

On the other hand, unresolved emotional needs of people may foster a totalitarian mentality, which essentially reflects excessive personal insecurities on a mass scale even though it often rationalizes them into economic slogans. Regardless of whether such a totalitarian mentality has its starting point and frame of reference in the lower or in the middle and upper classes and whether it presents itself in the Communist, Fascist, or any other shape, its successful spread sooner or later spells the death of any genuine movement for economic reform in advanced societies.

The fact that some types of totalitarianism profess "planning" should not confuse anybody. Economic planning, an integrated type of economic reform, need not be totalitarian. Planning of a strictly democratic type, however, does raise some new problems of personality and motivation. Any democratic planning stands or falls with its degree of success in selecting nonbureaucratic yet well-organized persons for its executive functions and in producing sufficient identification, involvement, and participation on the part of the population toward the reforms undertaken.

Basically, economic reform means a specific type of attitudinal change. Such a change will succeed only if it affects the perception pattern and value scale of the people, especially through influencing their reference groups and spiritual leaders, and sometimes the group structure itself as well. This applies, in somewhat different ways, to both underdeveloped populations and more advanced ones.

It is useless to argue whether the chicken or the egg comes first here—a change in institutions or a change in attitudes. New institutions are short-lived unless they are accompanied by attitudinal change, and the latter alone will not assure any lasting reform in the absence of the right institutional framework. There may occasionally be a time lag between these two aspects of reform, but in the long run only an integration of both will produce results. New economic institutions, in particular, do not necessarily or immediately produce a new mentality as long as other determinants of the latter are not ripe for such a change. If and when this is the case, however, institutional innovations may hasten the rise of new perception patterns and values. At the same time, a new attitude toward economic issues will remain ineffective as long as resources, education, or markets are missing that would permit translation of the attitude into practice. Institutions and attitudes in the field of economics are thus in constant, though sometimes lagging, interaction. Proposals for the application of this principle on the policy level are offered in Chapter V, pages 236–237.

Economists have good reason to feel more humble today than their predecessors did some decades ago. It will be good for this discipline to realize the basic reason why people have rarely followed its prescriptions for economic improvement: these prescriptions seldom took the attitudinal and emotional dynamics of economic reform into sufficient account, thus leaving a vacuum into which totalitarians have sometimes moved only too easily.

In order to be realistic, genuine economic reform in a free society must involve productive changes in human attitudes and emotions no less than in the intellectual equipment. Sometimes, as we have said, an attitudinal shift can be greatly facilitated by prior institutional innovations. In other cases, however, it is indispensable to act first upon the perception and value scale of reference groups in the population concerned. Only after such learning processes have taken place can we expect to carry through an institutional reform effectively, no matter how justified it may be from the theorist's point of view.

In summary, the existing variety of attitudes toward economic reform, especially in societies with relatively great freedom and responsibility of the individual, largely reflects differences in perception and values. Such differences sometimes, but not always, mirror objective "interests" or the class situation. Whether a person perceives as the most important issue of economics the needs of the common man, technological progress, individual initiative, or refinements of theory, depends largely on his personality traits. The incidence of the latter, as we have said, is greatly influenced by social arrangements of the past and present including the encouragement or discouragement of nonconformist thinking.

There is no good reason to assume that most human traits are immutable and that economic institutions should be adjusted to them once for all, or that economic society reforms itself all the time anyway so that meddling can only make things worse. One of the principal tasks ahead, therefore, is to channel the emotional needs of people into productive attitudes toward reform issues and to help everyone distinguish between genuine economic requirements and pseudoeconomic rationalization of unfulfilled emotional needs. This task is especially important for modern man, who lives in a society which is both freer and more confusing than were the more rigid societies of the past.

A high incidence of strong frustrations, insecurities, and fears will make for indifference in some cases, harmless but unrealistic rationalizations in others, devastating hatreds and totalitarian propensities in still others. As long as the course of society remains free, the choice lies between these groups and the people with productive orientation —those who manage to harness the prevailing frustrations of their period and to channel them into genuine reform attitudes.

Too often in our period have unrealistic images or destructive hatreds been disguised as programs for economic reform. The nineteenth century erred in assuming, to the neglect of the emotional problems involved, that economic reform was purely a matter of intellectual persuasion. The twentieth century is up against pseudo-reform attitudes which are guided by emotional needs of a hidden and unresolved nature, to the neglect of indispensable intellectual processes. From the preceding discussion emerge certain leads to a possible integration of "economic" and "psychological" approaches to needed reforms, on the levels of analysis and policy alike. These leads are summarized in the final chapter.

Chapter V

Summary and Conclusions

ESSENTIALLY, economic processes represent a specific kind of happenings in the human mind, followed up by corresponding actions of individuals and groups, with reference mainly to material aims. Any interpretation of economic processes as purely technical manipulation of lifeless resources misses the point and results in economic ideas which have little relevance to social reality. The same applies to any concept of economic processes as the implementation of objective laws of a logical if not transcendental character, to which human behavior is inexorably subjected by outside forces.

At the same time, only a fraction of the endless variety of human personality traits, attitudes, motivations, and behavior patterns can sensibly be associated with economics—only that fraction which is focused on material wants in a broad sense, including current choices among possible satisfactions and the institutional framework for efficient handling of such choices. The border line is somewhat vague, but it exists; color perception or psychosomatics, for instance, ordinarily have little connection on the social scale with savings or investment behavior, though there may be important points of contact in a specific individual.

Psychology cannot, of course, replace economics as a method of understanding processes of production, marketing, or finance in society, and any such aspiration on the part of the psychological discipline would lead the social sciences astray. But the economic discipline can afford just as little to disregard the explorations of psychology concerning personality, perception, nonconscious processes, and communication. Nor will it do for economics to proceed separately and then merely to "apply" the finished products of psychological research.

In other words, a reconstruction of economics—which is badly needed—should at all times integrate psychological approaches with its own, without ever allowing itself to be absorbed or replaced by psychology. Economics should give up any attempt either to do without psychology or to develop an armchair psychology of its own without reference to human reality as it emerges from the empirical research of psychologists. In utilizing psychological approaches continuously in the exploration of economic processes, due allowance should be made at all times for cultural variables, which influence the prevailing patterns of personality, attitudes, motives, and behavior in each historical society. Similar considerations, of course, apply to the general need for continuous integration of economic research with that of the other social disciplines such as anthropology, sociology, and history.

With these principles in mind, the results of the preceding investigation may be summarized as follows, in an inevitably diluted way:

I. BUSINESS ACTIVITY EXPRESSES EMOTIONAL FACTORS THAT UNDERLIE THE OVERT DRIVE FOR PROFIT

1. Far from representing timeless traits of human nature or the only normal approach to economic situations, the business mentality in the contemporary American sense is a distinctly limited phenomenon in historical and geographical terms alike. Even in North America this mentality is still new and by no means universal, and in many parts of the world it is nonexistent. European capitalism, older than its counterpart in America, has thus far been more exclusive, tradition-bound, restrictionist, and exploitive than the latter.

2. Business today ranges all the way from small owner-manager

firms to the professionalized management of large corporations. The attitudes, motives, behavior patterns, and personality requirements of business vary accordingly. Although the little grocer, the farmer, and the A & P management all meet in the same market, they do so with different psychological propensities. This applies especially to long-term aspects of profit orientation, to security aims, and to expansion interests.

3. *While expected profit is usually the most immediate and conscious incentive for business activity, it is not necessarily the ultimate determinant of such activity in the psychological sense.* This is true at least above a certain minimum of family income and assets. From that point on, profit making serves largely the purpose of self-assertion and status wherever profit or money are culturally considered an important standard of success or a safeguard of security. In large corporations in our society, executives pursue profit in a professionalized way mainly for their company, not for themselves; but there, too, the desire for continuity of production, financial stability, or expansion is often more influential than a striving for immediate and definite profit, though long-range aims of profit may be involved in a more general way.

4. *Specific traits of personality including those acquired through family background and early experiences, rather than mere accident or luck, are decisive in determining who goes into business and who makes a success of it under given economic conditions.* The traits that are conducive to doing business and succeeding in it vary according to the culture and socioeconomic situation. Vanderbilt and Morgan might have remained unknown or might have failed had they been born either abroad or fifty years earlier or later in America. Specifically, paternal attitudes, creative urge, aggressiveness, or acceptance needs transformed into salesmanship may bring about business success in one society, period, or assignment, but failure in another.

5. *Economic competition, far from representing a universal propensity of man, merely expresses one kind of self-assertive need—a need which varies greatly in its intensity, forms, and manifestations according to the cultural value scale, group standard, and personality concerned.* Some societies encourage competition *outside* the economic sphere, or find noncompetitive outlets for aggressive drives.

Our own society is characterized by a network of economic rivalries—
often but not always expressed in market competition—but even here
social and ethical standards have constantly been changing.

6. *The actual conduct of business in our society is greatly influenced
by factors that underlie the overt desire for profit and money, and
sometimes by factors that are at odds with it: personality traits of
owners or executives, assertive and security needs, traditions, habits,
myths, symbols.* This applies, especially, to many decisions on industrial location, investment, pricing, and labor relations. Such factors,
of course, are often rationalized into profit considerations. The opposite process also occurs but is likely to remain closer to the surface
level.

7. *Business attitudes toward the government are often characterized
by strong emotional influences, especially resentment against the implied challenge to social leadership by business as a group.* A severe
contradiction thus develops between the frequent cry for public aid
to specific industries and the attitudinal hostility of business toward
government action in general—a contradiction which is usually subject to extensive rationalizations. In particular, many business groups
and individuals show an uneasy urge to rationalize pressure-group
demands into claims of social utility.

8. *The codes of business conduct have been changing historically,
especially in the United States; long-range considerations and social
identification and responsibility are more widespread than they were
half a century ago.* Despite the lag of language behind the social facts
on the part of defenders and critics of business alike, the actual motivation of business activity has changed considerably and it has also
become better understood. The identification of business activity with
a direct drive for short-range profit may further diminish in the future
without necessarily leading to a reduction of economic efficiency if
and when other motives for the latter become more influential.

The period of industrialization, market competition and rivalry,
financial expansion, and corporate growth has also been a period of
disastrous depressions, world wars, and inflations. Modern methods
of production and distribution brought to a rapidly increasing world
population the technological possibility of higher living standards;
in North America and a few other areas these methods succeeded in

raising the standards remarkably. Even in prosperous countries, however, security feelings have been greatly impaired by economic and political troubles, either actual or feared. Most of the people now alive have grown up in an environment that is unstable even when it is prosperous. However great may have been the economic successes of modern business methods in some countries, no basic feeling of security has followed them in the populations concerned, including the business groups themselves.

II. INSTABILITY IN ECONOMIC AND SOCIAL LIFE INTERACTS WITH THE INCIDENCE OF PERSONAL INSECURITIES

1. The development of modern industry and business forms has greatly increased the technological efficiency and living standards in some parts of the world, but only at the price of manifold new instability in economic and social life. The competitive process as such, swings from deflation to inflation and vice versa, the threat of unemployment, housing shortages, the growing problem of old-age groups, the socioeconomic effect of scientific and technological innovations, and the impact of industrialized warfare long before any actual outbreak of military hostilities have all combined to produce a general condition of instability in society, especially in economic affairs.

2. The atmosphere of confidence, which modern production and marketing require in order to reach full efficiency, is thus constantly disturbed by the instability of basic economic processes. Such a disturbance may either take place directly and consciously or it may be effective below the surface level of personality. It varies in its forms according to the social group concerned without ever being completely absent in our period.

3. The concurrent frequency of strong personal insecurities has been striking even allowing for the fact that they are often difficult to measure or to trace. The most conspicuous forms or manifestations of such insecurities are neuroses; some psychosomatic disturbances; suicides; some types of alcoholism, drug addiction, crime, accidents; family disruption including divorces; excessive job mobility; and, last but not least, the wide appeal of quacks, especially totalitarian-minded agitators.

4. Some widespread insecurities are the result of specific childhood experiences which have entered into the personality formation of

many individuals. This includes experiences that were due to the socioeconomic instability which prevailed during the formative period of these individuals. In particular, family disruption due to unemployment or uncontrolled inflation, or loss of parental prestige in the wake of economic failure, may affect deeply the personality formation of a child even though such effects may not come out into the open until much later.

5. *A general atmosphere of insecurity affects every group in society, though the upper classes are affected by it in different ways than the lower.* The latter suffer mainly from the lack of a reliable financial basis for family life and from their unsatisfactory status in society; the former may be bothered by collective guilt feelings with reference either to their responsibility for running the society or to religious and moral codes.

6. *Conformity requirements, either overt or implicit, which characterize many societies assume a confusing and disturbing effect in a society which is officially pledged to freedom of individual initiative and intellectual choice.* The expectation by such a society of voluntary, internalized conformity on the part of the individual—far beyond the indispensable phase of his initial socialization during childhood—thus contributes to the rise of personal insecurities.

7. *Value conflicts between the requirements of economic competition or rivalry and the codes of religion or ethics contribute greatly to personal insecurity.* This dilemma is exemplified by the frequency of ambivalent attitudes toward money—attitudes which are characterized by glorification and guilt feelings at the same time.

8. *Far-reaching interaction between socioeconomic instability and personal insecurity is thus indicated by impressive if incomplete evidence.* Socioeconomic instability tends to breed a wide incidence of personal insecurities, either directly or through its ultimate effects upon personality formation; and such insecurities may then backfire upon economic and social attitudes and behavior, thus making economic society even more unstable.

In the past, economic reform has been associated mainly with institutional change. Our investigation of that fateful interaction between instability and insecurity indicates that an integrated action both upon existing institutions and prevailing attitudes is required in order to make any intended reform effective and durable.

III. ECONOMIC REFORM MEANS ATTITUDINAL CHANGE

1. The attitude of an individual toward given economic institutions, and toward any alternatives to them, is related to his general ideology; the latter, in turn, reflects essential traits of his personality. At the same time, the incidence of specific kinds of personality—and thereby, ideologies and economic ideas—is greatly influenced by the cultural, socioeconomic, and group setting. In our period the decisive difference in socioeconomic attitudes stems from the prevalence of either totalitarian or democratic traits in the existing personalities.

2. Whether an individual is basically conservative, reform-minded, or indifferent depends on his degree of independence or conformity in relation to the prevailing ideology of his environment during the formative years and to his cultural and group setting. In our society such basic attitudes are likely to be focused on economic ideas because of the central position of economic happenings in our period.

3. The economic ideas of a person thus represent part of a belief system which reflects his total personality. When contrasting economic ideas are confronted, therefore, this conflict seldom takes place on the intellectual level alone; usually it involves strong emotions. These emotional traits of economic arguments, however, often remain below the conscious level, and intricate rationalization processes are frequent in such debates.

4. Among the persons whose belief systems and basic attitudes appear to favor extensive economic change, the decisive difference is that between productive and destructive orientation, between reform and revolt. Genuine reform attitudes emphasize concrete and realizable goals; a revolt attitude, on the other hand, is basically (though often unconsciously) directed against everything and everybody, especially the rebel's own self. The real yardstick is not in institutional programs but in attitudinal traits.

5. In labor movements, both types of basic attitude have been known to exist. The conflicts among and within labor organizations in various countries, especially those of Europe, have largely reflected this attitudinal difference between reform and revolt. In both cases, it is true, organization as such has often raised the worker's feelings of belonging and self-assertion and has thus in a sense meant economic reform. In the United States the labor movement has traditionally disavowed any reform aims on the conscious level but has actually promoted far-reaching changes of an economic and psychological character, both among its members and in the national economy.

6. *Totalitarian mentalities of both the left-wing and right-wing varieties have often used pseudo-labor or pseudo-reform slogans in order to rationalize deeper emotional needs—needs for an all-embracing, exclusive creed which would relieve those affected of otherwise unbearable fears and insecurities.* Although the totalitarian mentality of today tends to appear in the guise of programs for economic reform, it actually represents a substitute religion of a primitive and barbaric type. This applies equally to Communist and anti-Communist (or ex-Communist) types of totalitarian mentalities. They are all closely related to each other psychologically despite important differences in their social roots and despite violent quarrels on the verbal level. An essential task of our generation is to replace totalitarian propensities of all kinds by genuine striving for needed reforms.

7. *Historically some types of economic planning have been connected with totalitarianism, but other types are compatible with democratic institutions. In all cases, however, economic planning involves distinct problems of personality, motivation, and incentives— not merely institutional adjustments.* This is true regardless of the degree of private ownership that is preserved. Economic planning differs from other types of reform in that it attempts to integrate new measures with one another and with existing institutions. If such planning is to be both democratic and realistic, it presupposes planners and policies that constantly take into account the cultural traits, attitudes, motives, and community patterns of the population affected. The actual selection of executive personnel, however, depends on the political groups in power and the social forces behind them.

8. *Generally, any kind of intentional economic change must be based on awareness of the prevailing value scales, perception patterns, and motivational processes in order to promise success.* This applies especially to that great assignment of our period, the economic progress of underdeveloped areas. It is no less true of other fields of

international aid. No one prescription for economic development is applicable to every culture and population group. The greatest improvements in technology may do more harm than good unless they are accompanied by understanding of the attitudes and motives affected.

What does this investigation add up to? Not by any means to a general theory of economic psychology. The intellectual aspiration of this book is far less ambitious. Not only have essential areas of this new discipline unavoidably been omitted from the discussion altogether—industrial relations and consumer motivation, for instance— but the author feels no more ready to present any such theory than do most other researchers right now. He is also uncertain whether the disciplines concerned have cleared the way toward it sufficiently at this juncture.

In particular, no attempt can be made here to decide the respective merits of the various approaches to psychology, or to integrate these approaches. At this point several schools of psychological thought can make important contributions to the understanding of economic processes: the Gestalt psychology through its concept of a psychological "field," its studies in perception and learning, and its level-of-aspiration theory; analytic psychology through its exploration of unconscious factors and rationalizations, of the range and meaning of "irrational" behavior, and of the impact of early childhood experiences upon personality; biopsychology through the elaboration of psychophysical connections, especially the effect of physical conditions (such as nutrition) upon the human mind; and various studies in communication and information through their applications to the economic scene.

Despite the methodological limitations mentioned, some conclusions and suggestions on essential tasks of psychological approaches to economics may be ventured in the interest of further research and analysis. The essential principle indicates, above all, that fundamentally human beings do not function differently in their economic roles than they do in other life situations. Their economic actions under certain objective conditions are guided by the general drives of man supplemented by the specific traits of their own personalities. The incidence of specific personalities in a given society is interconnected with the prevailing pattern of perception and values, the education process, and the economic institutions of that society. Analytic isolation of "economic" behavior can be a useful device only as long as it is not at odds with known psychodynamic traits of man, and as it avoids unhistorical generalizations to the neglect of the cultural, institutional, and psychological diversity that has characterized people and societies.

The kind of generalizations that economic analysis *can* hope to develop with fruitful results concerns human action in one kind of situations—those involving decisions on material factors mainly. In other words, it is the type of situation that distinguishes economic actions from other actions, not the basic psychodynamics underlying individual or group actions in general. In addition, economic analysis can elaborate through logical deduction a set of normative rules that can be applied *if and when* people desire to stress material goals of action, to the possible neglect of others. To this extent there is room for economic analysis as a discipline of its own; but such analysis should complement psychological theory, not try to supersede or disregard it.

This is not the place to attempt a reformulation of the functions of economic analysis, but any such attempt should allow for the following distinctions: first, between those economic actions that are actually based on "economic" motives in the conventional sense and those that are guided by "noneconomic" motives but lead to similar results; second, between both of these kinds of actions and "noneconomic" or "nonrational" actions in economic situations; third, between different *degrees* of rationality, and between different thresholds of economic decisions, depending on the psychological structure of the individuals and groups concerned; fourth, between four main levels of economic generalization: (a) human traits of really universal character, (b) a more limited cultural setting, scale of values, and basic personality, (c) a still more limited socioeconomic order, framework of historical institutions, and stratification, and (d) even more specific, situational constellations; and, fifth, between generalizations derived from any of these four levels of experience and purely normative propositions derived from hypothetical assumptions that are carried through by logical processes, without any necessary aspiration to be related to social reality.

In the last case mentioned, *any* kind of psychological assumption is permissible in a country with free speech—conscious or unconscious, explicit or implicit, close to reality or incompatible with it. Analysis on this level becomes an exercise in intellectual gymnastics, which can claim to help in the formal training of the mind but not necessarily in the understanding of economic life. If any other approach to economic analysis is chosen, however, the relations between economics and psychology must be resolved in a different manner. In the psychological assumptions of economic analysis no less than in other assumptions, abstraction and hypothesis are valid procedures for specific purposes—especially for the formulation of testable propositions—whenever the abstraction is clean-cut and genuine, and whenever the hypothesis is a temporary tool that is not from the outset incompatible with reality or confounded with it. Even so, no practical conclusions or predictions should ever be attempted on this level of analysis. Only by introducing at the earliest possible point all the known data of sociohistorical factors, effective motive forces, and attitudinal and cultural variations can the hypothetical procedure of analysis be gradually converted for practical uses, especially predictions.

In Western societies it has often been assumed that the ordinary market behavior of people and, especially, the regular profit orientation of businessmen represent a fairly close approximation to the conventional "rationality" postulates of economic theory. Any such assumption looks extremely dubious in the light of psychological evidence. Every person on the contemporary economic scene—the owner manager, the corporation executive, the farmer, the worker, the union officer, the consumer, the saver, the investor—now emerges as an extremely complex figure whose attitudes, motives, and behavior vary from culture to culture, from society to society, from period to period, and from individual to individual.

Every one of the groups listed is deeply affected—not necessarily in the same way—by the socioeconomic instability that characterizes our period and by the high incidence of strong personal insecurities that goes with it. The reactions of individuals and groups to a given economic situation (for example, to consumer prices, the labor market, or investment opportunities) are thus greatly influenced by underlying factors of economic instability and personal insecurity and not merely by considerations of profit orientation or financial gain, though the latter influences are more likely than the former to stand out on the conscious level.

It is a vital assignment of reform in our period to help break the vicious circle of socioeconomic instability and personal insecurity. Reform should also help society to utilize such norms of efficient behavior as economic analysis offers. This is true even of countries that have managed to keep improving their productive and distributive efficiency with the help of natural wealth and resourceful initiative. It is a thousand times more true of that great majority of countries which, with archaic tools, have been trying to support an ever-growing population under the constant shadow of hunger, disease, and war.

Certain policy implications emerge from the preceding analysis of vital psychological aspects of contemporary economic life. In order to promise success, genuine economic reform in most Western societies today needs to combine the following institutional and attitudinal factors, with local variations according to culture, history, social structure, and resources:

Living levels which—despite inevitable differences according to productivity and cultural standards—always bear a clean-cut relationship to contemporary advances in technology and managerial organization, thus holding out hope for families in every population group of a desirable future for their children.

Facilities for health and education which suffice to establish the necessary framework for an ever rising productivity and, at the same time, to increase both the life space and the life energy of the people.

A real home for everybody or, at last, concrete hope for it as a result of housing policies which provide safe tenure and encourage the feeling of being settled or able to find a desirable home.

Economic stability to the extent of making people feel safe from any uncontrollable threat of runaway depressions or inflations, from bankruptcy waves, mass unemployment, or extreme poverty. Such provisions would include public and private policies designed to cushion business cycles; adequate social-security legislation; safeguards of minimum real income; and a declared responsibility of organized society to prevent excessive fluctuations in economic activity.

An atmosphere of equal opportunity, social mobility, and attention for individual initiative regardless of an individual's origin or status.

Diversity of recognized incentives for economic efficiency including pecuniary rewards and social recognition along with an appeal to personal satisfaction from worth-while work well done.

Conception of property as one tool of personal satisfaction among many, not as self-purpose.

Recognition of competition through actual performance as a valid method of self-assertion, in contrast to the kind of rivalry that aims at monopolistic exclusion of others.

Interpretation of occupational choice and activity as a way of life and a function in society, not as an undesirable burden, even though the range of choices and activities is inevitably narrower for some persons than for others.

Opportunity for enjoyment of work by most people resulting from real assurance regarding the specific social function and value of their contribution—not from mere rationalizations—along with sensible and satisfying patterns of leisure.

An old-age way of life which combines lessened material strain with continued voluntary activity and feelings of social utility.

Encouragement of co-operation on various levels of community life as a means of meeting people's needs for acceptance, status, and a feeling of belonging.

Technology harnessed to serve clearly human progress and happiness, not dark uncontrollable destruction.

Mobilization of warlike national energies and social coherence for *peacetime* goals; elimination of images of external threat as the only cement of national unity.

Feeling of co-responsibility for the well-being of other nations along with respect for the culture and history of each of them.

A great amount of research will be required to work out the specific features of reforms that are psychologically suitable for the various populations which need them as soon as possible. More studies will be necessary in order to put the policy decisions of the future— especially those of international impact—on a firmer basis of psycho-economic analysis than is available to our generation.

A hopeful beginning toward such analysis has been made by the investigations of the Survey Research Center and other institutions in such areas as the behavior of consumers, savers, and investors in contemporary American society. There is additional need for data and analyses which will be applicable to other populations over time and space, and which will thus permit broader generalizations than are possible today. Specifically, the following assignments, in addition to the tasks that were discussed in the preceding chapters (namely, research in business motivation, in the interaction between economic instability and personal insecurity, and in the attitudinal aspects of economic reform), await exploration by economic psychology during the years to come.

a. The business cycle: What kind of fluctuation? The economic processes of shrinkage and expansion that go with business fluctuations have now been subjected to minute research. It has brought out the great diversity of events that combine to form what looks to the *post-hoc* observer like cycles even though no two of them really resemble one another very much. Little reliable information, however, is available on the psychic processes that go with each of these fluctuations and that conceivably might be at the root of the whole historical phenomenon of business upswings and downswings.

What happens in the mind of investors and traders in the course of a stock-market panic? To what extent do such reactions (and optimistic or pessimistic expectations in general) mirror objective economic conditions such as a previous decline in industrial orders or a rise in inventories? Under what psychological conditions has the spread of such information an upsetting effect? In what concrete ways do rumors affect the markets, and what, in general, is the mechanism of communication in business life during cyclical turning points?

What makes investors and consumers, en masse, change their perception of the economic situation, and how much of a shock effect is required for such an attitudinal change? We cannot take it for granted that objective information alone is the basis of such shifts. What is the mechanism of fluctuations in "confidence" and what goes on in the minds of those affected by changes in it? What is the role of personality variables and cultural differences in these processes? To what extent does a great incidence of personal insecurities backfire upon economic life, thus increasing its propensity to fluctuate? In what ways does government action exert a stabilizing effect, not only directly through its financial effects but by providing a new framework for expectations and, perhaps, a feeling of paternal protection?

What attitudinal changes concerning the economic role of the government have occurred in various populations as a result of the Great Depression, war-born inflation, or new means of public information and communication? Some spadework has been done on many of these questions, but it awaits supplementation and integration.

b. Consumer motivation and behavior. This field has been studied in considerable detail, especially in the annual Surveys of Consumer Finances. There is much room, however, for research in additional directions. This applies, especially, to cultural variations in consumer preferences, which may lead to greater expenditures on food, for example, in one country and on housing elsewhere, despite similar income structures. The relative intensity of consumer wants, and the attitudinal roots of shifts in consumer preferences are likewise an important object of investigation in the interest of a foolproof theory of consumption.

The symbolic meaning of specific commodities to individuals, groups (for example, immigrants or religious minorities), or entire populations has seldom been explored systematically. There is also the entire area of group standards, role expectations, and status needs as they apply to consumption patterns. This includes the actual range of conspicuous consumption and of ascetic attitudes in various populations and groups. Finally, the psychological influence upon consumption patterns of the historical increase both in leisure time and in life expectation in many countries awaits more specific research.

c. Farmer versus peasant. It is widely known that the North American farmer differs in his economic behavior from the European or Asian peasant; the farmer is less tradition-bound, more businesslike, more market-minded. However, the attitudinal and motivational processes in each case need detailed investigation. In particular, land yields and farm prices do not "behave" according to rigid laws; it is people who behave in certain ways, and not necessarily in the same way under all conditions.

What is the emotional and symbolic meaning of land tenure in various rural populations? In what ways does this meaning influence the real-estate business, mortgages, inheritance, mobility, and occupational change from agriculture to industry or vice versa? Is the strong psychological and, thereby, political position of agrarian blocks in various countries due in any degree to the emotional (as well as the physical) connotations of food? To what extent is the mentality of either peasants or farmers, under varying cultural conditions, similar to that of businessmen and to what extent are they guided by a consumer mentality? All these questions await full investigation even though much scattered material is available.

d. Labor attitudes and types of labor movements. It is now widely recognized that earnings are not the only incentive to work—at least, to effective work. However, the exact relationship of work incentives to the income level, assets, and standard of living, to group norms and cultural value systems remains to be explored. Is there anything approaching Veblen's "instinct of workmanship," and if so, under what sociocultural and psychological conditions does it exist?

The psychic effects of prolonged unemployment have been examined to some extent, but here, too, there is need for further research. The area of studies in industrial morale and productivity now commands an impressive literature; at this point, however, far more of it is on a company scale than on the level of a general theory. Clinical psychology and psychotherapy can contribute much to research on the impact upon the labor market of work compulsions, occupational neuroses, and emotional inability to work for money.

The psychological patterns of the labor movement in various countries could be explored more fully, though there is a huge literature on specific aspects of labor organization. Labor movements range all the way from those with a pressure-group mentality and short-run emphasis to those with a missionary attitude of social revolution. In both extremes—and in the various intermediate forms—the overt aims usually offer a very incomplete picture of the actual psychodynamics of the movement. Group solidarity, organization as a self-purpose—in helping many individuals who need self-assertion and status—and personality factors in labor leadership likewise can stand much further research.

e. The psychology of international economic relations. The conspicuous failure of the industrial age to achieve an international division of labor, the frustration of many hopes for free trade and exchange, and the tenacity of protectionism can no longer be attributed merely to the aftereffects of wars or to the intellectual inability of people to learn the teachings of nineteenth-century economists. Research is needed on the emotional elements that are implicit in tariffs, the paternalistic factors in protectionism, and the monetary speculation process insofar as it appraises the value of foreign exchange on the basis of general hopes or fears. These research needs apply especially to the behavior of individuals and groups toward domestic goods and services compared with those of foreign origin. Some nations are more willing to give their products away for nothing than to accept foreign products in return. Economic analysis of such experiences needs integration with sociopsychological approaches.

Such integration is of particular importance in the entire field of studies concerned with the economic advancement of underdeveloped areas. Experiences with a purely technical approach to this problem have not been very encouraging. The best machines, seeds, chemicals, or information are ineffective if they are used in the wrong way (or not at all) once they have been supplied; in other words, if the motivation and perceptual readiness to learn their proper use are missing, or if such use seems to conflict with traditional values of the population concerned. In order to promise success, action for economic development requires applied knowledge of social norms, group dynamics, and cultural processes.

In each area of research, economic analysis should continuously utilize psychological explorations and findings on the formation and patterns of personality, on perception and the "field" in which it operates, on attitudes and motive patterns, on levels of aspiration, on the types and processes of decision making, on rationalizations, on the impact of unconscious factors upon behavior, and on the range and exact meaning of nonrational influences in facing economic situations.

Aside from the contributions that psychological approaches as such can make, several related disciplines in the social sciences should also be continuously consulted by economists in their search for an understanding of actual economic processes. Sociology and the intermediate discipline of social psychology have explored rather widely the area of social norms and group dynamics. The effect of political and ideological pressures upon economic decisions cannot be fully understood without such approaches, nor can industrial and administrative processes. Cultural anthropology now uses psychological or psychoanalytic methods on a considerable scale; it thus helps to put economic research into proper perspective by illuminating the types and differences of reality systems, projective processes, and value scales in various populations. This will help to prevent new attacks of the hidden ethnocentrism which has been so frequent in the history of economic thought. Finally, econometrics can be utilized in determining the extent to which behavior in economic situations, with its underlying attitudes and motives, can be measured and quantified.

To carry through these suggestions would involve a far-reaching re-examination of the entire approach to economic research that has prevailed in recent decades. But such an integration of economics with psychology and related disciplines is well worth the effort. It will help to make economics a more realistic and socially useful discipline than it has been in the past. It will increase greatly the contribution of economics to the understanding of man and his society, in the interest of continuous improvement in the condition of both.

Personal Factors
in Industrial Location

THE following statements, which stress various kinds of personal factors in the location of industries, were selected from a survey of industrial mobility in Michigan that was undertaken by the Survey Research Center in late 1950. It should be emphasized that this selection was made from a total sample that also included a great number of purely "economic" reasons given. On page 66 it was pointed out that rationalizations in both directions should be allowed for. Even so, many of the statements quoted have great illustrative value. The statements are divided into four groups according to the type of personal factor stressed, but some of the statements overlap inevitably.

1. Family Reasons and Community Belonging

Our transportation facilities in Michigan are certainly an advantage to every manufacturer in the state. . . . Outside of that, though, I'd say we are here because we are Michigan people, we like the state, we like living here and we are carrying on a tradition. . . . And I hope that someday I'll turn over the business to my son.

It's a great state to live in. Nice people, good recreation facilities. Nice little towns. And of course, we feel good about living here where my father started his business. It really gives us a big kick to look out at the little place where he started this business. This plant, you know, just grew like Topsy. Started in, and never stopped. Before we knew it, there'd be more business and we'd need more room. We're kinda sentimental about the place, and the business, and my father, too. . . . We could do business any place, but we're happy here, so we're not going to move.

I told you we're sentimental. So are other people, even if they don't admit it. Personal reasons certainly can swing a decision any day, provided you feel strongly enough one way or the other.

Well, one thing I think would enter into it is the fact that my father founded the firm here. I've lived here all my life and my people back a hundred years or more. You don't just brush those things off and move without some very serious reasons.

Personal reasons would enter into it. I wouldn't want to move far away from my home town. In fact I wouldn't want to move out of it at all. I spent 20 years in Detroit and was glad to get back home to X. But we would certainly not consider moving out of Michigan. We'd all have personal reasons against that. We all prefer to work in this state and preferably in X.

I believe there should be pretty close harmony among the various manufacturers in a town or community. [Why?] It gives you a better feeling, and it gives you a feeling of close fellowship. That's an important factor, but I don't think it has anything to do with production.

We'll stay right here. We'll move nothing. We're an institution here. . . . In a way, it's an asset to us to stay here and carry on the tradition, I guess.

Now you take this town. Before I came here, this town didn't want any new industries. I found them downright discouraging. . . . But I came here anyhow. Of course, I didn't get into the town, but I'm just as well off here, right where I am. . . . Those men are my friends, today. They'd come out here to work for me. They've told me so. And the town has changed toward me, too. Just lately, they have organized a Chamber of Commerce, and they asked me to join. I did, too. And they made me very welcome. Now, they want to bring other industries into the town. I feel very proud of that, because I think I had something to do with it. We spend money and we are quiet and respectful to them. All we want is their good will, and we want them to respect us, too. And today, I think they do. Else, would I be a member of the Chamber of Commerce?

We would like to be in a small town. We would prefer to be the one big industry in the town. We would like a town which needs industry, for that would mean the people would appreciate the cooperation and the contribution of the company. We'd like to let the community build around us, let the town get a new start, new life, new vigor.

We have a population of 1650 here. That's a good town for a business like ours. Not too much competition for labor, and it gives us a chance to fit into the townlife more, too. We know everybody in town, and they know us. We all work together, and it works out fine for everyone. If we were going to move, I think our firm would hunt for another town like this one, because they are so pleased with our results here.

I'd have to be welcome, or I wouldn't go into a town. Matter of fact, I'd want more than a welcome. They'd have to coax me a little bit. That way, I'd be sure of their friendship to start with, and I'd try and be worthy of it. I know this company can help a town. We've done it right here. This town has very few old-age claimants. We use them, if they are able to work at all. The town appreciates our giving them work, the people are happy and earning their own keep, not on a dole—and I'm happy because they do good work. So you see it's a great situation, no matter how you look at it. And that would be true of any place we moved. Only it takes time to know people and get them to know you. So if you are welcomed when you move into the town, that helps a lot. Makes things move faster.

Well, I guess I'll have to tell you again that I'm an egotist. The attitude of the community toward a new plant wouldn't scare me. I'd take my chances. I have found very often that resistance to any new industry arises just because of a misunderstanding. When we want to move into a town we go around and see the business organizations, the exchange club, the local politicians and the School Board. So far we have been able to sell ourselves so that when the plant was opened, we were very welcome. But you notice that we do all this before we actually make the move. We don't let misunderstandings stand. We try to be honest with the townspeople, and we expect them to be honest with us. We cooperate with them, and so far, they have cooperated with us all the way.

You can't tell anything about what productivity you are going to get from the people of this town or that town. It all depends on the relations between the company and the workers and the town. It's a three-way figure. A company can be good to the workers, but not cooperative in town matters, and it won't get as much productivity as if it is good to the employees and the town. That's psychology. Got to make the people happy while they're working, but you got to make them proud to be able to say they work for the company, too.

Nobody wants to leave home. I'd hate to leave X. Our real money wouldn't leave Detroit. I'd rather live in a satisfied community than make money.

If it becomes too bad, I'll close up shop and quit. There'll be no moving.

We came here because we wanted to stay in Michigan—our homes are here and all our families wanted to stay in the home state. Michigan is Michigan.

Our business is established here. We've been here 113 years. We can't throw that away and go where we're unknown.

2. *Liking the People, Way of Life, Town, or State*

Friendliness. Friendliness, start with—start at the top with the state governor and have it permeate right on down through the mayors and city councils. Friendliness.

We like a small town—that's why we came here. We have no wish to make this town any larger. Solid growth, we believe, is healthier than fast abnormal growth which upsets housing, taxes, schools and employment in any community.

I would say that I wouldn't want to see any industry come into the State if it would bring a lower laboring class with it. [Lower laboring class?] Foreign elements. There are very few of them here. [Why not?] Oh, we'd better skip that. I think you know.

We like Y. We still like it, much as it has deteriorated by the 10,000 bad-class Negroes and such. . . . Intrinsically, I told you I am a hick. I feel one can live a more nearly normal life in a small town.

Michigan has a lot of small industrial cities where people live, work, and are contented and happy. Take a pattern from those cities. We like a small town because the people are friendlier. Appreciate a job, and being treated like they were important. Small-town people don't go for agitators or troublemakers. But don't let any big industry go into a small town. There you'd change the character of the town, and you'd spoil it, both for the townspeople and for the manufacturer.

We would look for a medium sized town—a good town that had some religion in it.

It was on top of the American migration from New England and New York with a mixture of French Canadian and Southerners. It was largely Hollanders and Scandinavians. It was a hell of a good populace. I had been living in Chicago and I didn't like it. I am intrinsically a hick. Y. is not as desirable now, because of laborers brought in by the foundries, the southern Europeans, Mexicans, Negroes during the second World War, and the first World War, too, to some extent. They don't amount to much. They are minor offenders, all of them, and there are the poor whites.

I think it's about the right-size town—not too much dirty politics, not too much unionism; a good town to bring up a family and it has enough available mill supplies so you don't have to depend on Chicago or Detroit too much.

But living is cheaper, too, and the Country Clubs—you can belong to all the clubs in the Valley for the price of one in Cleveland. So that's the way it balances out.

Well, we like a small town for our business. Like the attitude of people in these small towns. Like the fishing and the chances for recreation for ourselves and for our workers, too. Now you take this section of Michigan. There are 115 lakes in this area. Good fishing, camping, bathing, fun. Schools in Michigan are good, too. Now, we don't really have enough schools in this section to say those facilities are really ideal. But what we have is good, and some day we'll have more of it. And we can get our materials in here easy and we can get our finished products out of here, don't forget.

Well, anything up to 20,000 is best for us. The smaller the town the better for us provided the help is available. [Why?] Hm-m, now maybe I can't answer that! Well, I think most industries prefer to operate in a smaller city if their other requirements are there. There is much less chance for labor trouble because the radical labor tends to be in the large cities. Transportation to and from work for your workers is simpler in a small place. It's just simpler living in a relatively small place. We sell on a national basis so it isn't important to be in a large city from the market standpoint.

In the main I think our climate makes working conditions perfect. For instance, the lack of that extended heat spell that some areas have. It's a known fact that a man can think better in a comfortable climate. They're much more alert in this part of the country than where it's hot and muggy. You can't do as good work mentally or physically farther South where it's humid. Michigan should boost up the fact of the leisure-hour advantages of employees and there's a lot of it with an eight-hour five-day week. . . . For at least six months of the year, our people are right on the threshold of the best of recreational facilities. All right, you got to keep your employees happy to make them do a good job. The leisure-hour welfare of its employees is becoming more of a major factor with all employers. Good leisure activity makes better workers.

We feel that if you expand too fast, you lose productivity. But if you operate at a steady rate and stop turnover, you get good productivity. We feel that you have to use psychology on your workers.

The size and character of the town is very important. We're in business to make money, but we also are living. I personally, and I know the boys here unless they are happy no amount of money can make any difference. [Why?] They are happier—just happier. They are more efficient if they are, and I think they will live longer.

The size of the town is of no importance whatever but the character is. [How is that?] Well, to go back to your availability of skills—if we have the skilled people in the town, it's o.k. The size alone is not important. The availability of labor is important. [Why is character of town important?] Well, because good housing, plenty of good schools, playgrounds and, in general, good living—that's all important, very important. [Why?] Because they are important to the character of the community as a whole. Happy people stick to their work so it is important to have good houses, playgrounds, etc. . . . We have to live in the community and we want good relations with people around us. However, I would rather have a good attitude from our employees than from the other business men! They're the ones who do the work for us.

It's a better place to live—if I can give that reason for the executives and the men. It is a *very* important reason. I wouldn't go back to Cleveland or New York on a bet! When I think of spending all that time going back and forth —now it takes five minutes from my house to my office. And the same with the Country Club and the Yacht Club. You have much more time to live and I think that's better.

I'd want to move to a small town. Not over 2500 people. Where the people were mostly farmers. Those people are happy. They're contented. They have peaceful lives. They appreciate the chance to earn some money. They give you a day's work for your money. They are sincere, and honest. The kind of people you like to deal with. That's the real American life—not the mixed-up mess you find in the big cities today.

3. Security Needs, Resentment, Inertia

We all have our likes and dislikes. And if we were considering a new plant, I'm sure that all the personal attitudes would be aired and considered before any final decision was made.

Whether to move the plant or change the product? [Yes. Laugh.] It would be an *awful* thing to do either one. I don't know. Oh, I would say—I don't know what to say on that—that's *really*—I would say about 50-50. It would be a terrible thing to do either one. Some people have done it, but I would probably say changing the plant would be the lesser of two evils.

We would change or adjust our product. [Why?] We don't run away from problems. We'd stick and fight it out.

We've not thought of moving, so we've never bothered to find out. If you find out about taxes in Alabama—so what? We're stuck with it here. It seems to me that these questions are directed to smaller firms who could move. We can't and so we're stuck here.

Very serious disadvantages in the labor rates. I can tell you that if I weren't a native of this state and already in business here, I'd never consider coming to Michigan to go into business.

I know that if I was on the outside looking in I would think a hell of a long time before coming in. This radical labor would scare hell out of me. All you read about is strikes and labor trouble.

My experience is that there is a certain way to handle men. In most cases it's the fault of the firm if they have trouble with the men and with the union. It's the way you behave as well as the way the men behave that is important.

They would *not* be in favor of bringing in an industry that would employ a lower type of labor. We have a pretty good class of worker. But in —— they've brought in an awful lot of Negroes. But we wouldn't go for that— but a good class—yes.

We didn't want a town where too many colored people have been brought in, by the way. That was the reason a couple of other towns in Indiana were discarded early in the plans. Those men were brought up from the South to work during the war, and after the war, they stayed in the towns. Somehow, it hasn't worked out very well. We thought we'd rather avoid the problem, if we could.

Some of the people in this line are drifting to the South. [Why?] I don't know, but I think it's for better labor conditions. As a matter of fact, we've been thinking of it ourselves. . . . The union agitation here, and the radical elements, and the government attitude starting at the city hall and going all the way up to Washington, and through Lansing [Attitude?] Anti-free enterprise. I'm not talking from hearsay. I've been in the thick of it for 15 years. [How does it show up?] From the standpoint of the labor boards whether state or national—they are too far pro-labor. You get a hearing just like you're being tried for insanity, and it's the same result every time. There's no difference, so why the hearing? Business has no representative on the boards. [Other reasons?] No. There might be a few minor ones, but those are offset by the advantages of staying here.

I think we'd be very careful of the town we'd go into. We'd go into the background of the town, the general religious outlook of the people. [Why?] I find it has a steadying effect on the people, and labor conditions are less likely to be disrupted, and there is practically no violence. There is a great deal of pride in keeping up their homes and property, and they dress their children well. There is a greater opportunity in a town like that to work in partnership with your employees than in a town that was a hard-bitten town. . . . Then, of course, the state and city tax situation, I suppose. Their attitude toward new industry, particularly toward new industry of our type. I don't mean we expect to be given everything—just that we be given consideration and the hope that we would prosper and be of value to the community. . . . I have the uneasy feeling about our present state government as far as taxes are concerned. I certainly have an uneasy feeling concerning the federal government. We've been able to grow and prosper, but it's a very difficult thing to plan and hold the ground that's gained. I don't think anyone minds paying taxes they could afford to pay. The important thing is—that those taxes are used effectively and soundly and that is not always done. That is where resentment is. [What about the attitude of the people?] That's awfully important. We've got a nice little plant and a wonderful spirit. A high percentage of the men are good men, and they have stuck with us. We've had a high labor turnover here, but with men who are floaters. When we came here there were about 7 to start with, and we gradually built that up and the fellows could see, after a year, a great deal of progress. . . . They began to be proud to be with us. With the reputation this plant had before, they were ashamed of it and had to apologize for us that first year. Now that has decreased, and the people in town are beginning to respect us.

4. Investment versus Caution

When a thing like this hits the country, no one can tell where it is going to lead. People of all grades accept the stories in advertising. They believe anything. . . . Got to give them a chance to try this new material, and learn for themselves about it. But it may have a big effect on my business, if it goes over big. Again, though, it may not cut in. . . . I'll get along, I guess. Maybe business will be better than ever, I really don't know.

Scarcely a month goes by but that we need additional working capital for a short period. Strangely enough, we've found out local financing puts you on your toes. I would have to have complete confidence in the bank however. [Why?] I mean in the character of the bank president and the men we would confide in. We'd be telling them our operations in our plant. They would know our financial conditions. There have been unscrupulous dealings in the past. We could be thrown into bankruptcy and squeezed unless the men were interested and cooperative with us.

We don't depend on "financing"—we don't go after it. [Why?] It's just a personal opinion. We like to feel even if we don't have a big plant it's ours. We have a feeling of security that *we* own it and not the finance company. We are often told we are foolish and that we shouldn't feel that way about borrowing money. We just feel more secure. We will be more satisfied to expand when finances are available.

A business like ours is very highly competitive, and any future profits depend on what any item adds to the basic costs, even as to pennies. As my father says, "We're in business for the fun of it, but there's no fun in it if you don't make any money."

We follow the policy of self-containment. If that means anything to you. [Not much right now.] This is a family-owned industry. No stock is owned by outsiders, and therefore business in general has been satisfactory to the owners and they haven't tried to expand, to spread themselves out and sell stock. It is a personal attitude and hasn't anything to do with the climate, the state, or anything else. We've weathered a couple of depressions by having money in the bank, our feet on the ground, and by not being spread all over the territory.

We are constantly expanding. After the war ended we were faced with a decision. We knew we had to sink a lot of money in this plant or we had to give up. We're not going to give up. So we had to expand. We had to buy new equipment. We had to modernize. We had to introduce new ideas. . . . When my father started out here, he had just that one little building you see out there. He expanded a lot, but we've been carrying on for him, too. We intend to be able to expand, so we want the land. Remember what I said about zoning, though? The people who built houses up in this section had the railroad running through, but they didn't expect that this plant would spread until they were really living in the factory grounds. So we decided we didn't want to have them think we were spoiling their properties. We went to them and told them we planned to expand over the years, and we offered to buy the houses so we'd have the land, and they could think about where they were going to build their new homes. Most of them took us up on the offer.

I told you that our one idea is to bring out something new and radically different at least once in two years so that the women will feel they have to have new window hardware. That's what this business is built on. We're at it all the while.

We hope to make many changes. I'm scouting all the time for new ideas. Trying to make the women feel they are old-fashioned and have to change. We'll keep bringing out new ideas or old ideas, but we'll go after the business. We have to get our share of the money that is around. You see we've discovered over the years that we're about one year behind on booms and busts. If business booms, in about a year we feel the results of the boom. If it busts, then we're good for one more year of good business before it hits us. So we're pushing the market now, and will push it. And just when the bust comes, then we'll put out a radically different idea.

Appendix II

The Case of Mrs. X

THE person referred to in this statement underwent prolonged psychotherapeutic treatment for a disorder diagnosed as character neurosis, in this case an obsessive character with compulsive ambivalent attitudes toward money, work, art, and men. This disorder resulted in severe conflicts with recurrent states of anxiety, fear of failure or rejection, spells of depression, rather heavy drinking with aggressive and even violent behavior, and severe guilt feelings and inferiority complexes, especially with reference to the opposite sex and to her children.

The written materials on which the following statement is based were made available to me with all the identification marks removed. The identity of the persons concerned is thus unknown to me.

One need not be a social scientist in order to notice immediately the enormous importance of socioeconomic codes and value systems in the personality development of the patient. This, however, should not be interpreted as an invitation to neglect any other factors in her personality. We cannot hope to resolve here the question as to what extent socioeconomic factors may have had a conditioning, rather than a determining, effect in this case and to what extent such factors may have served merely to express or mirror disturbances of an essentially personal nature, which might have found other outlets in a different social atmosphere. In other words, in any individual case we need to beware of socioeconomic overdetermination no less than of the traditional neglect of such factors. With this qualification in mind, the case of Mrs. X certainly provides a striking example of the interaction discussed.

1. *The Value Standing of Money*

Mrs. X was brought up in an environment in which attitudes toward money were definitely "guilt-charged." Father was a society painter and mother also had artistic interests. The patient likewise became an artist and so did her two sisters. In the family atmosphere, money was not to be spoken of, the implication being that such mentioning of an essentially sinful thing was almost obscene. Only part of this attitude could be explained by the fact of lost family wealth, although Mother did start nagging each time financial decline made headway. The effects of this attitude upon Mrs. X were far-reaching. She speaks of a "financial neurosis," which she connects in part with posing for her father's paintings without being paid. The assumption was that the child-parent relationship was "priceless" anyway, especially in terms of the "sinful" money; but the child was sufficiently influenced by the prevailing market-exchange standards to feel gypped by her father.

This conflict between theory and practice keeps affecting her. Money comes to represent guilt factors in the existing society, for it symbolizes materialism and, perhaps, exploitation. One implication is that money "spoils" children, who live in a "natural" world without classes, but not grown-ups, who live in a "rational," sophisticated world with class divisions. Mrs. X was imbued with the feeling that she "had no right to demand an honest reward for her devoted labor," yet she participates in a prize for a painting.

She marries John partly for his money—or at least she lets Mother assert this repeatedly. Both of them drink heavily; the marriage is a failure, quite possibly in part as a result of the repulsiveness of money due to childhood conditioning. The dichotomy of the value standing of money in her childhood environment and in the economic society in which she lives throws her into recurrent conflicts. "I am able to marry a man with money, ask for no money from him, yet accept a larger settlement than I would have received as a divorce if I had named the sum, remain unmarried partly to keep control of the money, and then go into a violent emotional tailspin when he dies and leaves me his money, and having a great guilt-complex, feel that I must spend almost all of it on the children, though it was left to me with no strings attached. And yet I criticize my poor mother for her financial ambivalence."

What, however, are the deeper social roots of the family attitude toward money and of its conflict with other social standards which have such an upsetting effect upon Mrs. X's vulnerable personality?

2. Survival of Feudal Standards in a Capitalist System of Values

She had been brought up with constant admonitions to adopt "ladylike" behavior in a competitive world. Competition with "inferiors" is to be avoided. The parents are unique—actually knights in shining armor. She mentions the "charming aristocratic egoism" of her mother; her likewise charming grandparents "exacted service without pay." The financial extravagance of her mother caused financial catastrophes in the family; yet Mother's socioeconomic position later on, as a wealthy and well-groomed widow, did not suffer from this fact very much.

Mother reminds her of Tolstoi, in her "confused and unsuccessful attempts at world salvation and self-abnegation." Actually Tolstoi's guilt feelings came from his unhappy realization that he belonged to an aristocratic class of exploiters in a doomed feudal society. In Mother's case it is a *phony* feudal world in which she lives. The same phony system of outmoded feudal values characterizes the Victorian tradition by which the mother is so strongly influenced. Mrs. X is quite aware of the hypocrisy that is implicit in such pseudo-feudal codes in the midst of a capitalist society, but she shows little awareness of the real root of such peculiar longing for the feudal past on the part of a new capitalist upper class—namely, guilt feelings about the materialism and other features of this new society, combined with a hopeless attempt to escape from them into the past, at least on an individual or family scale.

Grandfather had "great schemes to save the world," yet Mrs. X has also been taught that "if you love you are despised." In other words, she is brought up under constant conflict among at least three social value standards: a precapitalist, feudal one, which she rationally recognizes as outmoded; a capitalistic, money-oriented one, due chiefly to influences *outside* her family, though she also discerns it in some financial practices of her parents; and one of unrealized social criticism in connection with guilt feelings of her family about the society within which they live in a privileged position. Both the survival of precapitalist value standards and an inner conflict felt to exist within the capitalist society (between its money-oriented materialism and its own ethicoreligious claims) result in Mrs. X's being constantly torn by conflicts of social value systems. This applies to every sphere of life, especially her relations to men. She does not accept anything tangible from a man; it throws her into a "storm of terror," for it would be against her Victorian "ladylike" code, or Cant. However, "common women can be more candid," they are allowed to accept gifts from men and are even supposed to attract men "by a vast hypocrisy." Again the desire for individual escape in the midst of an otherwise unladylike world.

These conflicts of social value systems are symbolized by the "complexity and unhealthiness or ambivalence of Mother's attitude toward money," the "possessive quality of someone who wished to be a female St. Francis." Mother has a capitalist profit urge plus precapitalist guilt feelings about it; she is actually caught in a conflict between the socioeconomic and the ethical standards of "success" in existing society. "The fallacious Victorian philosophy on which our training was based" also included admonitions to self-sacrifice and negation, which symbolized the economic drive toward thrift, "abstinence" in the interest of capital formation, which is characteristic of an early capitalism but not a modern, Keynesian one.

As far as Mrs. X is concerned, "my parents both had the natural vitality to throw most of this [the Victorian values] out of the window as far as their actions, if not their words, were concerned," thus bringing out into the open the value conflict mentioned. She also mentions a friend who was forbidden by her husband (a painter) to paint, or to work in general; "he was one of those people who are a little too good for their financial station in life," but who do not mind being supported instead of selling their works without hypocrisy on a competitive market. In this case the husband was evidently afraid of the competition of his wife, who was a better painter than he; but Mrs. X also hints at the guilt feelings of the artist (and she is one herself) about the profit motive, which is at odds with the artistic scale of values.

Mother was always "most anxious and neurotic" about finances: "if you loved and trusted God enough there would be no need for private property." Capital and interest were wrong, and so was insurance. All this is very reminiscent of the usury prohibitions of the Church Fathers; it is criticism of capitalism from a feudal system of values (and not pseudo-communism as Mrs. X thinks). This also applies to Mother's verbal interest in "charity," as opposed to a collectivistic drive for organized economic security. Anyhow, the child was "unable to reason all this out," and was puzzled and upset by a mother who "constantly flouted her own dictums" and who was "parsimonious to an incredible degree alternating with extravagance."

3. Socioeconomic Instability and Personal Insecurity

During Mrs. X's childhood the family always lived "under the shadow of some great calamity." This was true despite a substantial degree of objective financial security in the family, aside from occasional crises. Apparently that shadow of some great calamity actually reflected the malaise in the society as a whole and the vicissitudes of a competitive economy in general, rather than concrete financial problems of this particular family.

This socioeconomic instability affects Mrs. X's personality in various ways. She "conceives of success as *dangerous*." "It is far safer all round to be a failure, practically and emotionally." "What I was taught to believe as a child was that love was a cannibalistic impulse." The quest for "safety" leads her to the absurd conclusion that she should avoid success. This may in part be the primitive method of protective incantation designed to ward off failure by admitting it in advance; however, it also bears a striking resemblance to what stock-market technicians call profit taking. You cash in a modest gain and trade the possibility of further profit against security.

Possibly her "dislike of recognizing the relationship between cause and effect" (that is, indirectly, a refusal to recognize and accept a "rational" order of economic life) also has something to do with fear of socioeconomic instability, but the connection is not quite clear here. It seems clearer in her dreams, which are often connected with a childhood *house.* "Property," in the narrow sense of real-estate holdings, in many people's minds is a symbol of security, which, of course, it is not at all in terms of the objective facts of economic life. A house appears to many as a tangible value, as something which cannot evaporate like money, for instance. Mrs. X wants to show off toward her husband and others, wants to prove that she has "*something* of her own," and something safe; however, in her dream no one admires it as much as she feels they should. This symbolizes another failure, cushioned (or rationalized) by a feeling that "happiness cannot last and that it is safer to destroy it oneself than to allow it to be destroyed by someone else"—another reminder of the vicissitudes of a competitive economy, of periodic business fluctuations, and of profit taking. She is "frightened of *change* in anyone I knew," for change means uncertainty and thus instability.

4. Cutthroat Competition

Despite the precapitalist and sociocritical influences mentioned, there is also an especially forceful heritage of "rugged individualism." It represents in part the underlying philosophy of early capitalism. It thus leads to an additional source of conflict in her mind—a conflict between the attitudes of early capitalism and the inevitably more subtle, more complex, and more socially responsible standards of a developed, wealthy, and partly oligopolistic capitalism in the America of the mid-twentieth century. To *some* extent the conflicts in her mind mirror the general difference between the social environment and values of her childhood years and those of her adult period.

During her childhood people within her family "were each bent on the others' destruction"; her parents were "cannibals in their wellbred and hideous way." This looks like the unrestricted competition of an early capitalist society, applied to the family scale. She resents the "exploitation" of her childhood talents by her mother in order to show off; she was "flogged on to further efforts." Mother "probably could have sold hot-air furnaces in hell." The child was the object of a displaced parental urge for self-assertion on the competitive market.

The same mother who at times strove toward Franciscan purity "had an attachment almost morbid to *things,* objects . . . and set great store of them, becoming furious if they were lost or broken." That sounds partly like Marx's *Eigentumsbestie,* partly like a quest for greater economic stability. There is, in addition, a preindustrial element in it, the threat of famine. In fact it is a most interesting combination of precapitalist (both primitive and feudal) elements with those of an early capitalism; for the training for self-denial, for the accumulation of durables at the expense of consumption—a training which in Mrs. X's case resulted in resistance to labor during her first childbirth owing to unconscious reluctance to yield anything from her physical possession—had become a very important virtue at the time of switchover from feudal to early capitalist economy. From mere farsighted providence it had developed into the basic virtue of a society which needed capital formation more than anything else. Her mother's attitude shows some elements of Calvinist thrift, which, of course, paralleled the capital needs of early capitalism. Mother's attitude also shows elements of the famous abstinence theory of Nassau W. Senior, who explained the institution of interest as a reward for abstinence from immediate consumption. But in other respects Mother was a great advocate of spending, another unresolved contradiction.

Nowadays, under the influence of Lord Keynes, thrift is often considered more of a threat and mistake than of a virtue and hope. Western society has piled up enormous capital resources without always knowing how to utilize them in peacetime. Such considerations, however, could not be expected to guide the mind of Mrs. X's mother around the turn of the century, or Mrs. X's mind later on either.

She considers herself "fiercely competitive . . . in the wrong way"; she applies this judgment to her competition with men in intellectual achievement, among other things. Her dreams "usually have to do with vast and overpowering houses" which dwarf the people—presumably a bow to the prevailing cult of bigness in a material sense at the expense of the human being or, at least, the common man. Her revolt against the parents' scale of values leads to inability "to work for something I care for," though she works well when she *expects* refusal and thus does not *risk* anything. She shuns the market place, the competitive game and risk; she works best in its absence. She is capable of the "most grinding labor and conscientiousness in a matter in which I have no personal interest or where someone else is to reap the benefit." She is, in other words, just as afraid of profit as of the market place itself; she feels basically that something is wrong with the whole setup.

She does not think, altogether, that financial incentives are very strong with her; while she rationalizes her enjoyment of financial security into interest in the future of her children, she feels guilty because she is better off than "more deserving members of the human race." She has lived at various financial levels of security and insecurity, enjoys potentially the idea of financial recognition of the value of her writing: "it is almost the only prestige that most people can recognize." Yet she wants "a clear conscience about the genuineness of the goods I offered regardless of their price or scale" and is "frightened of being successful." She is constantly torn between the conventional money standard of success in a competitive economy and an artist's realization that her own standard of success hardly ever coincides with the former.

5. Children and Social Values

Out of such conflicts she tries to find shelter in the only world which, to her mind, is relatively unaffected by the contradictions and hypocrisies discussed—that of children. She loves "to talk to young people in their teens, as the shades of the prison house begin to close, but before they are too much hampered by compliance with the rules," but she is "promptly bored by the pretensions of most 'adult' society." She was as a child "obsessed with the cruelty and stupidity of most 'grown-ups.'"

What she really means is that children are not at first as rigidly defined in terms of a given historical society as adults are; or, to put it in a different way, children are not as clearly committed as adults are to a given scale of social values and are "normally" unspoiled enough to question constantly society's institutions and norms—the good and the bad ones alike. That is why, as Mrs. X remarks, so many adults "fear and hate children"; the latter are only too often penalized (unconsciously, as a rule) for being social critics, for asking so many why's. Mrs. X remarks keenly that their understanding and intelligence is often obscured and ruined by "life," by being taught "right" and "wrong"; but she does not see the historically relative and changing character of these concepts and codes. Therefore she speaks of "the sad and futile and perpetual children . . . those who have followed those examples too well."

Basically she would like to return to her childhood condition, that is, the one that prevailed *before* social repression took place. This appears to be at least one important cause for her overdrinking; she apparently feels that society makes alcoholics—they are simply people who want to get away from the artificial personality which society has forced on them—and that getting drunk gets you more or less back to your outspoken independence of childhood days. In short, the drunkard has a kind of license to criticize society, which a sober person is denied. "The superego teaches us to 'get on in the world' according to its frequently stupid and irrational rules and conventions." This may be true to some extent, but she assumes an overstrict and purely negative superego developed for the protection of a given order of things and overlooks the positive element involved.

In summary, she makes it clear that both the wish to stay on the "immaturity level" of childhood, or to go back to it, and the desire to get drunk may often result from a wish to discard the social restrictions (whether good or bad is a matter of judgment) and to regain the comparative license which children and drunkards enjoy in our society—the freedom of a modernized court jester.

Speaking of certain fits, Mrs. X says, "One knows more at these times than sane people can *afford* to remember or take into account." . . . "One cannot continue to live and communicate with the workaday world on such terms. Unbalanced people and children can have a wisdom that is very inconvenient and thus eventually becomes neutralized (because for their protection it must) by the essential mediums of exchange of the civilized world: money, politeness, convention or what have you." She thinks, therefore, of the psychotherapist as "a man well trained in a certain aspect of mankind's ailments, ready and willing to clarify," a "wise and trained and impartial observer and interpreter."

The conflict, in Mrs. X's mind, of social codes from various periods of economic society suggests that in this case psychotherapy might stress an awareness of the changing and historically limited character of the codes in question, codes which the parents had perceived as permanent. This, indeed, presupposes a psychotherapist who does not take the social framework and norms of his own period for granted and who does not interpret his role toward the patient as that of a virtual attorney of a given social order even though the therapist inevitably represents "society" in a formal and clinical sense.

6. Mother's Book

When Mrs. X was a child, her mother wrote an anonymous book on personal aspects of financial problems, especially the cost of living. The book was printed privately, apparently for a very limited circulation. It is a very revealing document in terms of what happened to the child later on. To read this book is an ordeal: its sentences are endless, very often in the literal sense; most of it is incredibly repetitious and unbearably conventional. In its excessive saintliness it inevitably arouses the sneaking suspicion of hypocrisy, of which indeed the author's daughter is fully convinced. Perhaps it might better be characterized as whimsical fuzzy-mindedness.

Its setting certainly is interesting. The first part of it (which is also most confused) was written on the eve of the first World War, the remainder during the war itself. The latter part is clearer and sharper, and has some surprising psychological insights, at least for a while. It is pretty clear that the war crisis of Western society precipitated the expression of certain fears and guilt feelings which may have been there long before.

a. Social guilt complex. The mother (let us call her Mrs. Y), at least at the time of writing this book, suffered agonies from the conflict between the business code of "her" society and group, on the one hand, and Christianity on the other. Her starting point is the high cost of living, which she interprets both as punishment and as cause for more fears, though she also claims that "evil apprehension" may be the *cause* of the high cost of living, rather than vice versa. It is a vicious circle for her in any case. It may, indeed, be "sanely treated"; we shall see how.

The whole book teems with statements of guilt feelings about the conflict between "economics" and "Christianity," or about modern civilization, which for her amounts to the same thing. She criticizes materialism and money drives in the churches, has guilt feelings about employing other people, and sees mankind paying penalties for economic exploitation. Of special interest are her repeated references to debt as breeding (or representing) sin and to "forgiveness," again in the financial *and* in the moral sense, as being a necessity.

Mrs. Y's supposed ideal is Christ, "a man without visible means of support," though she creates a nice escape clause through "just" use of wealth. Similarly, in one place she blames social evils on "infidelity to God." In short, she feels deeply guilty—as a member of her social group—for the conflict of codes and tries meekly to save her own soul from this conflict.

b. Economic insecurity and the cure. The kind of fears generated by economic insecurity bother Mrs. Y especially. Her big idea is that everybody should give up personal thrift and, especially, insurance, and that instead everybody should rely on God for economic security and not try to organize it individually. Her program represents a very convenient justification of personal spending.

She despises the attitude that children should be taught to think early of security both for themselves and for their parents' old age. Apparently she imbued her daughter with this feeling, thus leading to the latter's attitude toward money. "We suffer from the terror which is seizing us for our own life and the life of every one we are for," but the judgment belongs to God and not to the insurance companies. Only God can relieve her from her responsibility; in fact, God should be the only insurance.

She keeps harping on the fact that insurance expresses fear, that people take it out in order to "feel rich," thus allaying their fears; but that without insurance their confidence would really be stronger. Christian Scientists have some good points, she thinks, but they are trying to reach their aim in an insecure society. And she herself really persuaded her husband to give up insurance.

c. Retour à la nature. Mrs. Y's criticism of the moral conflict in her society is basically a precapitalist one. In it at least two historical elements are combined: a glorification of primitive, "sinless" ways of life, and a distorted tradition of mediaeval, feudal chivalry and nobility. Lack of generosity makes you feel uncomfortable, and the selfishness which is at the root of a competitive society is "ignoble."

Yet "charity" likewise does not satisfy her, especially if it is for future "profit," as religion claims. "Doing simple kindnesses" is insufficient, for there is much more wrong with society and only reliance on God can really cure it. She feels very uneasy about the motives of economic activity in her period and would like to escape into the past (an imaginary one, to be sure).

There are, however, some elements of a more "radical" anticapitalism; she criticizes the profit system, competition, and "capital." She glorifies the common people, but she does not like co-operation either, since people should have "the strength to stand alone." She even enjoyed the entrance of the United States into the first World War for a while, as it would set an end to profit! She is for "selfless action," but against abuse of charity as a mere pretext to make money first. In short, Mrs. Y feels extremely uncomfortable about the society she was born into and is groping for some avenue of mental escape from it.

d. Spending versus saving. "I have spent what I had." Why? "For fear of losing it." Here we are. Her spending theory has in fact two roots: first, economic insecurity (she is afraid that unless she spends her money promptly the rising cost of living or other factors will deprive her of it); and, second, the role of money as a symbol of an economic setup about which she feels guilty (as Mammon). Actually she feels guilty about property in general, but especially in the conspicuous form of money. Although she dislikes a "butterfly existence" too and indicates that men should suffer for improvidence, she hates the godless habit of hoarding and thrift. She thus appears to rationalize both her underlying feeling that money (as a symbol of an unjust economic society) is sinful and also her ordinary female wish to spend money freely. Perhaps there is also a vague anticipation of an economic philosophy which explains business fluctuations from inadequate spending, although she claims, amazingly, that the cost of living would drop if there were *no* saving. Anyway, she considers herself a "crank."

It is especially interesting, in terms of her social guilt complex, that she claims that saving makes you responsible for the use of your money by the banks. "Spending wisely" makes you stop worrying and start living, while saving throws you into "fictitious importance." But do not give money to the poor, for it would make them servants of the devil; just spend it according to your own fancy. What a convenient rationalization! What is not spent is lost.

e. Causes and effects of Mrs. Y's attitudes toward money. She mentions that she has personally "experienced the horror with which the dreaming child awakens to the apparent need of serving money." Perhaps this is the key to her attitude, insofar as individual factors are concerned. In addition, she also refers to an earlier primitive idealism which she apparently abandoned when she made her debut in society or when she married. These are scanty indications of the roots of her own attitude. It is safe to say, however, that her attitude reflected the

malaise which characterized her generation and class to the extent that
this group began to realize conflicts of codes between business life and
religion.

It would have been a miracle if the mother's social malaise had not
affected the daughter in her childhood years—and indeed it did. Whatever *additional* factors—organic or constitutional—may have influenced the personality formation of Mrs. X, the way in which she, as an
individual, was reared by Mrs. Y and by other family members was
very important. Mrs. Y's theories and practices concerning the education of her children reflected, in turn, the cultural, historical, and economic setting of her own class and the value conflicts by which Mrs. Y,
as an individual and as a group member, found herself torn. In certain
respects Mrs. X's personality disorder—like any other patient's—must
have been of an individual, unique nature, but at the same time some
aspects of the disorder were evidently rooted in the long-range impact
of cultural and socioeconomic conflicts as they affected her parents'
attitudes and behavior toward their children.

Notes

Introduction

1. Albert Lauterbach, *Economic Security and Individual Freedom* (Ithaca, N.Y., 1948).

Chapter I

1. Erik H. Erikson, *Childhood and Society* (New York, 1950), pp. 112f.; and Ruth Benedict, *Patterns of Culture* (New York, 1934), ch. 6.

2. Abram Kardiner, *The Psychological Frontiers of Society* (New York, 1945), pp. 107ff., 163ff.

3. Geoffrey Gorer, *The People of Great Russia* (London, 1949), p. 203. This quotation of a keen observation should not be interpreted as an endorsement of the dubious approach of this book in general. See also Margaret Mead, ed., *Cooperation and Competition among Primitive Peoples* (New York, 1937); and M. Zborowski and E. Herzog, *Life Is with People: The Jewish Little Town of Eastern Europe* (New York, 1952), pp. 65ff.

4. Muzafer Sherif, *Outline of Social Psychology* (New York, 1948), pp. 270ff.

5. United Nations, *Measures for the Economic Development of Underdeveloped Countries* (New York, 1951), p. 13.

6. Clare E. Griffin, *Enterprise in a Free Society* (Chicago, 1949), p. 83. See also Miriam Beard, *A History of the Businessman* (New York, 1938); E. N. Saveth, "What Historians Teach about Business," *Fortune,* April 1952;

and Fritz Redlich, *History of American Business Leaders* (Ann Arbor, 1940); *The Molding of American Banking* (New York, 1947), and "The Business Leader as a 'Daimonic' Figure," *American Journal of Economics and Sociology,* January 1953.

7. Max Weber, *The Protestant Ethic and the Spirit of Capitalism* (New York, 1930); Werner Sombart, *Der Bourgeois* (Munich, 1913); R. H. Tawney, *Religion and the Rise of Capitalism* (New York, 1926); and Franz Borkenau, *Der Uebergang vom feudalen zum buergerlichen Weltbild* (Paris, 1934).

8. Sombart, *op. cit.,* pp. 24, 170f.

9. W. T. Easterbrook, "The Climate of Enterprise," *American Economic Review, Papers and Proceedings,* May 1949; J. A. Schumpeter, *Capitalism, Socialism, and Democracy,* 3d ed. (New York, 1950), part II, esp. ch. 6; and Karl Polanyi, *The Great Transformation* (New York, 1944).

10. Wilder Hobson, "Before the Wars," *Fortune,* January 1946.

11. G. W. Stocking and M. W. Watkins, *Monopoly and Free Enterprise* (New York, 1951), esp. p. 11 and ch. 10. For a critique, see Neil H. Jacoby, "Perspectives on Monopoly," *Journal of Political Economy,* December 1951.

12. Robert A. Gordon, *Business Leadership in the Large Corporation* (Washington, 1945); Harry W. Laidler, *Our Changing Industrial Incentives* (League for Industrial Democracy pamphlet, New York, 1949); and Johannes Alasco, *Intellectual Capitalism: A Study of Changing Ownership and Control in Modern Industrial Society* (New York, 1950).

13. D. S. Landes, "French Business and the Business Man: A Social and Cultural Analysis," in E. M. Earle, ed., *Modern France* (Princeton, 1951).

14. W. S. Schlamm, "European Business Is Different," *Fortune,* February 1950; and U. Stille, "European vs. U.S. Industrialists," *The Reporter,* January 8, 1952.

15. *Survey of Current Business,* August 1958. See also Stocking and Watkins, *op. cit.,* esp. ch. 2.

16. Lewis H. Kimmel, *Share Ownership in the United States* (Washington, 1952). Compare "Who Owns Business?" *Fortune,* September 1952.

17. See, for instance, Elliott Jaques, *The Changing Culture of a Factory* (London, 1951), esp. part III.

18. S. H. Hayes, Jr., "Some Psychological Problems of Economics," *Psychological Bulletin,* July 1950, pp. 311ff.

19. M. A. Adelman, "Is Big Business Getting Bigger?" *Fortune,* January 1952.

20. Gordon, *op. cit.,* pp. 309, 322, 336.

21. Alfred Marshall, *Principles of Economics,* 8th ed. (London, 1938), pp. 285ff., 315ff.

22. Chester I. Barnard, *The Functions of the Executive* (Cambridge, Mass., 1938); E. P. Learned, D. N. Ulrich, and D. R. Booz, *Executive Action* (Cambridge, Mass., 1951); Alasco, *op. cit.,* ch. 2; Oswald W. Knauth, *Managerial Enterprise* (New York, 1948), esp. pp. 11ff.; Joel Dean, *Man-*

agerial Economics (New York, 1951); Melvin T. Copeland, *The Executive at Work* (Cambridge, Mass., 1951), ch. 12; and Austen Albu, *Management in Transition* (London, 1942).

23. "What Makes the Boss Work?" *Fortune*, April 1948.

24. Arthur M. Schlesinger, Jr., *The Vital Center* (Boston, 1949), p. 12.

25. Thorstein Veblen, *The Theory of Business Enterprise* (New York, 1904), pp. 42f.

26. Chester I. Barnard, *Organization and Management* (Cambridge, Mass., 1949), pp. 14ff. See also Griffin, *op. cit.*, pp. 404ff.; Talcott Parsons, *The Social System* (Glencoe, Ill., 1951), pp. 243ff.; Paul H. Douglas, "The Reality of Non-Commercial Incentives in Economic Life," in R. G. Tugwell, ed., *The Trend of Economics* (New York, 1924); and J. Marchal, "The Construction of a New Theory of Profit," and S. Enke, "On Maximizing Profits," *American Economic Review*, September 1951.

27. Peter F. Drucker, *The New Industrial Society* (New York, 1949), p. 72, and *Concept of the Corporation* (New York, 1946), pp. 236ff. Compare Robert Triffin, *Monopolistic Competition and General Equilibrium Theory* (Cambridge, Mass., 1940), pp. 184ff.

28. Henry Ford II in *U.S. News and World Report*, January 25, 1952, p. 35. See also R. L. Heilbroner, "The Fabulous Ford Foundation," *Harper's*, December 1951.

29. George Katona, *Psychological Analysis of Economic Behavior* (New York, 1951), ch. 9.

30. B. F. Fairless, president of the U.S. Steel Corporation, *Dedication to Success*, address in Duncansville, Pa., on October 18, 1951.

31. Melville Herskovits, *Man and His Works* (New York, 1948), p. 284.

32. D. W. Brogan, *American Themes* (New York, 1949), pp. 38ff.

33. R. S. and H. M. Lynd, *Middletown* (New York, 1929), p. 52.

34. Sombart, *op. cit.*, pp. 253–268; and F. W. Taussig and C. S. Joslyn, *American Business Leaders* (New York, 1932). Compare "The Nine Hundred," *Fortune*, November 1952.

35. Sherif, *op. cit.*, p. 454. See also Gardner Murphy, *Personality* (New York, 1947), esp. chs. 22, 33; and C. Wright Mills, "The Competitive Personality," *Partisan Review*, September–October 1946.

36. Erich Fromm, *Man for Himself* (New York, 1947), ch. 3, part 2. See also the first two articles by H. A. Murray and C. Kluckhohn in their volume *Personality in Nature, Society, and Culture*, 2d ed. (New York, 1956).

37. Compare A. H. Kornhauser, "Analysis of Class Structure of Contemporary American Society," in G. W. Hartmann and T. Newcomb, eds., *Industrial Conflict: A Psychological Interpretation* (New York, 1939); and C. Wright Mills, *White Collar: The American Middle Classes* (New York, 1951), esp. chs. 1, 4, 5.

38. William Miller, ed., *Men in Business* (Cambridge, Mass., 1952), esp. ch. 11; William Miller, "The Recruitment of the American Business Elite," *Quarterly Journal of Economics*, May 1950, and "American Historians and

the Business Elite," *Journal of Economic History,* November 1949; also "The Thirty Thousand Managers," *Fortune,* February 1940, and L. P. Lessing, "The World of Dupont," *Fortune,* October 1950.

39. Bernard Baruch, according to the *New York Times,* October 27, 1950.

40. Andrew Carnegie and others, *Personality in Business* (Chicago, 1907), pp. 26ff.

41. Frederick Lewis Allen, *The Great Pierpont Morgan* (New York, 1949), p. 282.

42. William C. Richards, *The Last Billionnaire* (New York, 1948), p. 196. See also Henry Ford, *My Life and Work* (Garden City, 1922), followed by other autobiographical writings; Keith Sward, *The Legend of Henry Ford* (New York, 1948); Harry Bennett, *We Never Called Him Henry* (New York, 1951); and Allan Nevins, *Ford: The Times, the Man, the Company* (New York, 1954).

43. Learned, *op. cit.,* pp. 64ff.; Gordon R. Taylor, *Are Workers Human?* (New York, 1952), pp. 101f.; Gordon, *op. cit.,* pp. 276f.; W. E. Henry, "The Business Executive: Psychodynamics of a Social Role," *American Journal of Sociology,* January 1949; and *Fortune* Magazine, *The Executive Life* (New York, 1956).

44. F. W. Taussig, *Inventors and Money-Makers* (New York, 1915), esp. pp. 1ff., 57, 78, 113; and Thorstein Veblen, *The Instinct of Workmanship* (New York, 1914).

45. Barnard, *The Functions, passim.*

46. For a psychiatric critique of Miller's play, see Frederic Wertham, "Let the Salesman Beware," *New York Times Book Review,* May 15, 1949. Compare the following articles from *Fortune:* "Salespeople Aren't Selling" (October 1949) and "The Sales Bosses" (June 1950); also the more conventional approach of Franziska Baumgarten, *Die Psychologie im kaufmaennischen Berufe* (Zurich, 1943), esp. ch. 2.

47. Robert R. Updegraff, *The Subconscious Mind in Business* (New York, 1929), p. 28; and L. Urwick, "For Management, Too—An Optimum Workweek," *Management Review,* January 1952.

48. W. H. Whyte, Jr., "The Wives of Management" and "The Corporation and the Wife," *Fortune,* October 1951 and November 1951; "Manifesto from a Corporation Wife," *Fortune,* March 1952; and "The New Rich," *Fortune,* January 1952.

49. "Avery Criticized by Trust Official," *New York Times,* April 11, 1950.

50. Knauth, *op. cit.,* pp. 37, 45, 173. Compare Cyril O'Donnell, "The Source of Managerial Authority," *Political Science Quarterly,* December 1952.

51. Max Weber, *Wirtschaft und Gesellschaft* (*Grundriss der Sozialoekonomik,* vol. III; Tuebingen, 1925), I, 140ff., II, chs. 9 and 10.

52. E. and F. Jennings, "Making Human Relations Work," *Harvard Business Review,* January 1951. See also F. J. Roethlisberger, *Management and Morale* (Cambridge, Mass., 1946); F. J. Roethlisberger and W. J. Dickson,

Management and the Worker (Cambridge, Mass., 1947); Benjamin M. Selekman, *Labor Relations and Human Relations* (New York, 1948); and Neil W. Chamberlain, *The Union Challenge to Management Control* (New York, 1948), esp. ch. 3.

53. John R. Commons, *Institutional Economics* (New York, 1934).

54. Kardiner, *op. cit.*, p. 422. See also Mead, *op. cit.*, Clyde Kluckhohn, *Mirror for Man* (New York, 1949), p. 190.

55. Bertrand Russell, *The Conquest of Happiness* (New York, 1951), p. 30.

56. E. A. G. Robinson, *Monopoly* (New York, 1941), esp. p. 29. See also C. P. Kindleberger, "Group Behavior and International Trade," *Journal of Political Economy*, February 1951.

57. D. Krech and R. S. Crutchfield, *Theory and Problems of Social Psychology* (New York, 1948), p. 390.

58. Karl Mannheim, *Freedom, Planning, and Democratic Power* (New York, 1950), p. 194.

59. Meyer Berger, in the first of a series of articles on gambling, *New York Times*, December 3, 4, 5, 6, 7, 1951. See also, Murray Schumach in the *New York Times*, January 15, 1950; and dispatches in the same newspaper on Jan. 28, 1950, and May 16, 1951. For a more comprehensive discussion of various aspects of gambling, see M. Ploscowe and E. J. Lukas, eds., "Gambling," special issue of the *Annals of the American Academy of Political and Social Science*, May 1950.

60. Robert K. Merton, "Social Structure and Anomie," *Social Theory and Social Structure* (Glencoe, Ill., 1949).

61. Edmund Bergler, *Money and Emotional Conflicts* (Garden City, 1951), p. 67.

62. Jean Giraudoux, *La Folle de Chaillot* (Paris, 1946), pp. 151f.

63. Georg Simmel, *Philosophie des Geldes*, 5th ed. Munich, 1930), esp. ch. 3, part 2, and ch. 5; Albert G. Hart, *Money, Debt and Economic Activity* (New York, 1948), esp. p. 385; Katona, *op. cit.*, ch. 12, and *War without Inflation* (New York, 1942); F. D. Graham and C. R. Whittlesey, *Golden Avalanche* (Princeton, 1939); and P. Nichols, "Political Distortion of International Monetary Relations," *Proceedings of the American Philosophical Society*, vol. 92, no. 6, 1948.

64. Sigmund Freud, *Collected Papers* (London, 1924), vol. II, ch. 4; Bergler, *op. cit.*; R. M. Griffith, "Dreams of Finding Money," *American Journal of Psychotherapy*, October 1951; and Otto Fenichel, *The Psychoanalytic Theory of Neurosis* (New York, 1945), pp. 281ff., 487ff.

65. Kardiner, *op. cit.*, pp. 165f. See also John Dollard, *Frustration and Aggression* (New Haven, 1939); and Fromm, *op. cit.*, pp. 89ff.

66. A. I. Hallowell, "Aggression in Saulteaux Society," in Kluckhohn and Murray, *op. cit.*, ch. 15.

67. Harry Stack Sullivan, *Conceptions of Modern Psychiatry* (Washington, 1947), p. 103.

68. Kluckhohn, *op. cit.*, pp. 242ff.

69. Knauth, *op. cit.*, pp. 180ff.

70. "Why Executives Drop Dead," *Fortune,* June 1950. Compare Sune Carlson, *Executive Behavior: A Study of the Work Load and the Working Methods of Managing Directors* (Stockholm, 1951).

71. Bergler, *op. cit.*, p. 42.

72. *New York Times,* December 21, 1949, January 24, 1952, February 1, 1952, March 2, 1952, March 20, 1952, December 3, 1957, February 15, 1958, and October 26, 1958.

Chapter II

1. John M. Clark, "Economic Means—To What Ends?" *American Economic Review,* December 1950, part II, p. 41. Compare Karl Mannheim, "Ueber das Wesen und die Bedeutung des wirtschaftlichen Erfolgsstrebens," *Archiv fuer Sozialwissenschaft,* vol. 63, no. 3.

2. J. R. Hicks, *Value and Capital* (Oxford, 1948), esp. pp. 124ff., 204ff. Compare, for the following paragraphs, George Katona, *Psychological Analysis of Economic Behavior* (New York, 1951), pp. 52ff., 198ff.; "Expectations and Decisions in Economic Behavior," in D. Lerner and H. D. Lasswell, eds., *The Policy Sciences* (Stanford, 1951); and M. J. Bowman, ed., *Expectations, Uncertainty, and Business Behavior* (New York, 1958).

3. A. W. Jones, "Fashions in Forecasting," *Fortune,* March 1949; and A. Cowles, "Can Stock Market Forecasters Forecast?" *Econometrica,* July 1933. Compare Oskar Morgenstern, *The Limits of Economics* (London, 1937); and M. Sapir, "Review of Economic Forecasts for the Transition Period," *Studies in Income and Wealth* (New York, 1949), vol. XI.

4. Frank H. Knight, *Risk, Uncertainty, and Profit* (Boston, 1921), esp. chs. 1, 7, 8, 9, 12; also Albert G. Hart, *Anticipations, Uncertainty, and Dynamic Planning,* 2d ed. (New York, 1950); F. H. Weston, "A Generalized Uncertainty Theory of Profit," *American Economic Review,* March 1950; Tibor Scitovsky, *Welfare and Competition* (New York, 1951), pp. 111ff.; and A. G. Papandreou, in B. F. Haley, ed., *A Survey of Contemporary Economics* (Homewood, Ill., 1952), vol. II, ch. 5.

5. See the papers by Forest D. Siefkin, Ralph E. Flanders, and Henry S. Dennison in the *American Economic Review, Papers and Proceedings,* May 1951; also Robert Tannenbaum, "The Manager Concept" and "Managerial Decision-Making," *Journal of Business,* October 1949 and January 1950. Compare P. E. Holden, L. S. Fish, and H. L. Smith, *Top-Management Organization and Control* (New York, 1951), esp. part C; W. E. Henry, "The Business Executive: The Psycho-Dynamics of A Social Role," *American Journal of Sociology,* January 1949; and J. E. Janney, "Company Presidents Look at Themselves," *Harvard Business Review,* May–June 1952.

6. R. F. Harrod, "Price and Cost in Entrepreneurs' Policy," and R. L. Hall and C. J. Hitch, "Price Theory and Business Behavior," *Oxford Economic Papers,* 1939, no. 2.

7. Edwin G. Nourse, *Price Making in a Democracy* (Washington, 1944), esp. ch. 4; Alfred R. Oxenfeldt, *Industrial Pricing and Market Practices* (New York, 1951), pp. 180ff., 290ff.; National Bureau of Economic Research, *Cost Behavior and Price Policy* (New York, 1943), esp. pp. 6, 42ff., 285f.; W. J. Eiteman, *Price Determination* (Ann Arbor, 1949); Katona, *Psychological Analysis,* ch. 10, and *Price Control and Business* (Bloomington, 1945); Stocking and Watkins, *op. cit.,* ch. 6; and A. D. H. Kaplan and others, *Pricing in Big Business* (Washington, 1958).

8. Knauth, *op. cit.,* pp. 118ff. See also Dean, *op. cit.,* chs. 7, 8, 9; and Jesse W. Markham, "The Nature and Significance of Price Leadership," *American Economic Review,* December 1951.

9. Survey Research Center, University of Michigan, *Industrial Mobility in Michigan* (Ann Arbor, 1951), esp. pp. 19, 32f. Also G. Katona and J. N. Morgan, "The Quantitative Study of Factors Determining Business Decisions," *Quarterly Journal of Economics,* February 1952.

10. H. S. Ellis, ed., *A Survey of Contemporary Economics* (Philadelphia, 1948), vol. I, chs. 1 (B. F. Haley) and 4 (J. S. Bain); D. C. Hague, "Economic Theory and Business Behavior," *Review of Economic Studies,* 1949–50. Compare G. F. Thirlby, "The Economists' Description of Business Behavior," *Economica,* May 1952; and the articles by R. H. Coase and T. Scitovsky in G. J. Stigler and K. E. Boulding, eds., *Readings in Price Theory* (Chicago, 1952), pp. 331–358.

11. Survey Research Center, *op. cit.* See also George Katona, with A. Lauterbach and S. Steinkamp, *Business Looks at Banks* (Ann Arbor, 1957), esp. p. 21.

12. I. Friend and J. Bronfenbrenner, "Business Investment Programs and Their Realization," *Survey of Current Business,* December 1950. Compare Walter W. Heller, "The Anatomy of Investment Decisions," *Harvard Business Review,* March 1951; and George Terborgh, *Dynamic Equipment Policy* (New York, 1949), pp. 225ff.

13. Thomas A. Sanders, *Effects of Taxation on Executives* (Boston, 1951); and Lewis H. Kimmel, *Taxes and Economic Incentives* (Washington, 1950), pp. 33, 99ff.

14. Sombart, *op. cit.,* pp. 49ff.

15. Bronislaw Malinowski, *Magic, Science and Religion* (Boston, 1948), esp. pp. 50ff.

16. Elmer L. Irey, *The Tax Dodgers* (New York, 1948), esp. chs. 1 and 10.

17. Thorstein Veblen, *The Theory of the Leisure Class* (New York, 1931) and many other writings; also Louis Schneider, *The Freudian Psychology and Veblen's Social Theory* (New York, 1948).

18. Gordon R. Taylor, *op. cit.,* ch. 16; P. Sargant Florence, *The Logic of Industrial Organization* (London, 1933), esp. ch. 2; and Merlin Thomas, "Sexual Symbolism in Industry," *International Journal of Psychoanalysis,* vol. II, 1951.

19. Knauth, *op. cit.*, p. 26; also John Ise, "The Futility of Trust Busting," *American Economic Review, Papers and Proceedings,* May 1948.

20. F. X. Sutton and others, *The American Business Creed* (Cambridge, Mass., 1956).

21. Malinowski, *op. cit.*, p. 79. See also Thurman W. Arnold, *The Folklore of Capitalism* (Garden City, 1937), esp. chs. 5, 11, 12.

22. Albert Lauterbach, *Economic Security and Individual Freedom* (Ithaca, N.Y., 1948), esp. pp. 52ff.

23. John Kenneth Galbraith, *American Capitalism: The Concept of Countervailing Power* (Boston, 1956), esp. pp. 84ff.; compare Benjamin Higgins, *What Do Economists Know?* (Melbourne, 1951), pp. 115ff.

24. Kimmel, *op. cit.*, pp. 101ff. See also A. A. Ballantine, "Psychological Bases for Tax Liability," *Harvard Business Review,* March 1949.

25. Sanders, *op. cit.*, esp. pp. 11ff.

26. D. M. Keezer, ed., "The Effectiveness of the Federal Antitrust Laws: A Symposium," *American Economic Review,* June 1949. Compare Robert E. Lane, "Government Regulation and the Business Mind," *American Sociological Review,* April 1951.

27. Jean Marchal, "The Construction of a New Theory of Profit," *American Economic Review,* September 1951; also J. J. Spengler, "Power Blocks and the Formation and Content of Economic Decisions," *American Economic Review, Papers and Proceedings,* May 1950; Ben W. Lewis, "The Effect of Businessmen upon Controls," *Michigan Business Review,* June 1951.

28. Sherif, *op. cit.*, chs. 9 and 10; also Vance Packard, *The Hidden Persuaders* (New York, 1957).

29. Thomas H. Sanders, "The Annual Report: Portrait of a Business," *Harvard Business Review,* January 1949; and Dean, *op. cit.*, ch. 6.

30. E. S. Turner, *The Shocking History of Advertising!* (London, 1952); Blake Clark, *The Advertising Smokescreen* (New York, 1944); and Charles S. Braden, *These Also Believe* (New York, 1949), ch. 2.

31. For example, Melvin S. Hattwick, *How to Use Psychology for Better Advertising* (New York, 1950); George B. Hotchkiss, *An Outline of Advertising,* 3d ed. (New York, 1950); and D. B. Lucas and S. H. Britt, *Advertising Psychology and Research* (New York, 1950).

32. *New York Times,* November 23, 1950.

33. Knauth, *op. cit.*, pp. 30, 67.

34. William H. Whyte, Jr., *"Is Anybody Listening?"* (New York, 1952); and William D. Patterson, ed., *America—Miracle at Work* (New York, 1953).

35. T. K. Quinn, *I Quit Monster Business* (New York, 1949), and *Giant Business: Threat to Democracy* (New York, 1953).

36. *New York Times,* April 5, 1951, and February 18, 1952.

37. See the following periodicals: *Good Business; Christian Economics;* and *Trends in Church, Education and Industry Cooperation* (National As-

sociation of Manufacturers). In addition, "The Moral History of U.S. Business," *Fortune,* December 1949; William Scarlett, ed., *The Christian Demand for Social Justice* (New York, 1949); Thorstein Veblen, "Christian Morals and the Competitive System," *Essays in Our Changing Order* (New York, 1934); A. Dudley Ward, ed., *Goals of Economic Life* (New York, 1953); Howard R. Bowen, *Social Responsibilities of the Businessman* (New York, 1953); and J. Whitney Bunting, ed., *Ethics for Modern Business Practice* (New York, 1953).

38. J. A. Schumpeter, "The March into Socialism," *American Economic Review, Papers and Proceedings,* May 1950, p. 448. See also his books *Capitalism, Socialism and Democracy,* part II, and *Essays* (Cambridge, Mass., 1951), pp. 216ff., 248ff.

39. Survey Research Center, University of Michigan, *Big Business as the People See It* (Ann Arbor, 1951). Compare Elmo Roper, "The Public Looks at Business," *Harvard Business Review,* March 1949.

Chapter III

1. Hugo Muensterberg, *Psychology and Social Sanity* (Garden City, 1914), p. viii.

2. A. Kardiner, *The Psychological Frontiers of Society* (New York, 1945), pp. 97f., 124ff., 416ff.; Ruth Benedict, *Patterns of Culture* (New York, 1934), ch. 5; and John Dollard, *Frustration and Aggression* (New Haven, 1939), ch. 8. See also C. S. Braden, *These Also Believe* (New York, 1949); and Carlo Levi, *Christ Stopped at Eboli* (New York, 1947).

3. "Social Policy and Social Research in Housing," *Journal of Social Issues,* 1951, nos. 1–2; and Robert K. Merton, "Social Psychology of Housing," in *Current Trends in Social Psychology* (Pittsburgh, 1948).

4. M. Grotjahn, "Some Analytic Observations about the Process of Growing Old," in G. Roheim, ed., *Psychoanalysis and the Social Sciences* (New York, 1951), vol. III; G. Lawton, "Meeting the Emotional Needs of Older Persons," in M. L. Reymert, ed., *Feelings and Emotions* (New York, 1950).

5. Elton Mayo, *The Human Problems of an Industrial Civilization* (Boston, 1946), esp. pp. 144ff.

6. Survey Research Center, *Public Responses to Peacetime Uses of Atomic Energy,* 2 vols. (Ann Arbor, 1951), mimeo.

7. Harry Stack Sullivan, *Conceptions of Modern Psychiatry* (Washington, 1947), pp. 87ff., 111.

8. Sigmund Freud, *An Outline of Psychoanalysis* (New York, 1949), pp. 76, 84.

9. Karen Horney, *The Neurotic Personality of Our Time* (New York, 1937); Rudolf Brun, *Die Neurose als kulturelles und soziales Problem* (Zurich, 1949); Marie Jahoda, *Toward a Social Psychology of Mental Health,* Research Center for Human Relations, New York University (New York, 1950); A. B. Hollingshead and F. C. Redlich, *Social Class and Mental Illness* (New York, 1958); J. Wilder and A. Lauterbach, "Economics and

Psychotherapy," in J. Masserman and J. Moreno, eds., *Progress in Psychotherapy*, vol. IV (New York, 1959).

10. See Joseph Wilder, "Facts and Figures on Psychotherapy," *Journal of Clinical Psychopathology*, October 1945. Compare T. A. C. Rennie and L. E. Woodward, *Mental Health in Modern Society* (New York, 1948), ch. 14.

11. 1957 Annual Report, National Association for Mental Health.

12. Benjamin Malzberg, *Social and Biological Aspects of Mental Disease* (Utica, 1940), pp. 280ff. Compare S. Kirson Weinberg, *Society and Personality Disorders* (New York, 1952), pp. 151ff., 511 ff.; Milbank Memorial Fund, *Epidemiology of Mental Disorder* (New York, 1950); "Mental Health in the United States," *Annals of the American Academy of Political and Social Science*, March 1953 (esp. R. H. Felix and S. W. Ginsburg); and H. Goldhamer and A. Marshall, *Psychosis and Civilization* (Glencoe, Ill., 1953).

13. House of Representatives, 79th Congress, Committee on Interstate and Foreign Commerce, Subcommittee Hearing, *National Neuropsychiatric Institute Act* (Washington, 1945); also S. A. Stouffer and associates, *The American Soldier* (Princeton, 1949), I, 130ff., II, ch. 9; and J. L. Woodward, "Changing Ideas on Mental Illness and Its Treatment," *American Sociological Review*, August 1951.

14. James L. Halliday, *Psychosocial Medicine* (New York, 1948), pp. 51, 60ff., 80ff., 164ff.

15. G. Zilboorg, "Differential Diagnostic Types of Suicide," *Archives of Neurology and Psychiatry*, February 1936. Compare Emile Durkheim, *Le Suicide* (Paris, 1897); L. I. Dublin and B. Bunzel, *To Be or Not to Be* (New York, 1933), esp. part VI, pp. 100ff.

16. Metropolitan Life Insurance Co., *Statistical Bulletin*, April 1949, July 1949, May 1950, September 1951, May 1953, December 1958; L. I. Dublin and A. J. Lotka, *25 Years of Health Progress* (New York, 1937), pp. 415ff.

17. Hermann Levy, *Drink: An Economic and Social Study* (London, 1951); Clarence H. Patrick, *Alcohol, Culture and Society* (Durham, N.C., 1952); Metropolitan Life Insurance Co., *The Alcoholic* (New York, 1951).

18. S. A. Stouffer and P. F. Lazarsfeld, *Research Memorandum on the Family in the Depression* (New York, 1937); and William J. Goode, "Economic Factors and Marital Stability," *American Sociological Review*, December 1951.

19. U.S. Department of Commerce, Bureau of the Census, *1950 U.S. Census of Population, Number of Inhabitants, U.S. Summary* (Washington, 1952).

20. Compare Eli Ginzberg and associates, *Occupational Choice* (New York, 1951), esp. chs. 14 and 15.

21. Benedikt Kautsky, *Teufel und Verdammte* (Vienna, 1948), p. 84. Compare Harold D. Lasswell, *Psychopathology and Politics* (Chicago, 1930), esp. chs. 4–7.

22. George Orwell, *1984* (New York, 1949), p. 213.

23. Marion L. Starkey, *The Devil in Massachusetts* (New York, 1950), p. 30. Compare Aldous Huxley, *The Devils of Loudun* (New York, 1953); Carey McWilliams, *Witch Hunt* (Boston, 1950), esp. p. 320; Leo Lowenthal and Norbert Guterman, *Prophets of Deceit* (New York, 1949).

24. M. Sherif, *Outline of Social Psychology* (New York, 1948), pp. 40ff. See also Hadley Cantril, *The Psychology of Social Movements* (New York, 1941).

25. Kluckhohn, *op. cit.*, p. 201; Erik H. Erikson, *Childhood and Society* (New York, 1950), p. 210; Horney, *op. cit.*, p. viii; Dollard, *op. cit.*, pp. 88f., 97ff., 107ff. See also L. K. Frank, *Society as the Patient* (New Brunswick, 1948), chs. 15, 16, 19; Gardner Murphy, *Personality* (New York, 1947), chs. 33–37; Midcentury White House Conference on Children and Youth, *Personality in the Making* (New York, 1952), ch. 5; Kurt Lewin, *A Dynamic Theory of Personality* (New York, 1935), chs. 3, 4; J. M. Hunt, ed., *Personality and the Behavior Disorders* (New York, 1944), esp. chs. 10 (K. Lewin), 21 (L. B. Murphy), 22 (P. Blanchard), 23 (G. Bateson), 24 (R. E. L. Faris), and 28 (W. Malamud); J. Dollard and N. E. Miller, *Personality and Psychotherapy* (New York, 1950), esp. ch. 10; and Wilder, *op. cit.*

26. Bradley Buell and associates, *Community Planning for Human Services* (New York, 1952), pp. 237ff., 264ff.

27. Joan Fleming, "Mental Hygiene Implications of the Effect of Unemployment on the Family and the Child," *Mental Hygiene Bulletin*, Illinois Society for Mental Hygiene, November–December 1949.

28. Sherif, *op. cit.*, p. 263. See also Mirra Komarovski, *The Unemployed Man and His Family* (New York, 1940); E. Wight Bakke, *The Unemployed Worker* and *Citizens without Work* (New Haven, 1940); M. Lazarsfeld—Jahoda and H. Zeisel, *Die Arbeitslosen von Marienthal* (Leipzig, 1933); Eli Ginzberg, *The Unemployed* (New York, 1943); R. S. and H. M. Lynd, *Middletown* (New York, 1929), pp. 58ff., and *Middletown in Transition* (New York, 1937), pp. 482ff.; P. Eisenberg and P. F. Lazarsfeld, "The Psychological Effects of Unemployment," *Psychological Bulletin*, June 1938.

29. L. Coch and J. R. P. French, Jr., "Overcoming Resistance to Change," *Human Relations*, vol. I, no. 4, 1948. Compare F. Zweig, *Men in the Pits* (London, 1949).

30. Hollingshead and Redlich, *op. cit.*, pp. 223, 238.

31. Norman Mailer, *The Naked and the Dead* (New York, 1948), p. 169.

32. Svend Ranulf, *Moral Indignation and Middle-Class Psychology* (Copenhagen, 1938). B. M. Spinley, *The Deprived and the Privileged: Personality Development in English Society* (London, 1953).

33. Carnegie Corporation of New York, *Report for 1950*, p. 15.

34. Richard Centers, *The Psychology of Social Classes* (Princeton, 1949), pp. 109ff., 148ff.

Notes

35. Erich Fromm, *Man for Himself* (New York, 1947), pp. 72ff. and 49; also *Psychoanalysis and Religion* (New Haven, 1950).

36. J. W. Eaton and R. J. Weil, *Culture and Mental Disorders* (Glencoe, Ill., 1956).

37. Robert K. Merton, in R. N. Anshen, ed., *The Family: Its Function and Destiny* (New York, 1949), p. 227.

38. Kurt Lewin, *Resolving Social Conflicts* (New York, 1948), p. 57. See also Karl Mannheim, *Freedom, Power, and Democratic Planning* (New York, 1950), ch. 8, pp. 303ff.

39. David Riesman, *The Lonely Crowd* (New Haven, 1950), pp. vff.; also *Faces in the Crowd* (New Haven, 1952). Compare Dorwin Cartwright, "Emotional Dimensions of Group Life," in Reymert, *op. cit.*

40. Edmund Bergler, *Money and Emotional Conflicts* (New York, 1951). Similarly, Theodor Reik, *The Secret Self* (New York, 1953), ch. 16.

41. Geoffrey Gorer, *The American People* (New York, 1948), esp. chs. 3 and 7.

42. Ruth Benedict, *op. cit.*, ch. 4. Compare H. J. Wegrocki, "A Critique of Cultural and Statistical Concepts of Abnormality," in C. Kluckhohn and H. A. Murray, eds., *Personality in Nature, Society, and Culture*, 2d ed. (New York, 1956).

43. Compare R. H. Felix and R. V. Bowers, "Mental Hygiene and Socio-Environmental Factors," *Milbank Memorial Fund Quarterly*, April 1948.

44. Sullivan, *op. cit.*, pp. 87ff.

45. Survey Research Center, *Public Evaluation of Life Insurance* (Ann Arbor, 1951), mimeo.

Chapter IV

1. Theodore M. Newcomb, *Social Psychology* (New York, 1950), p. 344, also part IV in general; Gardner Murphy, *Personality* (New York, 1947), esp. chs. 13, 19, 22, 30–37; C. Kluckhohn and H. A. Murray, eds., *Personality in Nature, Society, and Culture*, 2d ed. (New York, 1956), chs. 1, 2, 33; Kurt Lewin, *A Dynamic Theory of Personality* (New York, 1935), pp. 206ff.; and Karen Horney, *The Neurotic Personality of Our Time* (New York, 1937).

2. Abram Kardiner, *The Individual and His Society* (New York, 1939), esp. chs. 2, 4, 9, 10, and *The Psychological Frontiers of Society* (New York, 1945), esp. chs. 1, 2, 11, 14. For a critical viewpoint, see Clyde Kluckhohn, *Mirror for Man* (New York, 1949), pp. 200ff.

3. Kurt Lewin, *Field Theory in Social Science* (New York, 1951), pp. 81f., 285; also his book *Resolving Social Conflicts* (New York, 1948), ch. 1; Hadley Cantril, *Psychology of Social Movements* (New York, 1941), esp. pp. 37ff., 62ff.; and Talcott Parsons, *The Social System* (Glencoe, Ill., 1951), chs. 6–8.

4. Lewin, *Resolving Conflicts*, ch. 4; Erich Fromm, *Man for Himself* (New York, 1947), pp. 197ff.; Solomon E. Asch, *Social Psychology* (New York,

1952), part V; S. E. Asch, "Effects of Group Pressure upon the Modification and Distortion of Judgements," in G. E. Swanson, T. M. Newcomb, and E. L. Hartley, *Readings in Social Psychology*, rev. ed. (New York, 1952).

5. Harry Stack Sullivan, *Conceptions of Modern Psychiatry* (Washington, 1947), pp. 39ff., 96f. Compare Harold D. Lasswell, *Psychopathology and Politics* (Chicago, 1930), esp. chs. 4–8.

6. See Karl Mannheim, *Freedom, Power, and Democratic Planning* (New York, 1950), ch. 9; also the articles by Robert K. Merton and Margaret Mead in Kluckhohn and Murray, *op. cit.*, chs. 23 and 43; and Harold D. Lasswell, *Power and Personality* (New York, 1948), ch. 7. Compare Emil J. Walter, *Psychologische Grundlagen der geschichtlichen und sozialen Entwicklung* (Zurich, 1946), esp. ch. 6.

7. R. S. and H. M. Lynd, *Middletown* (New York, 1929), ch. 28. Compare A. W. Kornhauser, "Analysis of 'Class' Structure of Contemporary American Society," in G. W. Hartmann and T. M. Newcomb, eds., *Industrial Conflict* (New York, 1939).

8. "A Communist's Career," *New York Times*, May 22, 1949; and Gabriel A. Almond, *The Appeals of Communism* (Princeton, 1954).

9. National Planning Association, *Why I Am in the Labor Movement* (Washington, 1949).

10. Peter Viereck, *Conservatism Revisited: The Revolt against Revolt, 1815–1949* (New York, 1949), pp. 5f., 16. Compare Karl Mannheim, "Das konservative Denken," *Archiv fuer Sozialwissenschaft und Sozialpolitik*, vol. 57, 1927; A. B. Wolfe, *Conservatism, Radicalism, and Scientific Method* (New York, 1923); and William F. Ogburn, *Social Change* (New York, 1950), part III.

11. Sherif, *op. cit.*, pp. 296ff., 367f., 450ff. Compare Gordon W. Allport, *Personality* (New York, 1937), pp. 430f.

12. Ruth Benedict, *Patterns of Culture* (New York, 1934), p. 252.

13. Hendrik De Man, *Zur Psychologie des Sozialismus* (Jena, 1926). For a Marxian criticism of De Man, see Pierre Naville, *Psychologie, Marxisme, Matérialisme* (Paris, 1946), esp. pp. 35ff. See also Emile Vandervelde, *La Psychologie du Socialisme* (Brussels, 1928).

14. R. H. S. Crossman, ed., *The God That Failed* (New York, 1949), esp. pp. 18, 82; also Arthur Koestler's self-analytic autobiography *Arrow in the Blue* (New York, 1952) and many other writings by both Koestler and Silone.

15. Among the very sizable literature by ex-Communists and Soviet victims, see Alexander Weissberg, *The Accused* (New York, 1951); and Whittaker Chambers, *Witness* (New York, 1952), esp. pp. 92ff., 114ff., 209ff., 482ff.

16. Kardiner, *Psychological Frontiers*, pp. 371ff., 436ff.; Eduard Heimann, *Freedom and Order* (New York, 1947); Erich Fromm, *Escape from Freedom* (New York, 1941), ch. 3; W. Scarlett, ed., *The Christian Demand for Social Justice* (New York, 1949); Frank H. Knight, *Freedom and Reform*

280 *Notes*

(New York, 1947), esp. ch. 4; and A. T. Mollegen, "The Religious Basis of Western Socialism," in D. D. Egbert and St. Persons, eds., *Socialism and American Life* (Princeton, 1952), vol. I, ch. 3.

17. J. M. Keynes, *The General Theory of Employment, Interest, and Money* (New York, 1936), ch. 24, esp. pp. 383f. Compare J. A. Hobson, *Confessions of an Economic Heretic* (London, 1938), esp. chs. 1, 14; and, of course, John Stuart Mill, *Autobiography* (New York, 1924).

18. D. Krech and R. S. Crutchfield, *Theory and Problems of Social Psychology* (New York, 1948), pp. 150ff.

19. Karl Mannheim, *Ideology and Utopia* (London, 1946), esp, pp. 36f., 49f., 173ff., 206ff. Compare Erich Fromm, *Man for Himself* (New York, 1947), pp. 42ff.; and Rosa Mayreder, *Der typische Verlauf sozialer Bewegungen*, 2d ed. (Vienna, 1925).

20. J. A. Schumpeter, "Science and Ideology," *American Economic Review*, March 1949.

21. Eric Hoffer, *The True Believer: Thoughts on the Nature of Mass Movements* (New York, 1951). Compare Sebastian De Grazia, *The Political Community* (Chicago, 1948), part II; and Robert Michels, "Psychologie der anti-kapitalistischen Massenbewegungen," *Grundriss der Sozialoekonomik* (Tuebingen, 1926), vol. IX, no. 1.

22. Cantril, *op. cit.;* and Charles S. Braden, *These Also Believe* (New York, 1949).

23. Of the enormous literature on Marxism, we can mention only a few studies which deal especially with its psychological problems: Karl Marx, *Die deutsche Ideologie* (Moscow, 1942); Otto Bauer, *Die Nationalitätenfrage und die Sozialdemokratie*, 2d ed. (Vienna, 1924); Georg Lukacs, *Geschichte und Klassenbewusstsein* (Berlin, 1923); Max Adler, "Das Formalpsychische im historischen Materialismus," in *Marxistische Probleme* (Stuttgart, 1919); F. H. Bartlett, "Marxism and the Psychoanalytic Theory of the Unconscious," *Science and Society*, winter 1951–1952; Otto Rühle, *Karl Marx* (New York, 1929), pp. 371ff.; Vernon Venable, *Human Nature: The Marxian View* (New York, 1945); M. M. Bober, *Karl Marx' Interpretation of History*, 2d ed. (Cambridge, Mass., 1948), part II; and J. A. Schumpeter, *Capitalism, Socialism, and Democracy*, 3d ed. (New York, 1950), part I.

24. Paul Federn, *Zur Psychologie der Revolution: Die vaterlose Gesellschaft* (Vienna, 1919). On the other hand, Robert Lindner, *Prescription for Rebellion* (New York, 1952), would like to see more "rebellion" (in the attitudinal sense of awareness, responsibility, and remedial action) and less "adjustment" (which he apparently identifies with conformity).

25. Karen Horney, *Our Inner Conflicts* (New York, 1945), p. 115.

26. For a discussion of the concept and scope of economic progress, see Colin Clark, *The Conditions of Economic Progress*, 3d ed. (New York, 1957), ch. 1.

27. John Strachey, *Contemporary Capitalism* (New York, 1956).

28. International Labor Office, *Lasting Peace the I.L.O. Way* (Geneva, 1951).

29. Vilfredo Pareto, *Introduction aux Systèmes Socialistes,* 2d ed. (Paris, 1926).

30. Louis Lévy, ed., *Anthologie de Jean Jaurès* (London, 1947), pp. 159f.; and Socialist Union, *Socialism: A New Statement of Principles* (London, 1952), p. 47. See also Socialist International, Declaration of July 3, 1951, in Frankfurt, Germany, *Aims and Tasks of Democratic Socialism;* Austen Albu, *Socialism and the Study of Man,* Fabian Tract no. 283 (London, 1951); and C. A. R. Crosland, *The Future of Socialism* (New York, 1957).

31. Joseph A. Schumpeter, *Imperialism and Social Classes* (New York, 1951), part II. Compare Riesman, *op. cit.,* ch. 12.

32. For example, Benjamin M. Selekman, *Labor Relations and Human Relations* (New York, 1947); D. Katz and R. L. Kahn, "Some Recent Findings in Human-Relations Research in Industry," in Swanson, Newcomb, and Hartley, eds., *op. cit.,* pp. 650ff.; C. M. Arensberg and others, eds., *Research in Industrial Human Relations* (New York, 1957); and A. Kornhauser, R. Dubin, and A. M. Ross, eds., *Industrial Conflict* (New York, 1954).

33. Selig Perlman, *A Theory of the Labor Movement* (New York, 1949); and Adolf Sturmthal, "Comments on Selig Perlman's *A Theory of the Labor Movement,*" *Industrial and Labor Relations Review,* July 1951, and "National Patterns of Union Behavior," *Journal of Political Economy,* December 1948.

34. Frank Tannenbaum, *A Philosophy of Labor* (New York, 1951).

35. Compare F. J. Roethlisberger and W. J. Dickson, *Management and the Worker* (Cambridge, Mass., 1947), part V; and J. R. P. French, A. Kornhauser, and A. Marrow, eds., "Conflict and Cooperation in Industry," *Journal of Social Issues,* February 1946.

36. Karl Marx, *Alienated Labor* (New York, n.d.).

37. C. S. Golden and H. J. Ruttenberg, *The Dynamics of Industrial Democracy* (New York, 1942), esp. ch. 1; Neil W. Chamberlain, *The Union Challenge to Management Control* (New York, 1948); and Arnold M. Rose, *Union Solidarity* (Minneapolis, 1952).

38. J. B. S. Hardman and M. Neufeld, eds., *The House of Labor* (New York, 1951), esp. chs. 2, 45; C. Wright Mills, *The New Men of Power* (New York, 1948); Eli Ginzberg, *The Labor Leader* (New York, 1948); and Charles A. Madison, *American Labor Leaders* (New York, 1950).

39. Carlo Levi, "For Freedom, We Must Conquer Fear," *New York Times Magazine,* October 3, 1948. See also his book *Of Fear and Freedom* (New York, 1950).

40. M. Horkheimer, "The Lessons of Fascism," in H. Cantril, ed., *Tensions That Cause Wars* (Urbana, 1950), p. 230; T. W. Adorno and others, *The Authoritarian Personality* (New York, 1950); Else Frenkel-Brunswik, "In-

teraction of Psychological and Sociological Factors in Political Behavior," *American Political Science Review,* March 1952; B. Bettelheim, "Remarks on the Psychological Appeal of Totalitarianism," *American Journal of Economics and Sociology,* October 1952; and R. Waelder, "Authoritarianism and Totalitarianism," in G. B. Wilbur and W. Muensterberger, eds., *Psychoanalysis and Culture* (New York, 1951).

41. Weissberg, *op. cit.;* Marion L. Starkey, *The Devil in Massachusetts* (New York, 1949); and Carey McWilliams, *Witch Hunt* (Boston, 1950).

42. For a historical comparison, see J. L. Talmon, *The Rise of Totalitarian Democracy* (Boston, 1952), esp. pp. 249ff.

43. Weissberg, *op. cit.,* pp. 123f.

44. Hamilton Fish Armstrong, *Tito and Goliath* (New York, 1951), p. 157. Compare Jan Stransky, *East Wind over Prague* (New York, 1951), esp. part III. For other interesting aspects of Soviet mentality, see Barrington Moore, *Soviet Politics* (Cambridge, Mass., 1950), esp. pp. 390ff., 408ff.; Margaret Mead, *Soviet Attitudes toward Authority* (New York, 1951).

45. N. W. Ackerman and M. Jahoda, *Anti-Semitism and Emotional Disorder* (New York, 1950), pp. 25ff., 88ff.; Sherif, *op. cit.,* esp. ch. 14; Cantril, *op. cit.,* ch. 4; B. Bettelheim and M. Janowitz, *Dynamics of Prejudice* (New York, 1950), chs. 4 and 9; Hannah Arendt, *The Origins of Totalitarianism* (New York, 1951); T. W. Adorno, "Freudian Theory and the Pattern of Fascist Propaganda," in G. Roheim, ed., *Psychoanalysis and the Social Sciences,* vol. III (New York, 1951); and A. Forster and B. R. Epstein, *The Troublemakers* (New York, 1952).

46. Albert Lauterbach, *Economic Security and Individual Freedom* (Ithaca, N.Y., 1948).

47. Ferdinand Zweig, *Economic Ideas* (New York, 1950), pp. 136ff., and *The Planning of Free Societies* (London, 1942), pp. 240ff.; Carl Landauer, *Theory of National Economic Planning,* rev. ed. (Berkeley, 1947), ch. 4; and W. Arthur Lewis, *The Principles of Economic Planning* (London, 1949).

48. J. A. Hobson, *Incentives in the New Industrial Order* (London, 1922). Compare Karl Marx, *Randglossen zum Programm der deutschen Arbeiterpartei* (Leipzig, 1922), p. 17; and Harry W. Laidler, *Our Changing Industrial Incentives* (New York, 1949).

49. The Acton Society Trust, *Nationalized Industry,* pamphlet series (London, 1950–1952); Herbert S. Morrison, *The Peaceful Revolution* (London, 1949), ch. 4; E. F. M. Durbin, *Problems of Economic Planning* (London, 1949); R. H. S. Crossman, ed., *New Fabian Essays* (London, 1952); G. D. H. Cole, *Socialist Economics* (London, 1950); Ben W. Lewis, *British Planning and Nationalization* (New York, 1952); Robert L. Heilbroner, "Labor Unrest in the British Nationalized Sector," *Social Research,* March 1952; William A. Robson, ed., *Problems of Nationalized Industry* (New York, 1952); A. Sturmthal, "Nationalization and Workers' Control in Britain and France," *Journal of Political Economy,* February 1953; and Crosland, *op. cit.,* ch. 16.

50. F. A. Hayek, *The Road to Serfdom* (Chicago, 1944), ch. 10. Compare

Herman Finer, *Road to Reaction* (Boston, 1945); and Barbara Wootton, *Freedom under Planning* (Chapel Hill, 1945).

51. Schumpeter, *Capitalism,* pp. 205ff. Compare Merton, *op. cit.,* chs. 5, 6.

52. I. M. D. Little, *A Critique of Welfare Economics* (Oxford, 1950), esp. chs. 14, 15. Compare K. J. Arrow, "Little's Critique of Welfare Economics," *American Economic Review,* December 1951; and E. Ronald Walker, *From Economic Theory to Policy* (Chicago, 1943), chs. 11, 12.

53. *Guidelines for Point 4,* Recommendations of the International Development Advisory Board (Washington, D.C., June 5, 1952); also United Nations, *Measures for the Economic Development of Under-developed Countries* (New York, 1951), esp. ch. 3; Bert F. Hoselitz, ed., *The Progress of Underdeveloped Areas* (Chicago, 1952), esp. the articles by A. Gerschenkron, R. Linton, M. J. Herskovitz, and S. P. Hayes, Jr.; and S. Herbert Frankel, *The Economic Impact on Under-developed Societies* (Cambridge, Mass., 1953); also "Attitude Research in Modernizing Areas," *Public Opinion Quarterly,* special issue, fall 1958, and W. Arthur Lewis, *The Theory of Economic Growth* (London, 1955).

54. Kurt Lewin, *Field Theory in Social Science* (New York, 1951), ch. 9, p. 235; also Dorwin Cartwright, "Achieving Change in People," *Human Relations,* vol. 4, no. 4, 1951.

Bibliography

THE following bibliography, which is confined to books, is meant to be suggestive, rather than exhaustive. Furthermore, it does not attempt to classify the specific field of psychological factors in economics for which each book may have relevance. Additional references can be found in the notes to the respective chapters.

Ackerman, N. W., and Jahoda, M. *Anti-Semitism and Emotional Disorder.* New York, 1950.

Acton Society Trust. *Management Succession.* London, 1956.

Adorno, T. W., and associates. *The Authoritarian Personality.* New York, 1950.

Aftalion, Albert. *Monnaie, Prix et Change.* Paris, 1940.

Alasco, Johannes. *Intellectual Capitalism.* Boston, 1950.

Alexander, Franz. *Our Age of Unreason.* Rev. ed. Philadelphia, 1951.

Allen, Frederick L. *The Great Pierpont Morgan.* New York, 1949.

——. *Lords of Creation.* New York, 1935.

Allen, George H., ed. *Individual Initiative in Business.* Cambridge, Mass., 1950.

Allport, G. W., and Postman, L. *The Psychology of Rumor.* New York, 1947.

Almond, Gabriel A. *The Appeals of Communism.* Princeton, 1954.

Andrews, F. Emerson. *Attitudes Toward Giving.* New York, 1953.

Anshen, Ruth N., ed. *The Family: Its Function and Destiny.* New York, 1949.

Arendt, Hannah. *The Origins of Totalitarianism.* New York, 1951.

Arensberg, C. M., and others, eds. *Research in Industrial Human Relations.* New York, 1957.

Arnold, Thurman. *The Folklore of Capitalism.* New Haven, 1939.

Arrow, Kenneth J. *Social Choice and Individual Values.* New York, 1951.

Asch, Solomon E. *Social Psychology.* New York, 1952.

Bakke, E. Wight. *Citizens without Work.* New Haven, 1940.

——. *The Unemployed Worker.* New Haven, 1940.

Barghorn, Frederick. *The Soviet Image of the United States.* New York, 1951.

Barnard, Chester I. *The Functions of the Executive.* Cambridge, Mass., 1938.

——. *Organization and Management.* Cambridge, Mass., 1948.

Bastide, Roger. *Sociologie et Psychanalyse.* Paris, 1950.

Bauer, Otto. *Die Nationalitaetenfrage und die Sozialdemokratie.* 2d ed. Vienna, 1924.

Bauer, Raymond A. *The New Man in Soviet Psychology.* Cambridge, Mass., 1952.

Baumgarten, Franziska. *The Psychology of Human Relations in Industry.* New York, 1951.

Baumol, William J. *Welfare Economics and the Theory of the State.* Cambridge, Mass., 1952.

Beard, Miriam. *History of the Business Man.* New York, 1938.

Bendix, Reinhard. *Work and Authority in Industry.* New York, 1956.

——, and Lipset, S. M., eds. *Class, Status and Power.* Glencoe, Ill., 1953.

Bergler, Edmund. *Money and Emotional Conflicts.* New York, 1951.

Bingham, Alfred. *Man's Estate: Adventures in Economic Discovery.* New York, 1939.

Blake, Clark. *The Advertising Smokescreen.* New York, 1944.

Blum, Fred H. *Toward a Democratic Work Process.* New York, 1953.

Blum, Milton L. *Industrial Psychology and Its Social Foundations.* New York, 1949.

Borkenau, Franz. *Der Uebergang vom feudalen zum buergerlichen Weltbild.* Paris, 1934.

Boulding, Kenneth E. *The Image.* Ann Arbor, 1956.

——. *The Organizational Revolution: A Study in the Ethics of Economic Organization.* New York, 1953.

Bowen, Howard R. *The Business Enterprise as a Subject for Research.* New York, 1955.

——. *Social Responsibilities of the Business Man.* New York, 1953.

Bowman, Mary Jean, ed. *Expectations, Uncertainty, and Business Behavior.* New York, 1958.

Braden, Charles S. *These Also Believe.* New York, 1949.

Brady, Robert A. *Business as a System of Power.* Berkeley, 1943.

Brun, Rudolf. *Die Neurose als kulturelles and soziales Problem.* Zurich, 1949.

Bunting, J. Whitney, ed. *Ethics for Modern Business Practice.* New York, 1953.

Butters, J. K., Thompson, L. E., and Bollinger, L. L. *Effects of Taxation: Investments by Individuals.* Boston, 1953.

Cantril, Hadley. *The Politics of Despair.* New York, 1958.

——. *Psychology of Social Movements.* New York, 1941.

Carlson, Sune. *Executive Behavior: A Study of the Work Load and the Working Methods of Managing Directors.* Stockholm, 1951.

Carnegie, Andrew, and others. *Personality in Business.* Chicago, 1907.

Carr, E. H. *The New Society.* London, 1951.

Centers, Richard. *Psychology of Social Classes.* Princeton, 1949.

Chamberlain, Neil W. *Union Challenge to Management Control.* New York, 1948.

Chambers, E. G. *Psychology and the Industrial Worker.* Cambridge, England, 1951.

Chase, Stuart. *Men at Work.* New York, 1945.

——. *The Proper Study of Mankind.* New York, 1948.

——. *Roads to Agreement: Successful Methods in Human Relations.* New York, 1951.

——, and others. *The Social Responsibility of Management.* New York, 1950.

Childs, M. W., and Cater, D. *Ethics in a Business Society.* New York, 1954.

Christie, R., and Jahoda, M., eds. *Studies in the Scope and Method of "The Authoritarian Personality."* Glencoe, Ill., 1954.

Clark, Colin. *The Conditions of Economic Progress,* 3d ed. London, 1957.

Clark, John B. *The Philosophy of Wealth.* Boston, 1894.

Clark, John M. *Alternative to Serfdom.* New York, 1948.

——. *Preface to Social Economics.* New York, 1936.

Clark, Lincoln H., ed. *Consumer Behavior.* 2 vols. New York, 1954 and 1955.

Cole, Robert H., ed. *Consumer Behavior and Motivation.* Urbana, Ill., 1956.

Commons, John R. *Institutional Economics.* New York, 1934.

Copeland, Melvin T. *The Executive at Work.* Cambridge, Mass., 1951.

Cressey, Donald R. *Other People's Money: A Study in the Social Psychology of Embezzlement.* Glencoe, Ill., 1954.

Crossman, R. H. S., ed. *The God That Failed.* New York, 1950.

——, ed. *New Fabian Essays.* New York, 1952.

Current Trends in Social Psychology. Pittsburgh, 1948.

Dahl, R. A., and Lindblom, C. E. *Politics, Economics and Welfare.* New York, 1953.

Davis, Alison, and Dollard, John. *Children of Bondage.* Washington, 1940.

De Man, Hendrik. *Joy in Work.* New York, 1929.

——. *Zur Psychologie des Sozialismus.* Jena, 1926.

Deutsch, M., and Collins, M. E. *Interracial Housing: A Psychological Evaluation of a Social Experiment.* Minneapolis, 1951.

Dewey, John. *Human Nature and Conduct.* New York, 1930.

Dickinson, Z. C. *Economic Motives: The Psychological Foundations of Economic Theory.* Cambridge, Mass., 1922.

Dimock, Marshall E. *Free Enterprise and the Administrative State.* University, Ala., 1951.

Djilas, Milovan. *The New Class.* New York, 1957.

Dollard, John, and others. *Caste and Class in a Southern Town.* 2d ed. New York, 1949.

Donnison, C. P. *Civilization and Disease.* Baltimore, 1938.

Downs, Anthony. *An Economic Theory of Democracy.* New York, 1958.

Drucker, Peter F. *The End of Economic Man.* New York, 1939.

——. *The New Society: The Anatomy of the Industrial Order.* New York, 1949.

Dubin, Robert, ed. *Human Relations in Administration.* New York, 1951.

DuBois, Cora. *The People of Alor.* Minneapolis, 1944.

Duesenberry, J. S. *Income, Saving, and the Theory of Consumer Behavior.* Cambridge, Mass., 1949.

Durbin, E. F. M., and Bowlby, John. *Personal Aggressiveness and War.* London, 1939.

Durkheim, Emile. *Suicide: A Study in Sociology.* Glencoe, Ill., 1951.

Eaton, J., and Weil, R. *Culture and Mental Disorders.* Glencoe, Ill., 1956.

Edgeworth, Francis Y. *Mathematical Psychics.* London, 1881 and 1932.

Egbert, D. D., and Persons, S., eds. *Socialism and American Life.* 2 vols. Princeton, 1952.

Eiteman, W. J. *Price Determination: Business Practice versus Economic Theory.* Ann Arbor, 1949.

Ellis, Howard S., ed. *A Survey of Contemporary Economics.* Vol. I. Philadelphia, 1948.

Erikson, Erik H. *Childhood and Society.* New York, 1950.

Ernst, M. L., and Loth, D. *Report on the American Communist.* New York, 1952.

Essertier, Daniel. *Psychologie et Sociologie.* Paris, 1927.

Eysenck, H. J. *The Psychology of Politics.* New York, 1955.

Faris, R. E. L., and Dunham, H. W. *Mental Disorders in Urban Areas.* Chicago, 1939.

Fein, Rashi. *Economics of Mental Illness.* New York, 1958.

Feller, F. M. *Psycho-Dynamik der Reklame.* Berne, 1932.

Fellner, William. *Competition among the Few.* Berkeley, 1950.

Festinger, L., and Katz, D., eds. *Research Methods in the Behavioral Sciences.* New York, 1953.

Festinger, L., Schechter, S., and Back, K. *Social Pressures in Informal Groups.* New York, 1950.

Fisher, B. R., and Withey, St. B. *Big Business as the People See It.* Ann Arbor, 1951.

Florence, P. Sargant. *Economics and Human Behavior.* New York, 1927.

——. *The Logic of British and American Industry.* London, 1953.

Flubacher, Joseph F. *The Concept of Ethics in the History of Economics.* New York, 1950.

Ford, Henry. *My Life and Work.* Garden City, 1922.

Fortune Magazine. *The Art of Success.* Philadelphia, 1956.

——. *The Executive Life.* New York, 1956.

——. *Why Do People Buy?* New York, 1953.

Frank, Lawrence K. *Nature and Human Nature.* New Brunswick, 1951.

——. *Society as the Patient.* New Brunswick, 1948.

Frankel, S. Herbert. *The Economic Impact on Under-developed Societies.* Cambridge, Mass., 1953.

Fraser, Lindley M. *Economic Thought and Language.* London, 1947.

Freud, Sigmund. *An Outline of Psychoanalysis.* New York, 1949.

——. *Das Unbehagen in der Kultur.* Vienna, 1930.

Friedmann, Georges. *Où va le Travail Humain?* Paris, 1950.

Fromm, Erich. *Escape from Freedom.* New York, 1941.

——. *Man for Himself.* New York, 1947.

——. *The Sane Society.* New York, 1955.

Galbraith, John K. *The Affluent Society.* Boston, 1958.

——. *American Capitalism: The Concept of Countervailing Power.* Boston, 1956.

Gambs, John S. *Beyond Supply and Demand.* New York, 1946.

Gardner, B. B., and Moore, D. G. *Human Relations in Industry.* Chicago, 1950.

Gasser, Christian, ed. *Mensch und Betrieb.* St. Gallen, 1950.

Ginzberg, Eli. *Grass on the Slag Heaps: The Story of the Welsh Miners.* New York, 1942.

——. *The Unemployed.* New York, 1943.

——, and associates. *Occupational Choice.* New York, 1951.

——, and associates. *What Makes an Executive?* New York, 1955.

——, and Bray, D. W. *Effective Change in Large Organizations.* New York, 1957.

——, and Bray, D. W. *The Uneducated.* New York, 1953.

Girvetz, Harry K. *From Wealth to Welfare: The Evolution of Liberalism.* Stanford, 1950.

Giterman, Valentin. *Die historische Tragik der sozialistischen Idee.* Zurich, 1939.

Glover, J. D., and Hower, R. M. *The Administrator: Cases on Human Relations in Business.* Chicago, 1950.

Golden, C. S., and Ruttenberg, H. J. *The Dynamics of Industrial Democracy.* New York, 1942.

Gordon, Manya. *How to Tell Progress from Reaction.* New York, 1944.

Gordon, Robert A. *Business Leadership in the Large Corporation.* Washington, 1945.

Gorer, Geoffrey. *The American People.* New York, 1948.

——, and Rickman, J. *The People of Great Russia.* London, 1949.

Gouldner, Alvin W. *Patterns of Industrial Bureaucracy.* Glencoe, Ill., 1954.

Graham, Frank D. *Social Goals and Economic Institutions.* Princeton, 1942.

Gruchy, Allan. *Modern Economic Thought.* New York, 1947.

Halbwachs, Maurice. *Esquisse d'une Psychologie des Classes Sociales.* Paris, 1955.

Haley, Bernard F., ed. *A Survey of Contemporary Economics.* Vol. II. Homewood, Ill., 1952.

Halliday, James. L. *Psychosocial Medicine: A Study of the Sick Society.* New York, 1948.

Handlin, Oscar. *The Uprooted.* Boston, 1952.

Harrod, R. F. *Economic Essays.* New York, 1953.

Hart, A. G. *Anticipations, Uncertainty and Dynamic Planning.* 2d ed. New York, 1950.

Hartmann, G. W., and Newcomb, T., eds. *Industrial Conflict: A Psychological Interpretation.* New York, 1939.

Havighurst, R. J., and Morgan, H. G. *The Social History of a War-Boom Community.* New York, 1951.

Hayek, F. A. *The Counter-Revolution of Science: Studies on the Abuse of Reason.* Glencoe, Ill., 1952.

Hayek, F. A. *Individualism and Economic Order*. Chicago, 1948.

Hayes, Douglas A. *Business Confidence and Business Activity*. Ann Arbor, 1951.

Heimann, Eduard. *Freedom and Order*. New York, 1947.

———. *Sozialwissenschaft und Wirklichkeit*. Tuebingen, 1932.

Heller, W. W., Boddy, F. M., and Nelson, C. L. *Savings in the Modern Economy*. Minneapolis, 1953.

Heron, Alexander. *Why Men Work*. Stanford University, 1948.

Hersey, Rexford B. *Workers' Emotions in Shop and Home*. Philadelphia, 1932.

Herskovits, Melville J. *Economic Anthropology*. New York, 1952.

———. *Man and His Works*. New York, 1948.

Hession, C. H., Miller, S. M., and Stoddart, C. *The Dynamics of the American Economy*. New York, 1956.

Hetzer, Hildegard. *Kindheit und Armut*. Leipzig, 1929.

Hexter, Maurice B. *Social Consequences of Business Cycles*. Boston, 1925.

Hickman, C. A., and Kuhn, M. H. *Individuals, Groups, and Economic Behavior*. New York, 1956.

Hicks, J. R. *Value and Capital*. 2d ed. Oxford, 1946.

Higgins, Benjamin. *What Do Economists Know?* Melbourne, 1951.

Hirschman, Albert O. *The Strategy of Economic Development*. New Haven, 1958.

Hobson, J. A. *Economics and Ethics*. Boston, 1929.

———. *Incentives in the New Industrial Order*. New York, 1922.

———. *Work and Wealth: A Human Valuation*. New York, 1949.

Hoffer, Eric. *The True Believer: Thoughts on the Nature of Mass Movements*. New York, 1951.

Hogben, Lancelot. *The Retreat from Reason*. London, 1936.

Hollingshead, August B. *Elmtown's Youth: The Impact of Social Classes on Adolescents*. New York, 1949.

———, and Redlich, F. C. *Social Class and Mental Illness*. New York, 1958.

Hopkins, Pryns. *The Psychology of Social Movements: A Psycho-analytic View of Society*. London, 1938.

Horkheimer, Max. *Eclipse of Reason*. New York, 1947.

———, ed. *Studien über Autorität und Familie*. Paris, 1936.

Horney, Karen. *Neurosis and Human Growth*. New York, 1950.

———. *The Neurotic Personality of Our Time*. New York, 1937.

Hoselitz, B. F., ed. *The Progress of Underdeveloped Areas*. Chicago, 1952.

———, and Weisskopf, W. A., eds. *The Psychological Approach to the Social Sciences. American Journal of Economics and Sociology*, special issue. October 1952.

Hoslett, S. D., ed. *Human Factors in Management.* Parkville, Mo., 1946.

Hoyt, Elizabeth E. *The Income of Society.* New York, 1950.

——, and associates. *American Income and Its Use.* New York, 1954.

Husband, Richard W. *The Psychology of Successful Selling.* New York, 1953.

Hutchinson, T. W. *The Significance and Basic Postulates of Economic Theory.* London, 1938.

Ichheiser, Gustav. *Kritik des Erfolges.* Leipzig, 1930.

——. *Misunderstandings in Human Relations: A Study in False Social Perceptions.* Chicago, 1949.

International Congress on Mental Health. *Proceedings.* London, 1948. 4 vols. New York, 1949.

Irey, Elmer L. *The Tax Dodgers.* New York, 1948.

Ise, John. *Economics.* Rev. ed. New York, 1950.

Jaques, Elliott. *The Changing Culture of a Factory.* London, 1951.

Jöhr, Walter A. *Die Konjunkturschwankungen.* Tuebingen, 1952.

——. *Theoretische Grundlagen der Wirtschaftspolitik.* St. Gallen, 1943.

Jones, Alfred W. *Life, Liberty, and Property.* Philadelphia, 1941.

Jones, Ernest, ed. *Social Aspects of Psychoanalysis.* London, 1924.

Jones, Manley H. *Executive Decision Making.* Homewood, Ill., 1957.

Jung, Carl Gustav. *Aufsaetze zur Zeitgeschichte.* Zurich, 1946.

Kaplan, A. D. H. *Big Enterprise in a Competitive System.* Washington, 1954.

Kapp, K. W. *The Social Costs of Private Enterprise.* Cambridge, Mass., 1950.

Kardiner, Abram. *The Individual and His Society.* New York, 1939.

——. *The Psychological Frontiers of Society.* New York, 1945.

——, and Ovesey, L. *The Mark of Oppression: A Psychosocial Study of the American Negro.* New York, 1951.

Katona, George. *Psychological Analysis of Economic Behavior.* New York, 1951.

——. *War without Inflation.* New York, 1942.

——, and associates. *Business Looks at Banks.* Ann Arbor, 1957.

——, and Mueller, Eva. *Consumer Attitudes and Demand, 1950–1952.* Ann Arbor, 1953.

——, and Mueller, Eva. *Consumer Expectations, 1953–1956.* Ann Arbor, 1957.

Katz, E., and Lazarsfeld, P. F. *Personal Influence.* Glencoe, Ill., 1955.

Keilhau, Wilhelm. *Principles of Private and Public Planning: A Study in Economic Sociology.* London, 1951.

Kellner, Wolfgang. *Die Wirtschaftsfuehrung als menschliche Leistung.* Braunschweig, 1949.

Keynes, John Maynard. *General Theory of Employment, Interest, and Money.* New York, 1936.

Keynes, John Neville. *The Scope and Method of Political Economy.* London, 1904.

Kimmel, Lewis H. *Taxes and Economic Incentives.* Washington, 1950.

Kluckhohn, Clyde. *Mirror of Man.* New York, 1949.

——, and Murray, H. A., eds. *Personality in Nature, Society, and Culture.* 2d ed. New York, 1956.

Knauth, Oswald W. *Managerial Enterprise.* New York, 1948.

Knight, Frank H. *The Economic Order and Religion.* New York, 1945.

——. *The Ethics of Competition.* New York, 1935.

——. *Freedom and Reform.* New York, 1947.

——. *Risk, Uncertainty and Profit.* Boston, 1921.

Kolnai, Aurel. *Psychoanalyse und Soziologie.* Leipzig, 1920.

Komarovsky, Mirra. *The Unemployed Man and His Family.* New York, 1940.

Kornhauser, A. W., Dubin, R., and Ross, A. M., eds. *Industrial Conflict.* New York, 1954.

Kracauer, S. *Die Angestellten.* Frankfurt, 1930.

Krech, D., and Crutchfield, R. S. *Theory and Problems of Social Psychology.* New York, 1948.

Kuznets, Simon. *Economic Change.* New York, 1953.

Lane, F. C., and Riemersma, J. C., eds. *Enterprise and Secular Change.* Homewood, Ill., 1953.

Lane, Robert E. *The Regulation of Businessmen.* New Haven, 1954.

Laski, Harold J. *Liberty in the Modern State.* New York, 1949.

Lasswell, Harold D. *Psychopathology and Politics.* Chicago, 1934.

——. *World Politics and Personal Insecurity.* New York, 1935.

——, and Atkins, W. *Labor Attitudes and Problems.* New York, 1924.

——, and Kaplan, A. *Power and Society.* New Haven, 1950.

Lazarsfeld, Paul F. *The People's Choice.* New York, 1948.

Lazarsfeld-Jahoda, M., and Zeisel, H. *Die Arbeitslosen von Marienthal.* Leipzig, 1933.

Learned, E. P., Ulrich, D. N., and Booz, D. R. *Executive Action.* Cambridge, Mass., 1950.

Leavitt, Harold J. *Managerial Psychology.* Chicago, 1958.

Le Bon, Gustave. *The Psychology of Revolution.* London, 1913.

Lederer, Emil. *State of the Masses: The Threat of the Classless Society.* New York, 1940.

Bibliography 293

Leighton, Alexander H. *Human Relations in a Changing World*. New York, 1949.

——, Clausen, J. A., and Wilson, R. N., eds. *Explorations in Social Psychiatry*. New York, 1957.

Leites, Nathan. *A Study of Bolshevism*. Glencoe, Ill., 1953.

Lens, Sidney. *Left, Right, and Center*. Hinsdale, Ill., 1949.

Lerner, D., and Lasswell, H. D., eds. *The Policy Sciences*. Stanford, 1951.

Levy, Hermann. *Drink: An Economic and Social Study*. London, 1951.

——. *Nationaloekonomie und Wirklichkeit: Versuch einer sozialpsychologischen Begruendung der Wirtschaftslehre*. Jena, 1928.

Lewin, Kurt. *Field Theory in Social Science*. New York, 1951.

——. *Resolving Social Conflicts*. New York, 1948.

Likert, R., and Hayes, S. P. *Some Applications of Behavioral Research*. Paris, 1957.

Lindner, Robert. *Prescription for Rebellion*. New York, 1952.

Linton, Ralph. *The Cultural Background of Personality*. New York, 1945.

——, ed. *The Science of Man in the World Crisis*. New York, 1945.

Lipset, S. M., and Bendix, R. *Social Mobility in Industrial Society*. Berkeley, 1959

Little, I. M. D. *A Critique of Welfare Economics*. Oxford, 1950.

Lombard, George F. F. *Behavior in a Selling Group*. Cambridge, Mass., 1955.

Lowe, Adolphe. *Economics and Sociology*. London, 1935.

Lowenthal, Leo, and Guterman, Norbert. *Prophets of Deceit*. New York, 1949.

Lucas, D. B., and Britt, S. H. *Advertising Psychology and Research*. New York, 1950.

Lynd, Robert S. *Knowledge for What?* Princeton, 1939.

Lynd, R. S. and H. M. *Middletown*. New York, 1929.

——. *Middletown in Transition*. New York, 1937.

McDougall, William. *The Group Mind*. 2d ed. New York, 1920.

MacIver, Robert. *Social Causation*. New York, 1942.

MacKenzie, Norman, ed. *Conviction*. London, 1958.

McWilliams, Carey. *Witch Hunt*. Boston, 1950.

Madison, Charles A. *Labor Leaders: The Personalities and Forces in the Labor Movement*. New York, 1950.

Maier, Norman R. F. *Psychology in Industry*. Cambridge, Mass., 1946.

Malinowski, Bronislaw. *The Dynamics of Culture Change*. New Haven, 1945.

Mannheim, Karl. *Essays on Sociology and Social Psychology*. London, 1953.

Mannheim, Karl. *Freedom, Power, and Democratic Planning.* New York, 1950.
——. *Ideology and Utopia.* New York, 1946.
——. *Man and Society in an Age of Reconstruction.* New York, 1941.
Marchal, Jean. *Problèmes Economiques Contemporains.* Paris, 1950.
Marx, Karl. *Die deutsche Ideologie.* Moscow, 1942.
Masserman, J., and Moreno, J., eds. *Progress in Psychotherapy.* Vol. IV. New York, 1959.
Mayer, Martin. *Madison Avenue, U.S.A.* New York, 1957.
Mayo, Elton. *The Human Problems of an Industrial Civilization.* Boston, 1946.
——. *The Social Problems of an Industrial Civilization.* Boston, 1945.
Mead, Margaret. *And Keep Your Powder Dry.* New York, 1942.
——. *Soviet Attitudes toward Authority.* New York, 1951.
——, ed. *Cooperation and Competition among Primitive Peoples.* New York, 1937.
——, ed. *Cultural Patterns and Technical Change.* Paris, 1953.
Merton, Robert K. *Mass Persuasion: Social Psychology of a War-Bond Drive.* New York, 1946.
——. *Social Theory and Social Structure.* Glencoe, Ill., 1949.
Meyer, J. R., and Kuh, E. *The Investment Decision.* Cambridge, Mass., 1957.
Michels, Robert. *Psychologie der antikapitalistischen Massenbewegungen. Grundriss der Sozialoekonomik,* Vol. IX. Tuebingen, 1926.
Midcentury White House Conference on Children and Youth. *Personality in the Making.* New York, 1952.
Miller, James G., ed. *Experiments in Social Process.* New York, 1950.
Miller, William, ed. *Men in Business: Essays in the History of Entrepreneurship.* Cambridge, Mass., 1952.
Mills, C. Wright. *The New Men of Power: America's Labor Leaders.* New York, 1948.
——. *The Power Elite.* New York, 1956.
——. *White Collar: The American Middle Classes.* New York, 1951.
Mises, Ludwig. *Human Action.* New Haven, 1949.
Mitchell, Wesley C. *Lecture Notes on Types of Economic Theory.* 2 vols. New York, 1949. Mimeo.
Money-Kyrle, R. E. *Psychoanalysis and Politics.* New York, 1951.
Monnerot, Jules. *Sociology and Psychology of Communism.* Boston, 1953.
Montagu, Ashley. *On Being Human.* New York, 1950.
Moore, Wilbert E. *Industrial Relations and Social Order.* New York, 1951.
——. *Industrialization and Labor.* Ithaca, N.Y., 1951.
Morgan, James N. *Consumer Economics.* New York, 1955.

Morgenstern, Oskar. *The Limits of Economics.* London, 1937.

——. *Wirtschaftsprognose.* Vienna, 1928.

Morse, Nancy C. *Satisfactions in the White-Collar Job.* Ann Arbor, 1953.

Mosca, Gaetano. *The Ruling Class.* New York, 1939.

Muensterberg, Hugo. *Psychologie und Wirtschaftsleben.* Leipzig, 1922.

——. *Psychology and Social Sanity.* Garden City, 1914.

Murdock, George P. *Social Structure.* New York, 1949.

Murphy, Gardner. *In the Minds of Men: The Study of Human Behavior and Social Tensions in India.* New York, 1953.

——, ed. *Human Nature and Enduring Peace.* Boston, 1945.

Myers, Gustavus. *History of the Great American Fortunes.* New York, 1936.

Myrdal, Gunnar. *The Political Element in the Development of Economic Theory.* Cambridge, Mass., 1954.

——. *Rich Lands and Poor.* New York, 1957.

National Planning Association. *Causes of Industrial Peace under Collective Bargaining.* Washington, 1948.

Naville, Pierre. *Psychologie, Marxisme, Matérialisme.* Paris, 1946.

Nevins, Allan. *Ford: The Times, the Man, the Company.* New York, 1954.

——. *Study in Power: John D. Rockefeller, Industrialist and Philanthropist.* 2 vols. New York, 1953.

Newcomb, Theodore. *Personality and Social Change.* New York, 1943.

——. *Social Psychology.* New York, 1950.

Newcomer, Mabel. *The Big-Business Executive.* New York, 1955.

Nobelstiftelsen, ed. *Nobel: The Man and His Prizes.* Norman, Okla., 1951.

Nordskog, J. E., McDonagh, E. C., and Vincent, M. P., eds. *Analyzing Social Problems.* New York, 1950.

Nourse, Edwin C. *Price-Making in a Democracy.* Washington, 1944.

Noyes, C. Reinold. *Economic Man: In Relation to His Natural Environment.* New York, 1948.

Nyman, R. Carter. *Foundations for Constructive Industrial Relations.* New York, 1949.

Ogburn, William F. *Social Change with Respect to the Culture and Original Nature.* New York, 1950.

Ortlieb, H. D., and Schelsky, H., eds. *Wege zum Sozialen Frieden.* Stuttgart, 1954.

Osborn, Reuben. *Freud and Marx.* New York, 1937.

Oxenfeldt, Alfred R. *Industrial Pricing and Market Practices.* New York, 1951.

Packard, Vance O. *The Hidden Persuaders.* New York, 1957.

——. *The Status Seekers.* New York, 1959.

Pareto, Vilfredo. *The Mind and Society.* 4 vols. New York, 1942.

Parsons, Talcott. *The Social System.* Glencoe, Ill., 1951.

——, and Shils, E. A., eds. *Toward a General Theory of Action.* Cambridge, Mass., 1951.

Patrick, Clarence H. *Alcohol, Culture and Society.* Durham, N.C., 1952.

Pederson-Krag, Geraldine. *Personality Factors in Work and Employment.* New York, 1955.

Perlman, Selig. *A Theory of the Labor Movement.* New York, 1949.

Picard, Max. *Hitler in Our Selves.* Hinsdale, Ill., 1947.

Piettre, André. *Humanisme Chrétien et Économie Politique.* Paris, 1950.

Pigou, A. C. *The Economics of Welfare.* 4th ed. London, 1938.

——. *Essays in Economics.* London, 1952.

Pitkin, Walter B. *The Consumer: His Nature and His Changing Habits.* New York, 1932.

Polanyi, Karl. *The Great Transformation.* New York, 1944.

——, and others. *Trade and Market in the Early Empires.* Glencoe, Ill., 1957.

Potter, David M. *People of Plenty.* Chicago, 1954.

Powdermaker, Hortense. *Hollywood: The Dream Factory.* Boston, 1950.

Radin, Max. *Manners and Morals of Business.* Indianapolis, 1949.

Ranulf, Svend. *Moral Indignation and Middle-Class Psychology.* Copenhagen, 1938.

Recent Social Trends in the United States: Report of the President's Research Committee on Social Trends. 2 vols. New York, 1933.

Reder, Melvin W. *Studies in the Theory of Welfare Economics.* New York, 1947.

Redfield, Charles E. *Communication in Management.* Chicago, 1953.

Redlich, Fritz. *History of American Business Leaders.* Ann Arbor, 1940.

——. *The Molding of American Banking.* New York, 1947.

Reymert, M. L., ed. *Feelings and Emotions.* New York, 1950.

Reynaud, P. L. *Economie Politique et Psychologie Expérimentale.* Paris, 1946.

——. *Le Facteur Humain dans l'Evolution Economique.* Paris, 1942.

——, ed. *La Psychologie Economique.* Paris, 1954.

Reynolds, Lloyd G., and Shister, J. *Job Horizons: A Study of Job Satisfaction and Labor Mobility.* New York, 1949.

Rhys-Williams, Lady. *Taxation and Incentive.* New York, 1953.

Riesman, David. *Faces in the Crowd.* New Haven, 1952.

——. *The Lonely Crowd.* New Haven, 1950.

Robbins, Lionel. *An Essay on the Nature and Significance of Economic Science.* London, 1946.

Robertson, D. H. *Utility and All That, and Other Essays.* London, 1952.

Robinson, Joan. *Economics Is a Serious Subject.* Cambridge, England, 1932.

Roepke, Wilhelm. *The Social Crisis of Our Time.* London, 1950.

Roethlisberger, F. J. *Management and Morale.* Cambridge, Mass., 1946.

——, and Dickson, W. J. *Management and the Worker.* Cambridge, Mass., 1947.

Roheim, Geza, ed. *Psychoanalysis and Anthropology.* New York, 1950.

——, ed. *Psychoanalysis and the Social Sciences.* 3 vols. New York, 1947–1951.

Rohrer, J. H., and Sherif, M., eds. *Social Psychology at the Crossroads.* New York, 1951.

Rose, Arnold M. *Union Solidarity: The Internal Cohesion of a Labor Union.* Minneapolis, 1952.

——, ed. *Mental Health and Mental Disorder: A Sociological Approach.* New York, 1955.

Rostow, W. W. *The Process of Economic Growth.* New York, 1952.

Ruehle, Otto. *Karl Marx.* New York, 1929.

Ruesch, J., and Bateson, G. *Communication: The Social Matrix of Psychiatry.* New York, 1951.

Salz, Arthur. *Macht und Wirtschaftsgesetz.* Leipzig, 1930.

Sanders, Thomas A. *Effects of Taxation on Executives.* Boston, 1951.

Sargent, S. S., and Smith, N. W., eds. *Culture and Personality.* New York, 1949.

Scarlett, W., ed. *The Christian Demand for Social Justice.* New York, 1949.

Schilder, Paul. *Psychoanalysis, Man and Society.* New York, 1951.

Schmölders, G., Schröder, R., and Seidenfus, H. St. *John Maynard Keynes als Psychologe.* Berlin, 1956.

Schneider, Louis. *The Freudian Psychology and Veblen's Social Theory.* New York, 1948.

Schoeffler, Sidney. *The Failures of Economics.* Cambridge, Mass., 1955.

Schumpeter, Joseph A. *Capitalism, Socialism and Democracy.* 3d ed. New York, 1950.

——. *Essays.* Cambridge, Mass., 1951.

Selekman, Benjamin M. *Labor Relations and Human Relations.* New York, 1948.

——. *A Moral Philosophy for Management.* New York, 1959.

——. *Power and Morality in a Business Society.* New York, 1956.

Shackle, G. L. S. *Expectation in Economics.* Cambridge, 1949.

——. *Time in Economics.* Amsterdam, 1958.

Sherif, Muzafer. *An Outline of Social Psychology.* New York, 1948.

Sherif, Muzafer. *Psychology of Social Norms.* New York, 1936.

Simmel, Georg. *Philosophie des Geldes.* 5th ed. Munich, 1930.

Simon, Herbert A. *Administrative Behavior: A Study of Decision-Making Processes in Administrative Organization.* New York, 1947.

——. *Models of Man, Social and Rational.* New York, 1957.

Skinner, B. F. *Science and Human Behavior.* New York, 1953.

Smith, Henry C. *Psychology of Industrial Behavior.* New York, 1955.

Smuts, Robert W. *European Impressions of the American Worker.* New York, 1953.

Social Science Research Council. *Studies in the Social Aspects of the Depression.* 13 vols. New York, 1937.

Sombart, Werner. *Der Bourgeois.* Munich, 1920.

——. *Der Moderne Kapitalismus.* 4 vols. Leipzig, 1902–1927.

Sorokin, Pitirim A. *Society, Culture, and Personality.* New York, 1947.

Soule, George. *The Strength of Nations.* New York, 1942.

Speck, O. *Kinder erwerbstätiger Mütter.* Stuttgart, 1956.

Spicer, Edward H., ed. *Human Problems in Technological Change.* New York, 1952.

Spinley, B. M. *The Deprived and the Privileged.* London, 1953.

Staley, Eugene, ed. *Creating an Industrial Civilization.* New York, 1952.

Stanton, A. H., and Perry, S. E., eds. *Personality and Political Crisis.* Glencoe, Ill., 1951.

Starkey, Marion L. *The Devil in Massachusetts: A Modern Inquiry into the Salem Witch Trials.* New York, 1950.

Stouffer, Samuel A. *Communism, Conformity, and Civil Liberties.* Garden City, 1955.

——, and associates. *The American Soldier.* 2 vols. Princeton, 1949.

——, and Lazarsfeld, P. F. *Research Memorandum on the Family in the Depression.* New York, 1937.

Strachey, John. *Contemporary Capitalism.* New York, 1956.

Strong, Edward K. *Psychological Aspects of Business.* New York, 1938.

Sturmthal, Adolf. *Unity and Diversity in European Labor.* Glencoe, Ill., 1953.

Sullivan, Harry Stack. *Conceptions of Modern Psychiatry.* Washington, 1947.

Super, Donald E. *The Psychology of Careers.* New York, 1958.

Survey Research Center, University of Michigan. *Big Business from the Viewpoint of the Public.* Ann Arbor, 1951.

——. *Industrial Mobility in Michigan.* Ann Arbor, 1951.

——. *Public Evaluation of Life Insurance.* Ann Arbor, 1951. Mimeo.

Sutton, F. X., and others. *The American Business Creed.* Cambridge, Mass., 1956.

Swanson, G. E., Newcomb, T. M., and Hartley, E. L., eds. *Readings in Social Psychology.* Rev. ed. New York, 1952.

Sward, Keith. *The Legend of Henry Ford.* New York, 1948.

Taussig, F. W. *Inventors and Money-Makers.* New York, 1915.

——, and Joslyn, C. S. *American Business Leaders.* New York, 1932.

Tawney, R. H. *The Acquisitive Society.* New York, 1921.

——. *Religion and the Rise of Capitalism.* New York, 1926.

Taylor, Gordon R. *Are Workers Human?* New York, 1952.

Tead, Ordway. *Human Nature and Management: The Applications of Psychology to Executive Leadership.* 2d ed. New York, 1933.

——. *Instincts in Industry: A Study of Working-Class Psychology.* Boston, 1918.

Thomas, Dorothy S. *Social Aspects of the Business Cycle.* New York, 1927.

Thurnwald, Richard. *Economics in Primitive Communities.* London, 1932.

Tugwell, R. G., ed. *The Trend of Economics.* New York, 1924.

Twentieth Century Fund. *Partners in Production.* New York, 1949.

United Nations. *Measures for the Economic Development of Underdeveloped Countries.* New York, 1951.

Updegraff, Robert R. *The Subconscious Mind in Business.* New York, 1929.

Vandervelde, Emile. *La Psychologie du Socialisme.* Brussels, 1928.

Veblen, Thorstein. *The Instinct of Workmanship.* New York, 1914.

——. *The Place of Science in Modern Civilization.* New York, 1919.

——. *The Theory of the Leisure Class.* New York, 1934.

Venable, Vernon. *Human Nature: The Marxian View.* New York, 1945.

Villalon, Luis J. A., ed. *Management Men and Their Methods.* New York, 1949.

Viteles, Morris S. *Motivation and Morale in Industry.* New York, 1953.

Wagemann, Ernst. *Beruehmte Denkfehler der Nationaloekonomie.* Bern, 1951.

Walker, Charles R. *Steeltown.* New York, 1950.

——, and Guest, R. H. *The Man on the Assembly Line.* Cambridge, Mass., 1952.

Walker, E. Ronald. *From Economic Theory to Policy.* Chicago, 1943.

Walter, Emil J. *Psychologische Grundlagen der geschichtlichen und sozialen Entwicklung.* Zurich, 1946.

Ward, A. Dudley, ed. *Goals of Economic Life.* New York, 1953.

Warner, W. L., and Abegglen, J. C. *Big Business Leaders in America.* New York, 1955.

Warner, W. L., and Abegglen, J. C. *Occupational Mobility in American Business and Industry.* Minneapolis, 1955.

Warner, W. L., and associates. *Democracy in Jonesville: A Study in Quality and Inequality.* New York, 1949.

Warner, W. L., and associates. *Social Class in America.* Chicago, 1949.

Warner, W. L., and Low, J. O. *The Social System of the Modern Factory.* New Haven, 1947.

Warner, W. L., and Lunt, P. S. *The Social Life of a Modern Community.* New Haven, 1941.

Warner, W. L., and Lunt, P. S. *The Status System of a Modern Community.* New Haven, 1942.

Weber, Max. *The Protestant Ethic and the Spirit of Capitalism.* New York, 1948.

——. *The Theory of Social and Economic Organization.* New York, 1947. Originally, *Wirtschaft und Gesellschaft. Grundriss der Sozialoekonomik,* vol. 3. Tuebingen, 1925.

——. *Zur Psychophysik der industriellen Arbeit. Gesammelte Aufsaetze zur Soziologie und Sozialpolitik.* Tuebingen, 1924.

Wecter, Dixon. *The Saga of American Society: A Record of Social Aspiration 1607–1937.* New York, 1937

Weinberg, S. Kirson. *Society and Personality Disorders.* New York, 1952.

Weisskopf, Walter A. *The Psychology of Economics.* Chicago, 1955.

White, Leonard D., ed. *The State of the Social Sciences.* Chicago, 1956.

Whitehead, T. N. *The Industrial Worker.* 2 vols. Cambridge, Mass., 1938.

Whyte, William F. *Money and Motivation.* New York, 1955.

——. *Pattern for Industrial Peace.* New York, 1951.

——, ed. *Industry and Society.* New York, 1946.

Whyte, W. H., Jr. *The Organization Man.* New York, 1956.

——, and *Fortune. Is Anybody Listening?* New York, 1952.

Wicksteed, P. H. *The Common Sense of Political Economy.* 2 vols. London, 1933.

Wiener, Norbert. *The Human Use of Human Beings: Cybernetics and Society.* Boston, 1950.

Wilbur, G. B., and Muensterberger, W., eds. *Psychoanalysis and Culture.* New York, 1951.

Williams, James M. *Human Aspects of Unemployment and Relief.* Chapel Hill, 1933.

Wolfe, A. B. *Conservatism, Radicalism, and Scientific Method.* New York, 1923.

Wood, Margaret Mary. *Paths of Loneliness.* New York, 1953.

Wootton, Barbara. *Lament for Economics.* New York, 1938.

——. *Testament for Social Science.* London, 1950.
Wortis, Joseph. *Soviet Psychiatry.* Baltimore, 1950.
Znaniecki, Florian. *Social Actions.* New York, 1936.
Zweig, F. *The British Worker.* Harmondsworth, Eng., 1952.
——. *Men in the Pits.* London, 1949.
——. *Productivity and Trade Unions.* Oxford, 1951.

Index of Names

Index of Names

Index of Subjects

309

Index of Subjects

Index of Subjects